D0238382

SCHOOL OF ORIENTAL AND AFRICAN STUDIES
University of London

Please return this book on or before the last date shown

Documen
umentari(
and Fog,
Back. Wil
themes im
"texts" of
readings a
book is b
suitable f(
broader fi

Long loans and One Week loans may be renewed up to 6 times
Short loans & CDs cannot be renewed
Fines are charges on all overdue items

E-mail: librenewals@soas.ac.uk   Phone: 020-7898 4197 (answerphone)

Documentary Film Classics

Documentary Film

Classics

William Rothman
University of Miami

Published by the Press Syndicate of the University of Cambridge
The Pitt Building, Trumpington Street, Cambridge B2 1RP
40 West 20th Street, New York, NY 10011-4211, USA
10 Stamford Road, Oakleigh, Melbourne 3166, Australia

First published 1997

Printed in the United States of America

Library of Congress Cataloging–in–Publication Data

Rothman, William.
Documentary film classics / William Rothman.
p.   cm.—(Cambridge studies in film)
ISBN 0-521-45067-5 (hbk)   ISBN 0-521-45681-9 (pbk)
1. Documentary films—History and criticism. I. Title.
II. Series
PN 1995.9D6R69   1997
070.1'8—dc20
96–14029   CIP

A catalog record for this book is available from the British Library

ISBN 0-521-45067-5 hardback
       0-521-45681-9 paperback

CAMBRIDGE STUDIES IN FILM

GENERAL EDITORS
Dudley Andrew, University of Iowa
Henry Breitrose, Stanford University
William Rothman, University of Miami

OTHER BOOKS IN THE SERIES

Film and Phenomenology, by Allan Casebier

Metaphor and Film, by Trevor Wittock

The Gorgon's Gaze: German Cinema, Expressionism, and the Image of Horror, by Paul Coates

The "I" of the Camera: Essays in Film Criticism, History, and Aesthetics, by William Rothman

Nonindifferent Nature: Film and the Structure of Things, by Sergei Eisenstein (Translated by Herbert Marshall)

Constructivism in Film: The Man with the Movie Camera, by Vlada Petrić

Inside Soviet Film Satire: Laughter with a Lash, Andrew Horton, editor

Melodrama and Asian Cinema, by Wimal Dissanayake

Film at the Intersection of High and Mass Culture, by Paul Coates

Another Frank Capra, by Leland Poague

Russian Critics on the Cinema of Glasnost, Michael Brashinsky and Andrew Horton, editors

Projecting Illusion: Film Spectatorship and the Impression of Reality, by Richard Allen

Contents

Preface

Documentary Film Classics consists primarily of close readings of a number of major landmarks of documentary film: Robert Flaherty's *Nanook of the North* (1921), Luis Buñuel's *Land without Bread* (1932), Alain Resnais's *Night and Fog* (1955), Jean Rouch's and Edgar Morin's *Chronicle of a Summer* (1961), Richard Leacock's and Joyce Chopra's *A Happy Mother's Day* (1963), and D. A. Pennebaker's *Don't Look Back* (1967). These are films that are all but obligatory for any course surveying the documentary tradition, films I have been thinking about and teaching for many years, films I am continually rediscovering through my students' responses as well as my own.

The critical readings that comprise this book are meant to guide readers through the cinematic "texts" of these classic documentaries – sequence by sequence, sometimes shot by shot – in a way that leads to a fuller appreciation both of their historical significance and their aspirations and achievements *as films*. In the spirit of my earlier books, *Hitchcock—The Murderous Gaze* and *The "I" of the Camera*, these readings, individually and together, also sustain philosophical investigations of a number of interrelated issues and themes.

Despite the inclusion of accomplished documentary filmmakers in so many university film faculties, the field of film study has only recently begun to show significant interest in documentaries.[1] Even now, there remains a striking dearth of serious critical studies of documentary films. The work of Frederick Wiseman, the subject of more than one excellent book-length critical study, has been the main exception to this pervasive neglect.[2] Wiseman's films clearly merit the thoughtful and sympathetic attention they have received. But there are many documentary filmmakers whose work is capable of rewarding serious criticism.

In part, the scarcity of critical studies of documentary films is indicative of film study's general neglect of criticism, a consequence of the revolution undergone in the past two decades by a field that has come to accord precedence to what it calls "theory" and (more recently) what it calls "historiography." There has been a special animus, though, in film study's resistance to devoting sympathetic critical attention even to the most significant works within the documentary tradition. It derives from the claim sometimes made on behalf of documentary films – less often by their makers or admirers than by detractors who invoke the claim only with the intention of repudiating it – that documentaries are capable of directly "capturing" reality. From the standpoint of the dominant contemporary film theories, which take "reality" to be an illusory ideological construct, such a claim seems intolerably naive or disingenuous.

Within contemporary film study, it is generally supposed that there is a clear distinction to be drawn between the American films discussed in this book (*Nanook of the North, A Happy Mother's Day, Don't Look Back*), which are presumed guilty of making the naive claim that they capture reality directly, and the European films (*Land without Bread, Night and Fog, Chronicle of a Summer*), which are taken to be far more sophisticated about philosophical issues of reality and representation, and hence exonerated. *Land without Bread*, for example, tends to be viewed – and taught – as if it were a mock documentary, not really a documentary at all; *Night and Fog* as a demonstration that the medium of film is not capable of representing the true dimension of the death camps; and *Chronicle of a Summer* as employing a wide range of sophisticated strategies to deny that the new method of filming it exemplifies (which Rouch, echoing Vertov, dubbed "cinéma-vérité") is a direct and truthful way to "document" the world as it is.

Within contemporary film study, these European films are viewed as if they simply repudiated documentary's traditional aspiration of revealing reality, as if they were antidocumentaries, in effect. As the readings in this book demonstrate, however, although *Land without Bread, Night and Fog* and *Chronicle of a Summer* are, indeed, sophisticated critiques of documentary modes of representation in film, they are also major achievements *as documentaries*. They do not deny the possibility of revealing reality in the medium of film; they achieve such revelations even as they reflect on the conditions that make their revelations possible.

As these readings also demonstrate, such classic American cinéma-vérité documentaries as *A Happy Mother's Day* and *Don't Look Back* – I find the distinction between "cinéma-vérité" and "direct cinema" prejudicial and unhelpful, and have no qualms about applying the term "cinéma-vérité" to the films of Leacock and Pennebaker as well as those of Rouch – likewise achieve revelations of reality and at the same time reflect seriously on the conditions of the film medium that make their revelations possible. To a surprising degree, this is true, as well, of their famous progenitor *Nanook of the North*. These American films address the same philosophical issues of reality and representation as their European cousins, and do so in ways that are no less sophisticated, philosophically. Indeed, all the films I address are revealed, in the readings that follow, as bearing far more intimate relationships to one another – as having far more in common, philosophically – than has ever been suggested.

When I proposed to Cambridge University Press a book of readings of classic documentaries, I envisioned writing twice as many chapters as the present volume contains. There were to be readings of all the films that are, in fact, included, and also chapters on Lumière and "primitive" cinema; on Dziga Vertov's *Man with a Movie Camera*; on Leni Riefenstahl's *Triumph of the Will* and Humphrey Jennings's *Listen to Britain*; on Frederick Wiseman's *High School*; on Edward Pincus's *Diaries: 1971–1976*; on Ross McElwee's *Sherman's March*; and on Errol Morris's *Thin Blue Line*. I kept wishing to add more titles (one of Trinh Minh-ha's films, for example), for I was well aware how problematic it is for any small handful of works to stand in for the vast diversity of films we call "documentaries." Not until I was well along in the writing of this book did its eventual trajectory begin to reveal itself to me. And not until I was well along in the writing of the last chapter was I certain that this *was* the last chapter, that from my readings of an even smaller handful of works than I had anticipated addressing a book had emerged that was coherent and complete unto itself, a book that accomplished what I had set out to accomplish – and more.

When I sat down to write this book, I did not anticipate that it would culminate, intellectually and dramatically, in such an extended reading of Pennebaker's *Don't Look Back*, or conclude so festively with an account of the ending of *Monterey Pop*. I had no idea that half the book's chapters – fully two-thirds of its pages – would be devoted to the historical moment represented by the first generation of cinéma-vérité filmmakers (Rouch, Leacock, Pennebaker). In thinking about documentary film over the years, I had devoted little attention to Leacock and Pennebaker, practitioners of a strict cinéma-vérité discipline that requires them to wait silently, from their place behind the camera, for other people – the camera's subjects – to reveal themselves. I had focused more on the younger generation of American filmmakers (among them Edward Pincus and his students – they were also Leacock's students – at the M.I.T. Film Section) who, in the spirit of the counterculture that emerged in the late sixties, undertook in the seventies and eighties to effect what they understood to be a radical, liberating break with that discipline.

The aspiration of Pincus's monumental *Diaries: 1971–1976*, for example, was to film the world without withdrawing from the world, to overcome or transcend the inhuman aspect of the cinéma-vérité filmmaker's role by filming his own everyday life and thereby transforming filming into an everyday activity. To this end, Pincus felt he had to be revealed, to reveal himself, in his acts of filming in ways not allowed by the discipline practiced by the first generation of American cinéma-vérité filmmakers. He felt he had to free himself, when filming, to speak and be spoken to and even on occasion to step in front of the camera, to let others film him. Yet in *Diaries*, a conflict emerges between the filmmaker's project, which only Pincus can call his own, and the demands of others (wife, children, parents, lovers, friends, fellow teachers, students) who call upon him to acknowledge them as human beings separate from him – and from his film.

Diaries concludes, symbolically, on the eve of Yom Kippur, the Jewish Day of Atonement (ironically, it is also the first day of the Vermont hunting season; in the distance, we hear gunfire). Yom Kippur is the day of all days to remember that no human being writes the book of his or her own life, and to atone for having forgotten this. Warning his son not to knock it over, Pincus lays his camera on the ground. It continues to roll as his wife, Jane, trims his almost hippie-length hair. We sense a possibility of renewal – but only if the filmmaker stops filming his life, abandons his project or, perhaps, acknowledges that his filming has been completed, has arrived at the possibility of a new beginning. On film, he has a melancholy air, as if he believes in his heart that he has failed in his aspiration to overcome or transcend the inhuman aspect of filming. Yet a final judgment is not his to make.

In the films of Pincus's gifted students (among them Steve Ascher, Joel DeMott, Jeff Kreines, Ross McElwee, Robb Moss, Mark Rance, and Ann Schaetzel), too, the aspiration is to overcome or transcend the inhuman aspect of the filmmaker's role by filming the world without withdrawing from the world. And in these films, too, there are central conflicts between filming one's life and living it in a fully human way.

Ross McElwee's grand epic *Sherman's March* and its sequel *Time Indefinite* are one culmination, to date, of the work of Pincus's students. From start to finish, *Diaries* takes the filmmaker and his project utterly seriously; editing his film, Pincus never explicitly distances himself from his former self behind (sometimes in front of) the camera, never claims he has changed since he put his camera down, that he has become Other to his filmed and filming self. McElwee's films, begun a full decade after Pincus shot *Diaries*, assert an ironic perspective on its filmmaker's project – a perspective the films reveal their maker to have lacked when living and filming the events the films enable us to view.

In their ironic perspective, McElwee's films are strikingly reminiscent of Leacock's *A Happy Mother's Day*. The conditions of the act of filming are not fundamentally altered, *Sherman's March* and *Time Indefinite* declare, even if the filmmaker breaks his or her silence behind the camera; even if people directly address the filmmaker in the act of filming; and even if the camera is pointed at the filmmaker who becomes an on-screen presence on a par with the camera's other subjects.

It is only in the course of writing this book that I have come fully to recognize the magnitude of the continuity between the first and second generations (and between the second and third generations) of American cinéma-vérité filmmakers, the centrality and depth of the acknowledgment of the filmmaker's role in films such as *A Happy Mother's Day*, *Don't Look Back*, and even *Nanook of the North*. It is a central concern of films like *Diaries*, *Sherman's March,* and *Time Indefinite* to acknowledge and thereby overcome or transcend the withdrawal from the world, the withdrawal of the world, that is a condition of the world's appearing on film at all. It turns out that this is a central concern of their American predecessors, too, as it is of Luis Buñuel's *Land without Bread*, Alain Resnais's *Night and Fog*, and Jean Rouch's (and Edgar Morin's) *Chronicle of a Summer*, the European films that *Documentary Film Classics* addresses at length.

Not coincidentally, all these films, as they emerge in these readings, share a common overall form or trajectory, a trajectory that (also not coincidentally) turns out to be shared by my writing as well (by each of the following readings, and by the book as a whole). All of these films assume the form of a literal and/or mythical journey in which the camera penetrates deeper and deeper into an ostensibly alien region. Upon penetrating to the heart of this region, at once a geographical and spiritual "place," each film simply ends, in every case without envisioning a way back, as if to imply that there is no world outside this region, no reality outside the world on film.

There is no particular feature or set of features that distinguishes the world on film from the real world, and yet the world projected on the movie screen does not exist (now). As Stanley Cavell has observed, the role reality plays in movies makes the world on film a moving image of skepticism, but the possibility of skepticism is internal to the conditions of human knowledge. That we cannot know reality with absolute certainty is a fact about human knowledge, a fact about what, for human beings, knowledge and reality *are*. It does not follow from this fact that in reality there are no truths about the world, or about ourselves, that we are capable of knowing, or acknowledging.

André Bazin believed it was the wish for the world re-created in its own image that gave rise to the emergence of film in the late nineteenth century, hence that, starting with Lumière, a realist strand runs the length of the fabric of film history. In *The World Viewed*, Cavell gave Bazin's idea a crucial dialectical twist by reflecting on the fact that it is precisely because the medium's material basis is the projection of reality that film is capable of rendering the fantastic as readily as the realistic. Reality plays an essential role in all films, no more so in the ones Bazin privileged as "realist" or even the ones we call "documentaries." But in no film is the role reality plays simply that of being recorded or documented. The medium transforms or transfigures reality when the world is revealed, reveals itself, on film. And reality itself, in our experience, is already stamped by our fantasies.

Documentaries are not inherently more direct or truthful than other kinds of films. But from this fact it does not follow that documentaries are too naive to take seriously unless they repudiate the aspiration of revealing reality. What particular documentary films reveal about reality, how they achieve their revelations, are questions to be addressed by acts of criticism, not settled a priori by theoretical fiat. What makes this principle especially pertinent is the fact that the documentaries addressed in this book, by virtue of their commitment to reality, challenge the theoretical frameworks that dominate contemporary film study, which thus may be said to have an interest in discrediting these films, an inherent bias against them. Then what critical approaches, what terms of criticism, do these works call for if their seriousness is to be taken seriously, if their revelations are to be acknowledged? How are we to acknowledge what separates what we call "documentaries" from what we call "fiction films" without denying what they have in common? (What they have in common, first and foremost, is the medium of film.)

If this book is to prove useful to the serious study of film, its usefulness must reside in its particular critical discoveries, which I hope readers will find fruitful. But the book's potential usefulness also resides in the critical approach it aspires to exemplify. My writing aspires to exemplify the value – all but forgotten in contemporary film study – of criticism that is rooted in experience and expressed in ordinary language, in words we hold in common, words capable of enabling us to achieve a perspective from which a clear understanding can be reached.

In accepting this double obligation, my writing is inspired and guided by the work of Stanley Cavell, who in turn relies on philosophical procedures associated with the names of Ludwig Wittgenstein and J. L. Austin. An analytical philosopher proceeds by abstract analysis or by defining technical terms to be given special uses. Cavell proceeds by appealing philosophically to what we ordinarily say and mean, by relying on the precision and clarity of ordinary words in their appropriate contexts. Self-knowledge is a paradigm of the kind of knowledge Cavell's philosophical procedures are designed to pursue. Without knowing oneself, one cannot know what self-knowledge is. And without knowing – that is, acknowledging – our own experience of film, we cannot know the roles films play in our lives, we cannot know the reality of the world on film, we cannot know what films are.

In writing *Documentary Film Classics*, my goal is to give voice to my experience of these particular films – to find a way of saying, in my own words, what my experience of these films has enabled me to know (about film, about the world, about myself) – and thereby to encourage readers to give voice to their experience, too. My writing continually turns in on itself, turns us to ourselves, aspires to make us mindful of who we have been, who we are, and who we are capable of becoming. In aspiring to remind us of the value of turning to our experience, the book aspires to remind us of the importance of expressing ourselves with conviction and passion and the equal importance of acknowledging one another's words. It aspires to remind us of the value of conversation.

When I was a doctoral student in the Harvard Philosophy Department in the late sixties, and when I returned to Harvard to teach film history, criticism, and theory from the mid-seventies to the mid-eighties, I reaped the rewards of conversations about their work with the many distinguished documentary filmmakers who lived in the Boston area. Apart from those conversations, this book would not have been mine to write. Robert Gardner and Alfred Guzzetti (and, later, Ross McElwee and Robb Moss) were valued colleagues at Harvard; Edward Pincus and Dusan Makavejev (whose work straddles documentary and "fiction") were among those who taught at Harvard for a year or more; for several summers, Jean Rouch taught an intensive seminar on ethnographic film, which my wife, Kitty Morgan, coordinated; there was constant interaction between faculty and students at Harvard and at the M.I.T. Film Section (co-founded by Leacock and Pincus), then the world's foremost training ground for cinéma-vérité filmmakers; the Boston area was home to the world-class documentary filmmakers Frederick Wiseman and John Marshall; and there were more gifted students than it is possible for me to name here who found themselves inspired to venture out with cameras on their shoulders to embark on the adventure of filming the one existing world.

Nor would this book have been mine to write apart from conversations over the years with nonfilmmaker friends, colleagues, and students who share a love of film and a belief in the importance of finding our own words, words we can stand behind, to account for the value of our experience of movies. Along with my wife, Kitty, the closest of these intellectual companions have been Stanley Cavell and Marian Keane. All of their comments on drafts of these chapters have been, as always, immeasurably fruitful.

I am also deeply indebted to a number of other readers whose responses to portions of this manuscript have proved invaluable to me. These include (in alphabetical order) Gus Blaisdell, Alan Cholodenko, Barry Grant, Jay Hollenbach, Ira Jaffe, Michael Lydon, Ellen Mandel, Gilberto Perez, Charles Warren, and David Woods.

I am grateful to Pennebaker Associates for permission to use frame enlargements from *Don't Look Back*, *Monterey Pop*, and *A Happy Mother's Day*; to Corinth Films for permission to use frame enlargements from *Chronicle of a Summer*; and to Bob Dylan for permission to use the quotations from song lyrics that appear in Chapter Six.

Finally, I would like to express my appreciation and thanks for the gracious support and friendship provided to me by the faculty, staff, and students of the University of Miami School of Communication, and by Beatrice Rehl, Fine Arts and Media Studies Editor of Cambridge University Press in New York.

Documentary Film Classics

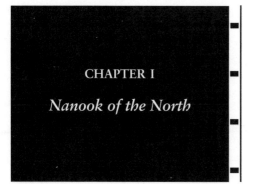

CHAPTER I

Nanook of the North

The widely distributed video cassette of *Nanook of the North* prefaces the film with a title that states, accurately enough, that the film "is generally regarded as the work from which all subsequent efforts to bring real life to the screen have stemmed." The implied contrast is with ordinary movies, of course – so-called fiction films with scripted stories, actors, and directors. Presumably these are something other than "efforts to bring real life to the screen" – efforts, perhaps, to bring to the screen the life of the imagination, the imaginary life of fantasy and myth.

Yet ordinary movies, too, may be said to bring "real life" to the screen. For example, in Griffith's *True Heart Susie*, a film contemporaneous with *Nanook of the North*, the character Susie and the world she inhabits may be imaginary, but it is the real-life Lillian Gish who is the subject of the camera. And so-called "documentaries," too, may be said to bring the life of the imagination to the screen, as we shall be reminded throughout this book.

Such facts have led some theorists to deny that in the medium of film there is a meaningful distinction between what we call "fiction films" and "documentaries." Without denying the truth in this suggestion, it is also important not to deny that there are, in fact, significant differences between them. And *Nanook of the North* is an appropriate place to begin reflecting on those differences. First, because virtually all documentary filmmakers have claimed its inheritance. Second, because Flaherty's pioneering work marks a moment before the distinction between fiction and documentary was set, before the term "documentary film" was coined.

As has often been remarked, Flaherty did not, in the manner of a cinéma-vérité filmmaker, simply film Nanook and his family going about their lives. Many actions on view in the film were performed for the camera and not simply "documented" by it. The filmmaker actively involved his subjects in the filming, telling them what he wanted them to do, responding to their suggestions, and directing their performance for the camera. As Gilberto Perez puts it, "The Eskimos in *Nanook of the North* were knowing actors in the movie and active collaborators in its making."[3]

Much of what is on view is typical behavior for Nanook and his family (lighting campfires, paddling kayaks, trapping foxes, making igloos). Some is not. For example, for the sake of his film Flaherty called upon Nanook

1

and some other men to revive a traditional – and dangerous – method of hunting walrus with harpoons, a tradition Nanook's people abandoned as soon as they became able to trade pelts for guns and ammunition.

Although the film faithfully illustrates certain aspects of the way people like Nanook actually live, it consistently underplays both the complexity of the social structures, different from ours, specific to Nanook's cultural traditions (Nanook appears to have more than one wife, for example, but no title acknowledges that Nyla is not the only woman who shares his bed). And the film equally consistently underplays the extent to which Western civilization has encroached upon those traditions, the extent to which modern society gives Nanook and his family no choice but to accommodate themselves to it, to become part of the modern world, not a self-contained universe separate from it.

Flaherty tends to portray Nanook's way of life as natural – unchanging, timeless, unthreatened – when, in reality, the way of life portrayed in the film was not only threatened but was already succumbing to that threat (or, more accurately, that way of life never really existed, for no real way of life is unchanging, timeless, unthreatened). And, in reality, nature itself, the natural environment on breathtaking display in *Nanook of the North*, was – is – facing a mortal threat.

To be sure, Flaherty may be said to have a vested interest in portraying his subjects' way of life as unchanging and timeless. For if the fabric of Nanook's way of life is being destroyed by the social and economic structures of Western civilization, the filmmaker's project is implicated in that destruction. The video version of *Nanook of the North* contains a title noting that "the film was made possible by the French fur company Revillon Frères," but Flaherty's own titles credit the making of the film only to the "kindliness, faithfulness and patience of Nanook and his family," omitting all reference to his corporate sponsor. Paired with his failure to acknowledge that his film was sponsored by a fur company, the filmmaker's acknowledgment of his subjects' participation in the making of *Nanook of the North* may strike us an act of bad faith, as a guilty denial that his own relationship with Nanook, his family, and his people was a fatally compromised one. On the other hand, there is no reason to doubt Flaherty's sincerity when he expresses appreciation of his subjects' admirable human qualities or when he declares that he could not have made *Nanook of the North* without their active participation. In any case, who are we to pass judgment on Robert Flaherty?

If Flaherty paints a distorted picture of the real way of life of Nanook and his family, in part he does so deliberately in the interest of telling the particular story he wishes to tell. The story *Nanook of the North* tells is one about its protagonist's struggle for survival against the elemental forces of nature, his everyday efforts to keep his family alive in a harsh natural environment, not his conflict with villainous human forces or his quest for romantic fulfillment (or, for that matter, the destruction of his world by forces he does not perceive as a threat). It is thus quite different from the stories Flaherty's contemporary Griffith was telling in his films. But the story of *Nanook of the North*, no less than that of *True Heart Susie*, did not, perhaps could not, really happen – it is literally a *fiction*. And insofar as Flaherty's Nanook is the protagonist of such a story, he is no less a fictional character, no less a creature of the imagination, than Griffith's Susie.

It is a distinguishing feature of Flaherty's work, one that separates *Nanook of the North* from Griffith's films, that it claims that its protagonist is a "real person," not a fictional character. As opposed to playing a character, as Lillian Gish does when she plays Susie in *True Heart Susie*, Nanook appears as himself in *Nanook of the North*. However, as film theorists (and films) never tire of reminding us, real people, too, are characters within fictions (we are creatures of our own imaginations and the imaginations of others). And real people are also actors (we play the characters we, and others, imagine us to be, the characters we are capable of becoming). Thus perhaps it is more apt to say not that Nanook appears as himself but that he plays himself (as opposed to playing a character other than himself). Yet the "self" Nanook plays and the "self" who plays him do not simply coincide, any more than Lillian Gish and Susie simply coincide.

Flaherty's titles characterize Nanook in mythical, fantastic (and contradictory) terms; Nanook thus emerges as a character created by and for the film in which he appears, the way Susie does. In the face of the camera, Nanook, like Lillian Gish, is a human being of flesh and blood, however. The "real" Nanook – the subject Flaherty films with his camera – is a character, too, a creature of myth and fantasy, as Lillian Gish is, as all human beings are. But the "real" Nanook is not a character created by or for the film, not a fictional character who serves the purposes of a narrative and holds no further claims upon the author or the audience. The "real" Nanook is separate from Robert Flaherty, who films him, and separate from us – he is a human being who calls for acknowledgment.

Insofar as he is a real human being who participated in the making of *Nanook of the North*, the way Lillian Gish participated in the making of *True Heart Susie*, Nanook's relationship to the camera, the camera's relationship to him, is part of his reality, part of the camera's reality, part of the reality being filmed, part of the reality on film, part of the reality of the film. In reality, *Nanook of the North* is an expression of the real relationships between the camera and its human subjects, relationships that in turn are expressions of, hence are capable of revealing, both the camera and its subjects.

And yet Nanook also emerges in *Nanook of the North* as a fictional character, a figure who has no reality apart from the film that creates him. The fact of being filmed has no more reality to this fictional character, to Nanook in his fictional aspect, than it has to the fictional Susie. But this also means that the fictional Nanook, Nanook in his fictional aspect, has no reality in the face of the camera. (Between a fictional character and a real camera, what real relationship is possible – what relationship capable of expressing, hence capable of revealing, the subject's nature, or the camera's?)

Griffith's camera is capable of making no revelations about the fictional Susie that are not also revelations about the real woman who incarnates her, revelations that emerge through, that express and thus reveal, the relationship between the camera and Lillian Gish. *True Heart Susie*'s prevailing fiction is that it is Susie, not Lillian Gish, who is real. Or we might say that its fiction is that Lillian Gish is only acting, rather than revealing herself, when she incarnates Susie in the face of the camera, that the character Susie is only a mask she can put on or take off at will or upon direction.

What is fictional about *True Heart Susie*, in other words, resides in its fiction that it is only fiction. What is fictional about *Nanook of the North*, by contrast, resides in its fiction that it is not fiction at all. Strip away what is fictional about the two films, therefore, and there is no real difference between them. Both equally exemplify Stanley Cavell's maxim that in the medium of film the only thing that really matters is that the subject be allowed to reveal itself.

This chapter will reflect primarily on three passages in *Nanook of the North* that achieve such revelations: The film's opening, in which Nanook and Nyla are introduced; the disquieting scene in which the trader – "in deference to the great hunter," as a title patronizingly puts it – explains to Nanook "how the white man cans his voice"; and the thrilling passage in which Nanook, in the act of devouring the walrus he has killed, pauses to confront the camera's gaze.

The Introductions of Nanook and Nyla

Nanook of the North opens with a title that – in its use of capitalization and dashes and its straining for poetic effect – is (like so much else in the film) strikingly reminiscent of Griffith: "The mysterious Barren Lands – desolate, boulder-strewn, wind-swept – illimitable spaces which top the world – ." This title is followed by two views, evidently taken from a boat, of the sublime, melancholy Arctic landscape that, on film, is one of the enduring wonders of *Nanook of the North*.

These views testify to the reality of the wind-swept lands invoked by Flaherty's words. They also offer testimony, in effect, to the title's claim that these lands are "illimitable," "mysterious" – we see with our own eyes that they are as fantastic, as mythical, as any our imagination is capable of conjuring.

And the following title asserts that the human figures around which

Nanook of the North revolves, too, are at once as real and as fantastic, as mythical, as the lands they inhabit:

The sterility of the soil and the rigor of the climate no other race could survive; yet here, utterly dependent upon animal life, which is their sole source of food, live the most cheerful people in all the world – the fearless, lovable, happy-go-lucky Eskimo.

Eskimos, as this title characterizes them, survive by subsisting entirely on the flesh of the animals they kill. They are also fearless heroes who stoically endure rigors "no other race" could survive. Part primitive savage, part hero, they are at once "lower" and "higher" than we are. Eskimos are also like innocent children, the title patronizingly asserts ("lovable," "happy-go-lucky," "the most cheerful people in all the world"). That they are possessed as well of the noble qualities of the most civilized adults is asserted by the following title, which is anything but patronizing:

This picture concerns the life of one Nanook (The Bear), his family and little band of followers, "Itivimuits" of Hopewell Sound, Northern Ungava, through whose kindliness, faithfulness and patience this film was made.

This title, the first that refers to the film's specific *dramatis personae*, also characterizes the human figures to whom it refers, much as a Griffith title might. But there would seem to be a crucial difference: Flaherty's title not only characterizes Nanook and his family, posits attributes that define them as characters, it also asserts their real existence.

To be sure, the opening titles of *True Heart Susie* likewise assert, at least rhetorically, the reality of the characters around whom Griffith's story revolves. But in introducing Susie, the film's protagonist, Griffith's title also names the star who plays her (Lillian Gish), at once positing their identity (in the face of the camera, Susie simply is Lillian Gish; Lillian Gish is Susie incarnate) and acknowledging their separateness (Susie has no existence apart from *True Heart Susie*, but Lillian Gish exists apart from her incarnation in this or any film, and, as a movie star, is capable of being incarnated as any number of different characters). Flaherty's title, by contrast, posits character and star simply as one, like a Rin Tin Tin or a Lassie. Nanook really exists, the title declares, and it is he who stars in this film, he whose appearance before the camera is a necessary condition of the film's existence.

Beyond this, by acknowledging that the film was made through the "kindliness, faithfulness and patience" of Nanook and his family, the author of this title is declaring the reality of his act of filming them, the reality of his own existence and that of his camera within the world of the film. Flaherty's title says, in effect, "Nanook and his family actually exist, and thanks to their kindliness, faithfulness and patience I was able to film them." (If Nanook were really the mythical figure Flaherty's titles claim him to be – part primitive savage, part hero, part innocent child, part sage adult – who would the filmmaker have to be, mythically, to film him?)

Susie is – cannot but be – the character she is in *True Heart Susie*. However, this does not mean that we must accept all the claims the film's titles make about her. Griffith's titles literally bear his signature; he claims their words, their voice, as his own. But too often they manifest the obtuseness that is the other face of Griffith's insightfulness, his unwillingness or inability to acknowledge the silent mysteries his camera is singularly capable of revealing. The assertions Griffith's titles make about his characters are subject to being overruled, as it were, by the camera's revelations. And this is true as well of the claims about Nanook and his family that Flaherty asserts in his titles.

It may be taken to be a definitive feature of documentary films that they are to be viewed as making truth claims about the world, claims that are subject to being tested not only against the testimony of the camera, as is the case with all films, but also against reality as it may be known independently of the camera's testimony. For example, if "The hunting ground of Nanook and his followers is a little kingdom in size – nearly as large as England, yet occupied by less than three hundred souls" were a title in a conventional documentary, we would take it to be making a factual claim about the real world, about the size of Nanook's "hunting ground" in particular. (We would also take it to be claiming, implicitly, that the other Eskimo men who are sometimes on view but never identified by name are in reality what could be called "followers" of Nanook. Throughout the film, it might be noted, the titles have a tendency to inflate Nanook's importance – he is the "chief," the greatest hunter in all Ungava; others are merely his followers – as if it were necessary for Nanook to possess such credentials to validate the camera's attention to him, as if only special people, not ordinary ones, were worthy of that attention.) If it were a title in a fiction film, we would take it to be positing a fictional premise, one we are called upon to accept for the sake of the story, but whose real truth or falsity is of no consequence to the film.

By this criterion, *Nanook of the North* seems poised between documentary and fiction. (This is part of what we meant by saying that it marks a moment before the distinction between fiction and documentary is set.) For when Flaherty presents this title immediately preceding his introduction of Nanook, we take it that it does make a factual claim. But we are also being called upon to accept it as a premise of the film's story; whether in fact it is true or false is of no consequence to the film. In *Nanook of the North*, as we have suggested, the only "fact" that is of consequence is that Nanook and his family really participated in the making of the film.

This fact is acknowledged by the singular way Flaherty effects Nanook's introduction, I take it. He follows his next title (the charmingly Griffith-like "Chief of the 'Itivimuits' and as a great hunter famous through all Ungava –

Nanook, The Bear") with the film's first view of its star and protagonist, a medium close-up sustained for a very long ten seconds – in this shot, Nanook is a dead ringer for John Wayne, by the way – framed almost frontally against the white sky. Within this frame, Nanook looks down, looks up, his eyes wide, but without ever quite addressing the camera with his gaze.

Having just characterized his protagonist as a "great hunter," Flaherty
might be expected to show Nanook
for the first time performing some act
related to hunting. Rather, when we
first view Nanook he is doing nothing – nothing, that is, apart from
being viewed, allowing himself to be
viewed, by the camera.

It is not that Nanook is presenting
himself theatrically to the camera, but

neither does he seem unaware of its presence. The frontality of the framing as well as the camera's close proximity, combined with the fact that he is engaged in no activity other than being viewed, reinforce our impression that it takes an effort for him not to look at the camera, that he is, for whatever reasons, avoiding meeting the camera's gaze. And they reinforce our impression as well that we do not know Nanook's reasons, that they remain private. (For all we know, a reason for Nanook's avoidance of the camera may be that Flaherty, for his own private reasons, directed him not to meet its gaze. But then Nanook also has his private reasons, unknown to us, for accepting Flaherty's direction.)

In his initial encounter with the camera, Nanook does not flash the "cheer-ful" smile we might expect of an exemplar of a singularly "happy-go-lucky" race, but neither does he confront the camera with the threatening gaze we might expect of a "great hunter." Nanook does what perhaps can best be described as enduring the camera's scrutiny – otherwise we would not have this view, of course. He seems reserved, inscrutable, guarded, not expressing his feelings about, or to, the camera. Or perhaps his evident reserve is Nanook's expression of how he feels, at this moment, about being filmed.

Contrast our first view of Nyla. The
equally Griffith-like title "Nyla – The
Smiling One" is followed by a shot of
Nanook's beautiful young wife, smiling radiantly as she talks animatedly to
someone offscreen.

Un-self-consciously engaged in a
conversation that absorbs her, she
seems completely at ease in the presence of Flaherty's camera (as we have
seen, Nanook is absorbed in no such

activity when we first view him). The camera frames Nanook head-on, forcing him to choose between looking at it or making an effort not to do so.
Framing Nyla obliquely, the camera assmumes a less provocative position.
Unthreatened by a camera from which she withholds no intimacies, Nyla
appears open, warm, accepting of the condition of being filmed, in contrast
to the guarded Nanook, whose relationship to the camera, as he is introduced to us, appears much tenser.

Our initial views of Nanook and Nyla make no assertions about them,
do not attribute characteristics to them the way the titles that precede them
do. They simply say, in effect, "This is Nanook as the camera views him"
and "This is Nyla as the camera views her." If Nanook and Nyla are
nonetheless characterized by these views, as indeed they are, it is only
through what these views reveal, through what is revealed simply by their
being placed on view, by their placing themselves on view, within these
frames.

Having already declared them to be real people, not fictional characters,
and having acknowledged the reality of the camera in their world, the reality of his own acts of filming them, Flaherty authorizes us to take these initial views of Nanook and Nyla, and by extension all our subsequent views
of them, as "documenting" their encounters with a camera that was really
in their presence. (This is not to deny the possibility that Flaherty told
Nanook and Nyla how he wanted them to relate to the camera, that he
staged these encounters, in effect. The crucial claim is not that these encounters with the camera were spontaneous, only that they were real.)

By contrast, when Griffith presents us with our first view of Susie in *True
Heart Susie* – it is also our first view of Lillian Gish, of course – we are not
authorized to take it as "documenting" a real encounter between camera
and subject. As we have said, the film's prevailing fiction is that it is Susie,
not Lillian Gish, who is real, hence that there was no real encounter
between camera and subject, for the camera that filmed Lillian Gish has no
reality within Susie's world.

To act as if she were Susie, Lillian Gish must act as if no camera were
really in her presence. But how is it possible for Lillian Gish to have a real
relationship with Griffith's camera, a relationship through which Susie is
capable of being revealed, if in the face of the camera she must act as if no
real camera were present?

For Susie to act as if no real camera were present, there is no reality she
must deny. For Lillian Gish to act as if no real camera were present, on the
other hand, she must deny the reality of the camera that is in her presence,
the camera that is really filming her. To deny the reality of this camera's
presence, Lillian Gish must relate to it, acknowledge its presence, in a particular way. And if the camera is to sustain the fiction that it is Susie who is
real, it must relate to Lillian Gish in a particular way, too; it must be used in
a way that at once acknowledges her presence and denies her reality.

A camera is a physical object made of metal, glass, and (these days) plastic; a dog can acknowledge the reality of its presence by licking it. But when the camera is doing its singular work, when it is filming Nanook, for example, it is no mere object. Through its presence, viewers who are "really" absent are also magically present, as it were. In the presence of a camera, what is absent is also present, what is present is also absent. Not recognizing this, a dog does not recognize what is present – what is also absent – when a camera is present.

What makes it possible for Griffith to use the camera in a way that acknowledges Lillian Gish's presence even as it denies her reality is the fundamental condition of human existence that real human beings are also characters, imaginary creatures of fantasy and myth, and are also actors capable of becoming who they are imagined to be. What makes it possible, in turn, for Lillian Gish to acknowledge the presence of the camera even as she denies its reality is the equally fundamental condition of the medium of film that the reality of the camera's presence is also the reality of its absence, the absence of its reality.

Nanook's and Nyla's ways of relating to Flaherty's camera, their ways of acknowledging the reality of its presence, are also ways of acknowledging the absence that presence represents. They, too, recognize what the camera is, in other words; their recognition is revealed to, and by, the camera. By acknowledging that his film could not have been made without their active participation, the filmmaker credits the camera's subjects with this recognition, acknowledges their acknowledgment of his acts of filming. This is Flaherty at his most progressive. At his most regressive, as in the disquieting passage in which Nanook's family visits the "trade post of the white man," Flaherty attempts to deny that Nanook and his family are capable of participating as equals in the making of *Nanook of the North*, attempts to disavow rather than acknowledge what is revealed to, and by, his own camera.

The Visit to the "Trade Post of the White Man"

After effecting the introductions of Nanook and Nyla, Flaherty establishes the narrative present by the title "Nanook comes to prepare for the summer journey down river to the trade post of the white man and to the salmon and walrus fishing grounds at sea" followed by a shot of Nanook paddling a kayak.

Now located spatially and temporally within the narrative world, Nanook is reintroduced by a title ("Nanook..."). Then we see Nanook pulling one family member after another out of the kayak, which seems so impossibly small to contain so many people that the effect is comic. Each emerging family member is named by a title – the child "Allee"; "Nyla," who has already been introduced to us; the baby "Cunayou"; finally "Comock," the puppy. (This joking association between baby and puppy first sounds what will become a major theme in the film, which repeatedly associates Eskimos with the animal kingdom.)

9

In narrative terms, the following passage presents the family's preparations for the "long trek" to the "trade post of the white man" and then the journey itself. Consisting as it does of titles like "This is the way Nanook uses moss for fuel" and "The kyak's fragile frame must be covered with sealskins before the journey begins" paired with shots that serve as illustrations of the practices to which they refer, this is one of the most documentary-like passages in the film. It is also one of the most impersonal. It is Nanook whom we view "using moss for fuel," for example, but it might just as well be any other Eskimo; revealing Nanook's character through the way he relates to the camera is hardly a purpose of this shot.

This passage culminates in a spectacular image: Men carry a huge crate, evidently containing furs, across the foreground of a frame dominated by a high wall of hanging pelts, too numerous to count, framed perfectly frontal-

ly in the background, blocking out the sky. This is at once an awesome display of the glorious bounty of nature and an appalling testimonial to the magnitude of the slaughter sanctioned and exploited by the "white trader" (that is, by the fur trade that also sponsors Flaherty's film).

By following this haunting image with the title "Nanook's hunt for the year, apart from fox, seal and walrus, numbered seven great polar bears, which in hand to hand encounters he killed with nothing more formidable than his harpoon," Flaherty retroactively transforms it from an impersonal "illustration" of the Eskimo way of life – actually, what it "illustrates" is the modern world's catastrophic intervention in that way of life – into an astonishing revelation of Nanook's individual prowess as a "great hunter."

But, again, Flaherty's next title implies that his larger-than-life hero is also an innocent child: "With pelts of the Arctic fox and polar bear Nanook

barters for knives and beads and bright colored candy from the trader's precious store." This is followed by a shot of Nanook showing pelts to the "white trader."

In most of the ensuing shots, the trader remains offscreen. Even when he is visible within the frame, as he is in this shot, he is filmed very differently from Nanook. Indeed, the trader is framed in such a way as to identify

him less with the camera's subject than with the camera itself: According to the title, Nanook is displaying this pelt to the trader, but he is really – at least he is also – displaying it to the camera. This underscores our impression that the trader functions in this sequence as a kind of stand-in for the film-maker. (Within the narrative, they certainly are in league with each other.)

The next title – "Nanook proudly displays his young 'huskies,' the finest dog flesh in all the country round" – is followed by a shot of Nanook plopping a playful puppy on the ground, then by a close-up of said puppy. This is followed, in turn, by the title "Nyla, not to be outdone, displays her young husky, too – one Rainbow, less than four months old," then by a shot of her baby, who is hugging a puppy (perhaps the one from the previous shot).

Whether "Rainbow" is the baby's name or the puppy's is not clear, but it could not be clearer that the film is linking baby and puppy, reasserting the association between Nanook's family and animals (dogs, wolves, walruses). This analogy at once reduces Eskimos to animals and elevates animals, at least ironically, to the level of humans (dogs, too, are perfectly capable of showing off). In any case, this shot is followed by a longer one in which two puppies are beside the baby in the frame. The baby keeps petting the

puppy on the left, but Nyla clearly wants her child to pet the other as well, perhaps to appear not to love one more than the other.

In this shot, Nyla's pride in her child is evident, as is her wish to show the baby off to best advantage. Quite obviously, Nyla is proudly exhibiting her baby to the camera, but Flaherty's titles implicitly deny this by asserting that she is showing her baby off to the trader. It is as if Flaherty employs the trader as a stand-in for himself as a rhetorical device that enables him to bracket his original claim that Nanook and Nyla are full-fledged participants in the act of filming. For they are actively participating in an encounter with the trader, Flaherty's titles imply, *rather than* with the filmmaker and his camera.

This strategy becomes more pointed, and more disquieting, following the strikingly condescending title "In deference to Nanook, the great hunter,

the trader entertains and attempts to explain the principle of the gramophone – how the white man 'cans' his voice."

In the shots that follow, we see Nanook, bending forward, staring at the phonograph as the trader cranks it up. Nanook half gets up, peers at the machine, and laughs, directing a big, broad grin first to the trader, then to the camera.

Still grinning, Nanook puts his ear to the phonograph as the trader cranks it again, again looks at the camera, points to the mechanism at the base of the phonograph, then looks questioningly at the trader, who has removed the record and now hands it to him. Nanook looks it over, and then puts it in his mouth and bites it!

Nanook looks thoughtfully at the trader, bites the record again, looks up to communicate something to him, takes two bites this time, then turns to the trader yet again. They are locked in conversation as the image fades out.

Viewing all this, we have a strong sense that the trader and Flaherty – two "white men" – have conspired to expose the incredible naivete of this "great hunter" who does not even comprehend "how the white man 'cans' his voice." The clincher is when Nanook bites the record, tastes it, in an effort to determine what it is.

The moment has a comical edge to it because in our culture even a man who had never seen a record would not try to figure out what it was by putting it in his mouth and biting it; only a baby would do that – or a dog. But a man in Nanook's culture cannot survive without every day making discriminations that way. Nanook's gesture really reveals a cultural difference, a difference between Nanook's culture and the culture of the "white man," not a difference between having and not having a culture, between being civilized and being a primitive savage bound to a natural order whose only law is "eat or be eaten," as Flaherty's title would have us believe.

If we laugh at Nanook at this moment, as Flaherty seems to be encouraging us to do, if we think that this gesture reveals Nanook to be more like a child than we are, or more like an animal, that is really a mark of our naivete, not Nanook's. For when Nanook bites the record, I take it, he is confirming his own provisional hypothesis that this object is not, and does not literally contain, a living thing – the "canned" voice is not "in" the record the way the seal is "in" the as-yet-uncarved ivory, for example, or the way a man's soul is "in" his body (or the way Nanook-on-film is "in" Nanook). When Nanook first hears the "canned" voice, he breaks into a big, warm grin, amused that the "canned" voice is not a profound mystery but only a special effect, as it were. (Nanook has no way of knowing – has Flaherty? – the profound threat the white man's soulless technology poses to his world, his way of life.)

Nanook's laugh, addressed first to the trader and then directly to the camera, registers pure pleasure and at the same time a spontaneous impulse to share his pleasure with others. However condescending the title may have been that introduced Nanook as lovably "cheerful," through his relationship to the camera he now reveals himself in fact to be a man of good cheer.

Nanook's cheerfulness is revealed to be an expression of a winning sense of humor that, in combination with the admirable generosity of spirit that is also revealed at this moment, makes him "lovable" indeed – worthy of Flaherty's love, and ours.

What makes this passage so disquieting is that Flaherty's titles undertake to deny, disavow, precisely what has been revealed to, and by, his own camera. That denial takes the form of suggesting that Nanook is so naive that he cannot even comprehend what a phonograph is; by implication, this naïf must also be unable to comprehend what a camera is, unable to comprehend what Flaherty is doing when he films him. This implication is in conflict with the claim, crucial to *Nanook of the North* as a whole, that Nanook and his family are active collaborators in the making of the film. What gives a filmmaker the right to film the private lives of human subjects? We want to say: What is required is the subject's consent. But if a subject does not comprehend what the camera is, how can that subject give consent? For that matter, how can any subject give consent, how can anything a subject says or does count as consent, if it is a condition of the film medium that no one can know in advance – in advance of viewing the footage that results, that is – what revelations, if any, are fated to emerge from a particular encounter with the camera?

I do not doubt that Flaherty is being disingenuous, rather than naive, when he implies that Nanook does not know what the camera is. First, because Flaherty processed his footage on location and showed the dailies to Nanook; by the time he had this encounter with the phonograph, Nanook had already become quite familiar with the film image. Second, because *Nanook of the North* itself acknowledges this, not only in the introductory titles but in the extraordinary passage, late in the film, in which Nanook carves out a window for his new igloo, at the same time revealing himself to Flaherty's waiting camera, waving at it with another big grin.

Clearly, this business with the window was set up by Flaherty and Nanook working in tandem. They conspired to play a little practical joke on the film's audience (the way, within the narrative, Flaherty and the trader earlier conspired to make Nanook the butt of a joke). When Nanook waves and grins at the camera through his newly carved-out window, it is impossible for any viewer to doubt that this man understands no less than Flaherty (but also no more than Flaherty) what a camera ontologically is, impossible to doubt that Nanook understands that a film, in particular *this* film, is made to be viewed, that the camera filming him not only stands in for the visible filmmaker who is really in his presence, but also for viewers who are absent, invisible.

In any case, in the comic business that immediately follows Nanook's encounter with the phonograph, it is painfully evident that there is an element of exploitation in Flaherty's filming. The trader "banquets" Nanook's children with sea biscuits and lard, as a title puts it, but Allegoo "indulges to excess," and so the trader "sends for – castor oil!"

Under the circumstances, he may be justified in making the boy swallow this unpleasant medicine, but the trader is anything but innocent. Within the narrative, it is he who has plied the boy with sea biscuits and lard, after all. Far more seriously, it is the trader who is the representative of the fur trade that exploits Nanook's prowess as a hunter, tempts or compels him to take the life of creatures whose flesh his family does not need to eat in order to survive. Flaherty, too, is anything but innocent. Within the narrative, he conspires with the trader. And in his role as filmmaker – a role the largess of a fur company enables him to play (a sponsorship unacknowledged within the film) – he happily exploits the boy's misfortune, which gives rise to one of

the film's most magical, yet most compromised, moments. When the boy takes his medicine, he makes a face at the trader, then addresses to the camera a look so beseechingly woeful that we want to break out laughing.

Immediately following this memorable moment, and almost as if caused by it (by the boy's overindulgence of his animal appetite? by the trader's, or the filmmaker's, exploitation of the boy's innocence?), there is a change in the tone of the film, signaled by the title "Wandering ice drifts in from the sea and locks up a hundred miles of coast. Though Nanook's band, already on the thin edge of starvation, is unable to move, Nanook, great hunter that he is. . . ." The boy's overeating has a comical aspect to it, but at another level it is not funny at all, as this title acknowledges. For the boy and his family are "already on the thin edge of starvation," and what is at issue in this story, it is now being made clear, is whether Nanook's prowess as a hunter will enable him to stave off the terrible threat that looms over his family.

The Walrus Hunt

To be worthy of the humanity of his subjects, a filmmaker must acknowledge the revelations that emerge through filming them, through their encounters with the camera. As we have suggested, Flaherty at his most progressive proves willing and able to do so. But *Nanook of the North* also reveals the filmmaker's guilty impulse to deny his human bond with his subjects, to disavow what is revealed by, and to, his camera.

And yet Flaherty's impulse to deny his commonality with Nanook and his family is itself an expression of their commonality. For the filmmaker, no less than his "primitive" subjects, belongs to a natural order whose only law is "eat or be eaten." Although his weapon is a camera, not a harpoon, Flaherty, too, is a "great hunter." He may respect Nanook and his family, but they are also his prey, to be exposed to his camera, exposed by his camera, in all their vulnerability. Flaherty's acts of filming, all acts of filming, have a violent aspect. (This does not mean that filming is never justified, only that it always needs to be justified, that it is never innocent. Nanook is justified in hunting the walrus; his family needs to eat to survive. What justifies Flaherty in filming the hunt?)

The passage that most pointedly links filming and hunting, the walrus hunt, begins with the title, "For days there is no food. Then one of Nanook's look-outs comes in with news of walrus on a far off island. Excitement reigns, for walrus in their eyes spells fortune."

In a sequence of nine shots, we view Nanook and his "brother fishermen" gathering in the vicinity of a family of walruses bobbing in the sea. "With the discovery of a group asleep on shore," the next title reads, "the suspense begins."

The following shots present the group of walruses, including the "sentinel" ("A 'sentinel' is always on watch," a title explains, "for, while walrus are ferocious in water, they are helpless on land"); the four hunters, including Nanook; and a shot with walruses in the background and one of the hunters – Nanook? – creeping toward them in the foreground. Within this last frame, the sentinel suddenly rises and, followed by the other walruses, hurriedly lumbers toward the safety of the water. Nanook runs after them, followed by the other men who enter and rush through the frame. Then shots of the hunters tugging on a rope are alternated with shots of the walruses in the water, including one that has been impaled by a harpoon.

In the midst of this action, there is an unintentionally hilarious title ("Weighing as much as two tons and armored with an almost impenetrable hide, the walrus, when charging, tusks agleam and sounding his battle cry 'uk-uk,' is well called the 'tiger of the North'"). It is followed by a shot of the walruses bobbing in the waves, including the one wounded by the harpoon.

The title "While the angered herd snorts defiance, the mate of the harpooned walrus comes to the rescue – attempts to lock horns and pull the captive free" is followed by a view purporting to show this. This shot is followed in turn by the poignant title "Rolling the dead quarry from the undertow," then by a series of shots in which Nanook and another hunter subject the dead walrus to the indignity of being flipped over like a side of beef, culminating in

one last vision of the walrus, now definitively dead (and equally definitively *alone* in death), displayed for the camera.

What follows is a frontal medium shot of Nanook sharpening his knife, his attention fixed on what he is doing, until he suddenly looks up with a grin, as if to show off his sharp blade to the camera.

Nanook then leans into this frame, his face now hidden from view, and places his knife blade against the base of the walrus's neck. He starts slicing the beast's flesh, his body blocking the bloody carcass from our view.

The title "They do not wait until the kill is transported to camp, for they cannot restrain the pangs of hunger" is followed by a shot of three hunters standing in long shot, each eating the still warm flesh. Nanook is in the middle of this grouping, his big knife in clear view.

Then there is a cut to a medium close-up of Nanook, framed almost in profile, slicing off chunks of flesh, tearing meat off with his teeth, chewing.

Viewing Nanook at this moment, we feel that we are glimpsing a primordial scene, humanity shorn of its thin veneer of civilization, and we are at once repelled and fascinated by this vision.

Like a cat interrupted as it is devouring a bird, Nanook looks up. Not smiling now, his gaze locks with the camera's.

For the first and last time in the film, Nanook seems to be viewing the camera as a threatening intruder – a fellow hunter or, perhaps, a lowly scavenger. And, also for the first and last time in the film, his gaze, too, is threatening, as if this savage predator, his taste for blood unsated, might next attack Flaherty or us.

When he looks up at the camera at this moment, Nanook is not sharing his pleasure, as he so often does when he addresses the camera with his gaze. There is a fierceness to his look, as if this "great hunter" is warning that he will tolerate the camera's presence only as long as it keeps its distance, as long as it does not cross an invisible barrier. He is not denying his relationship to the camera, but he is declaring that this relationship has a limit, that this limit must be respected, and that this limit has now been reached.

And Flaherty does respect this limit here. When Nanook looks back down, takes another bite of walrus flesh, then repeatedly licks the blood off his knife blade, completely absorbed now in sating his hunger, the camera does not linger on him. Rather – I find this the most thrilling moment in the film – Flaherty cuts to a view of the sea. We can barely discern the members of the walrus family, heads still bobbing in the surf close to shore, as they wait for the father, himself a "great hunter," that is fated never to return.

Flaherty's gesture of cutting to the walrus family does not feel like a reproach to Nanook, but rather a homage at once to Nanook and to the "great hunter" he has killed, a homage to their bond. Nanook is a beast of prey, as Flaherty is; his kinship with the slain animal, and with the filmmaker, has been revealed to, and by, the camera. But the walrus family, too, possesses the qualities of "kindness, faithfulness and patience" that Flaherty has recognized as attributes of Nanook's family. If there is an element of reproach in Flaherty's gesture, as surely there is, it is addressed not to Nanook but to himself insofar as he has failed always to acknowledge his bond with his subjects, failed always to remember that no life is a jest, that filming is a sacred trust.

Flaherty follows the haunting shot of the forlorn surviving walruses with the one-word title "Winter . . .," then with two memorable views of swirling snow blowing like smoke over the desolate landscape into the unfathomable depths of the frame.

These two shots, the film's most sublime visions of the inhospitable "Barren Lands" in which Nanook and his family struggle to fend off starvation, are in turn followed by one of the few titles in the film whose language rises

to the poetic level of the camera's revelations: "Long nights – the wail of the wind – short, bitter days – snow smoking fields of sea and plain – the brass ball of the sun a mockery in the sky – the mercury near bottom and staying there days and days and days." This is not the Griffith-like purple prose of so many of the film's titles – not the words of an impersonal, god-like authority who claims to stand above or outside the world of the film, but words "spoken," almost confessionally, by a human being who is acknowledging that he has lived through winters like this that feel like dark nights of the soul that will never end.

In another of what I think of as the film's Shakespearean transitions, this passage signals a new, more somber mood, as the arrival of winter intensifies the threat of starvation. It is as if Nanook's killing of the walrus, or perhaps Flaherty's filming of it, "causes" nature to respond, "causes" the onset of winter (the way Lear's rage "causes" the tempest, or the way Allegoo's overeating "causes" the wandering ice to drift in from the sea, occasioning the first entrance in the film of the theme of starvation).

The remainder of *Nanook of the North* is not unrelentingly somber in tone, however. There is the comic interlude, to which we have already

referred, in which Nanook and his family build an igloo. This is followed by the warmest, tenderest, most intimate passage in the film, in which the family awakens the next morning, having spent the night within the igloo, snug and happy under one big sealskin blanket.

Even in this idyllic passage, though, there are reminders of the terrible threat of starvation that looms

18

over the family. Nanook has to make a separate little igloo for the puppies to keep them "warm all night and safe from the hungry jaws of their big brothers." These puppies, as cute and innocent as little Cunayou and Allegoo, have the blood of wolves flowing through their veins; if they survive, these puppies will grow up to become beasts so savage they will eat their own kind when the "blood lust" is upon them, as Nanook's boys will grow up to be "great hunters" like their father.

Indeed, when Nanook hunts "'Ogjuk' – the big seal," the smell of steaming flesh awakens within his "master dog" the "blood lust of the wolf – his forebear." In yet another Shakespearean transition, the resulting commotion among the dogs causes ". . . a dangerous delay. . . . By the time the team is straightened out, a threatening 'drifter' drives in from the north. . . . Almost perishing from the icy blasts and unable to reach their own snowhouse, the little family is driven to take refuge in a deserted igloo. . . . The shrill piping of the wind, the rasp and hiss of driving snow, the mournful wolf howls of Nanook's master dog typify the melancholy spirit of the North."

And, quite astonishingly, the film ends with a series of views of the dogs outside, hunkered down in the raging blizzard, alternated with wonderfully intimate views of the family inside the igloo, preparing for bed, slipping under the sealskin blanket, and drifting off to sleep. The film ends with a shot of Nanook's solitary "master dog," his "blood lust" long since abated, as he faithfully and patiently endures the dark, cold night, followed by a shot of the family, peacefully sleeping, and then a final view of Nanook, snug in bed, safe at least for the duration of *this* night.

In a Griffith film, the machinations of human villains – agents of the devil, as it were – threaten the direst consequences. In the narrative of *Nanook of the North*, the threat to Nanook and his family comes not from supernatural forces of evil, but from within the order of nature.

What is threatened is not a fate worse than death, but only death itself, an inalienable part of nature. And what saves the vulnerable human community from this threat, or, rather, grants them this reprieve, comes from within the order of nature, too (the ice of the igloo that provides shelter from the storm, the sealskin blanket, the bodily warmth of these huddled human animals). The dog, man's best friend, has wolf's blood flowing through his veins; the "blood lust" in his nature is what causes the near-catastrophe. Nanook is not exempt from "blood lust"; neither is Flaherty, and neither are we. But neither are human beings exempt from the dog's capacity for "kindliness, faithfulness and patience."

What is noble and what is savage, in human nature as everywhere in nature, are two faces of the same reality, the sublime and beautiful reality that is the subject of *Nanook of the North*. But this reality – nature itself – is also facing a mortal threat, a threat that cannot be said to come from within the order of nature, although it cannot exist apart from nature, either. *Nanook of the North* is torn between acknowledging and denying the reality of this threat, in which the film itself is implicated.

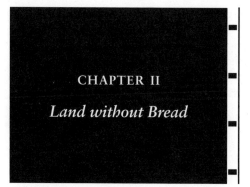

CHAPTER II

Land without Bread

Land without Bread (1932) is a twenty-two-minute film by Luis Buñuel whose ostensible subject is the Hurdanos, an impoverished people cut off from the rest of Spain by a range of high mountains. It is often referred to as the only documentary by the great Spanish filmmaker. However, all of Buñuel's films have a documentary aspect – his early surrealist classics *Un Chien andalou* and *L'Age d'or* and his late ironic comedies (*Tristana* and *The Discreet Charm of the Bourgeoisie*, for example) no less than the grimly naturalistic *Los Olvidados*. And, as we shall see, the documentary status of *Land without Bread* is itself a complex issue.

Land without Bread portrays the Hurdanos' way of life as a struggle for survival in a natural environment as inhospitable as the "Barren Lands" of *Nanook of the North*. "Nowhere does man need to wage a more desperate fight against the hostile forces of nature," one of Buñuel's opening titles reads. In *Nanook of the North*, nature may be harsh and unforgiving, but it is not hostile. Nature is sublime, as is the way of life, for all its rigors, of those who live as close to nature as Nanook and his family. In *Land without Bread*, by contrast, nature is a horror, at once cause and expression of the horror that is the Hurdanos' existence. But society, too, is implicated in this horror.

Remnants of the feudal system – an embarrassing anachronism for a self-proclaimed modern nation like Spain – now "unofficially" make the Hurdanos what they once were "officially," Buñuel's narrator asserts. Capitalism, the modern feudalism, reinforces their traditional status as "vassals" of the relatively prosperous inhabitants of the neighboring village of Alberca, who own the beehives the Hurdanos tend during the winter months. And in one of the film's most moving passages, we view "a group of twenty or thirty men with only a blanket on their backs" setting out for Castille and Estramadura "with the hope of getting work in the harvest," and then we view them, several days later, "returning as they went, with empty hands and empty stomachs."

Then, too, the narrator more than once reminds us of the enormous wealth of the Catholic church – long ago exhausted as a spiritual force – even in the midst of such poverty. "The only things of luxury in the Hurdano villages are the churches," we are told. Earlier in the film, we are

21

shown a "magnificent valley" between Alberca and the desperately poor Hurdano villages. For four centuries, this vast property has belonged to a religious order whose priests once actively "preached the gospel" to the Hurdano villages. Now the convent and chapels are in ruins, and in this luxurious garden within which grow "over two hundred varieties of trees" – how many Hurdanos could this verdant land save from starvation? – only one friar remains, his only companions "toads, adders and lizards." A shot of a snake slithering in the grass underscores that this Eden, standing in for the church itself, has been abandoned to the serpent.

Indeed, *Land without Bread* implicates all of society, society as a whole, in the horror that is the existence of the Hurdanos. For no element of society has taken effective action to alleviate their suffering. Even the Hurdanos themselves are implicated, for in their ignorance, their inability or unwillingness to change their traditional ways of thinking, these victims of society endlessly victimize themselves. (They "will endure the greatest hardships" in order to procure the wild strawberry tree, which "effectively produces an inferior kind of fertilizer," we are told in a passage that typifies the way the narrator portrays the Hurdanos as having the deck stacked against them and also stupidly misplaying the meager cards they are dealt. This "harmless-looking plant" is "a haunt of the deadly adder. The peasants are frequently bitten. This is seldom fatal in itself. But the Hurdanos generally infect the wound by their unhygienic efforts to cure it.")

The Spanish government, rather than assuring that the Hurdanos learn modern methods of farming and hygiene, sees to it that the famished Hurdano children "receive exactly the same primary education as children all over the world." What this means, the narrator makes clear, is that they are taught the rights of property and the "golden rule." That is, the government undertakes to indoctrinate the Hurdanos in the ideologies of capitalism and the church – ways of thinking that mandate that they accept their impoverishment as only natural or as supernaturally ordained, rather than rebel against it.

In light of all this, it is understandable that *Land without Bread* has over the years primarily been viewed – and taught – as a uniquely hard-hitting early example, indeed a paradigm, of the "social documentary." The Sadoul/Morris *Dictionary of Films*, for example, characterizing it as a "direct transcription of reality" and a "document of the monstrous conditions of life in the poorest district of northern Spain," judges Buñuel's film to be a "masterpiece of the social documentary, the first to be produced in Western Europe."[4]

The other famous "social documentaries" of the thirties (those made in Great Britain by John Grierson and his circle, for example, or in America by filmmakers like Pare Lorentz and Willard Van Dyke) are politically liberal films, as are virtually all their descendants. Society is imperfect, but society can perfect itself, such films promise. And they promise as well that the making or viewing of social documentaries is a mode of political action, a way of helping society solve its problems.

Land without Bread is different. It reveals a "social" problem for which it envisions no solution. Buñuel's film advocates no course of action, promises no relief for the horror that is the existence of the Hurdanos. Nor does it claim that our act of viewing this film, or even Buñuel's act of making of it, is a meaningfully *political* act. By refusing to endorse a course of political action, I take it, *Land without Bread* is implying that the existence of the Hurdanos is a problem so fundamental that no merely political solution is possible.

But a problem society cannot take action to solve cannot really be said to be a *social* problem, a problem *for* society. *Land without Bread* is thus not a "social documentary" at all. In Buñuel's film, the existence of the Hurdanos is not a problem *for* society; society *is* the problem. Society is the horror, as surely as nature is.

Then again, as the narration of *Land without Bread* makes clear, what we call "nature" and what we call "society" have become inextricably intertwined. Within the valley of the ruined convent, we are told, "there are many caves which have preserved traces of prehistoric life. On the walls have been found remarkably fine paintings of bees, goats and human beings." To the prehistoric artist, this wording suggests, human beings and the rest of nature were on a par (as they are on a par in Buñuel's film, another remarkably fine "painting" of "bees, goats and human beings"). When the church built the convent chapels, however, it also erected a wall to protect the friars "against the hordes of wolves and wild boars," that is, to keep nature out. But nature cannot be kept out. Wall or no wall, the lone remaining friar does not live apart from nature. The fellow creatures in his midst are serpents – that is all the difference the wall makes.

In the eyes of the narrator, the horror that is the existence of the Hurdanos most shockingly reveals itself in the "mirthless grins" of the "dwarves and morons" whose prevalence is due to "the terrible impoverishment of this race." They are not monsters, supernatural beings that exist beyond nature. They are what we call "freaks," that is, freaks *of* nature. They exist within nature. But they would not exist were it not for the impoverishment of the Hurdanos. Their existence is thus a sign that society has altered nature against itself, that we have rendered nature – hence ourselves – unnatural, a horror.

If *Land without Bread* is a radical film, as surely it is, its radicalness, like the radicalness of Nietzsche's writings, is not political but philosophical. And Nietzsche and Buñuel coincide in their diagnosis and prescription. Society must change, but society cannot change unless we change. And we cannot change unless our way of thinking changes. Repressive social institutions like feudalism and capitalism cannot be destroyed once and for all unless we uproot the way of thinking they express, the way of thinking that gives rise to them: our horror of nature, which is also our horror of our own nature, our horror of our own horror.

In the spirit of *Thus Spake Zarathustra*, *Land without Bread* aspires to awaken us to our desperate wish to change – to awaken us to, awaken us from, the horror to which we have condemned ourselves and our world. And the deepest source and expression of this horror, for both Nietzsche and Buñuel, is a degraded Christianity that denigrates the natural order of creation and destruction, denies that nature exists within us as we exist within nature, denies the blood that is on its hands even as it celebrates the inhuman, unnatural ideal of "conception without sin." (Near the beginning of the film, the narrator tells us that "over the threshold of most of the houses" in Alberca "is engraved the following inscription: 'Ave Maria the immaculate, who conceived without sin.'" And at the end of the film, after the death of a baby, an old woman – a Nietzschean herald if ever there was one – walks through the streets like a madwoman, tolling a bell and crying out into the night, "Awake, awake, lest the Angel of Death steal upon you unawares! Awaken and say an 'Ave Maria' that his soul may rest in peace!")

In *Land without Bread*, it is the whole earth, not merely the region inhabited by the Hurdanos, that is the "Unpromised Land," as an opening title puts it (clearly intending its mocking biblical echo). For all the extremity of their impoverishment, for all the unrelenting hardships they endure, the Hurdanos are not a "special case," are not really more "primitive" than we are. They are representative of humanity. Their lives are representative of ours. We inhabit a world "without bread," materially and spiritually, a world forsaken, abandoned, by God.

That the existence of the Hurdanos is also our existence, that the horror that is their existence is our horror, too – our horror of their existence, our horror of our own existence, our horror of everything that exists, our horror of existence itself – is a key to understanding *Land without Bread*.

■

In search of food, Nanook and his family penetrate deeper and deeper into the frozen wilderness until they reach its veritable heart. There "the melancholy spirit of the North" reveals itself in its purest form. And it is upon reaching this "place" – at once geographical and spiritual – that *Nanook of the North* ends.

Land without Bread follows a similar trajectory. The narrator – rhetorically, he is the filmmaker himself – and his companions depart from Alberca and cross the mountains into the land of the Hurdanos. Once there, they penetrate deeper and deeper into this impoverished region until the horror that is the Hurdanos' existence reveals itself in its purest form (to the narrator and thus to the camera, for rhetorically the filmmaker's camera is the narrator's camera).

Buñuel's film has no story other than this journey by the narrator/filmmaker to the heart of the region of the Hurdanos. The narration is in the first person and in the present tense as well, rhetorically underscoring, first, that the narrator is eyewitness to everything the camera "documents," that he is indeed the filmmaker, and, second, that the narrator does not know beforehand what will be revealed next, where this journey is leading him, or what he will discover when he gets there. And, as we have suggested, it is upon reaching its point of deepest penetration – this, too, is at once a geographical and spiritual "place" – that *Land without Bread*, like *Nanook of the North*, ends.

A prefatory title declares that *Land without Bread* may be considered as a "study" in "human Geography." The fact that these words are not spoken but presented in written form suggests that unlike the narration, which is in the present tense, they represent a mode of authorial address cognizant of the entirety of the film's trajectory. This suggests, in turn, that the "study" that constitutes Buñuel's film cannot simply be identified with the study of the impoverished Hurdanos that the narrator sets out on his journey in order to undertake. In *Land without Bread*, the narrator's study of the Hurdanos, its aspiration to scientific objectivity and detachment, is no less an object of Buñuel's "study" than are the Hurdanos themselves.

When evening falls and he and his companions depart from Alberca, the narrator observes that the inhabitants are all "tipsy" from the wine they were offered to celebrate the heroes of what he calls the "weird tournament of the cock." Evidently, the narrator himself refrained from partaking of the ceremonial wine, and presumably refrained as well from consuming the "wafers" whose offering is also part of the ceremony. The offering of wine and wafers makes it obvious that the "weird tournament of the cock" is a kind of parody of Holy Communion. The Albercans may inscribe "Ave Maria the immaculate, who conceived without sin" over the threshold of their homes, yet every year the town's bridegrooms ride on horseback through the central plaza, wrest the heads off living roosters that are hung by their feet high above the square, then triumphantly parade the severed heads as trophies before the assembled inhabitants, who celebrate their exploits. (In the English-language version Buñuel prepared when the Spanish government banned the film, he subtly underscores the sacramental aspect of the offerings of wine and wafers by allowing the expansive Brahms symphonic music he added to this version – an almost constant ironic counterpoint throughout the film – to cadence and momentarily become silent at the precise moment we are given our closest view of the pouring of the wine.)

Assuming the superiority of his sobriety to the "tipsiness" of the celebrants, the narrator excludes himself from the Albercans' "communion." And in this ostensibly more rational state he sets out to study the Hurdanos, whose "stolid silence" will reveal them to be, to his eyes, even less awake than the inebriated Albercans.

The film closes, however, with the narrator in the heart of the impoverished region of the Hurdanos, no way out envisioned, as the old woman walks through the streets tolling her bell and calling out her warning into the night. In the English-language version, the narrator lends his own voice to the old woman's cries. Hearing the narrator speak the words "Awake, awake, lest the Angel of Death steal upon you unawares!" conveys a sense that he has finally abandoned his attitude of superior detachment, that he is acknowledging his commonality with this old Hurdano woman. In the original Spanish version, the narrator falls silent – this is the only time in the film that he is silent – and we hear the old woman's own voice as she cries out her warning. The narrator's silence is an acknowledgment – the narrator's? Buñuel's? – of his commonality with this Nietzschean herald who is warning those who may be listening to awaken to their mortality. But the narrator's silence is also an acknowledgment – the narrator's? Buñuel's? – of his commonality with the Hurdanos in their homes, who may be listening, but who also may be sleeping through her warning.

Buñuel's term "human Geography" implies that human lives are affected by geographical considerations, that people lead different lives depending on where on Earth they happen to be. It also suggests that the human itself has a "geography," as it were, that the human condition, too, has uncharted regions. In *Nanook of the North*, "the North" is a literal place, a region of the earth, but it is also a state of mind or spirit – the "spirit of the North," typified by Nanook's "master dog," is a melancholy known or knowable by all human beings. In *Land without Bread*, the land of the Hurdanos is also a literal place, but it, too, is a spiritual state as well – a state of horror, not melancholy – known or knowable by all human beings.

The Hurdanos are not a "social" problem the narrator can study with scientific objectivity and detachment. Their existence is a horror. And the horror that is the existence of the Hurdanos is the horror that is the narrator's existence, too – an aspect of the condition of being human, a region of "human Geography" that Buñuel's film sets out to explore.

As we have observed, *Land without Bread* and *Nanook of the North* follow similar trajectories. Indeed, the endings of the two films are uncannily alike. Flaherty cuts back and forth between Nanook and his family,

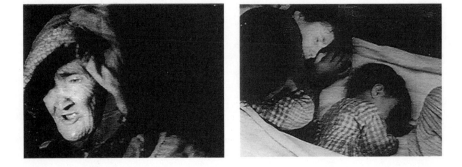

safe for now in their big sealskin bed, and the melancholy "master dog" enduring the long, dark night. In a gesture strikingly similar in effect and meaning, Buñuel cuts back and forth between the old woman crying out her warning like a walrus sentinel and the members of the bereaved family, who may or may not be listening as they huddle together in the bed that is their only luxury.

There is no counterpart in *Nanook of the North*, however, to the final shot of *Land without Bread*, a panoramic view of the range of lofty mountains that is the Hurdanos' domain.

In the opening of the film, Buñuel uses a series of ever tighter shots of a map of Europe to locate the land of the Hurdanos, to indicate its boundaries. This final panoramic view has the opposite effect. It declares that, no matter how lofty a position the camera assumes, from its viewpoint the land of the Hurdanos has no boundaries. The camera reveals no way out, no world "outside" this impoverished region.

Within the overall trajectory of *Land without Bread*, the narrator's horrific vision of the "mirthless grins" of the "dwarves and morons" represents a crucial development, coming as it does immediately after the shots of the advanced fever cases who suffer in "stolid silence" – "pitiful human wrecks," the narrator calls them – and immediately before the images of the dead baby whose funeral provides a rare break in the monotony of the Hurdanos' lives.

The shots of the fever sufferers, their bodies wracked with violent convulsions, are among the most harrowing in the film.

What strikes the narrator about these "human wrecks," what makes them so "pitiful" in his eyes, is not the severity of their physical symptoms but the passivity, the "stolid silence," with which they endure their suffering. Yet to the narrator, however "pitiful" the mute silence of these "human wrecks," the "mirthless grins" of the "dwarves and morons" are even more horrible.

At least the fever victims suffer, hence are to that extent aware. In the narrator's eyes, the "dwarves and morons" are so unaware of their condition, so unaware that their existence is a horror, that they do not even suffer, or they suffer unawares. There is no horror in their grins as they "play a sort of hide and seek" (with one another, with the narrator, with the camera). To the narrator's way of thinking, that is the measure of their unawareness. And in his eyes it is their unawareness, not their physical deformity, that is the horror "words cannot express." To the narrator these creatures are not "pitiful," not "human wrecks" like the fever sufferers. Their unawareness makes them horrors, not fully human beings.

And yet in the face of Buñuel's camera these "horrors" are revealed, reveal themselves, as human beings. To be sure, in their brief moments on the screen they do not emerge – none of the Hurdanos emerge – as full-fledged characters like Nanook or Nyla; in *Land without Bread* we never even learn a single Hurdano's name. But an aspect of Buñuel's mastery as a director is his ability to reveal in a flash, vividly and intensely, the humanity of the people he films.

Throughout *Land without Bread*, such revelations occur – in the shots of the children in the schoolroom, for example; the woman suffering from

goiter who the narrator says is only thirty-two years old; or the little girl he and his companions come upon, he tells us, lying ill in a deserted street.

Our glimpses of these people do not allow us to get "close" enough to feel we really known them, but their humanity is revealed to, revealed by, Buñuel's camera, which enables us, indeed compels us, to recognize that they are human beings, just as we are.

The horror the narrator finds in the existence of the Hurdanos is in his eyes, not theirs. Nor is this horror revealed to, by, Buñuel's camera. (Cameras are machines that automatically film everything they are made to film.

The camera's gaze cannot but be unflinching; in the face of a camera there are, there can be, no horrors.) Indeed, throughout *Land without Bread* there is a tension – the shots of the "dwarves and morons" bring it to a head – between the narrator's denials and the camera's revelations of the Hurdanos' humanity.

What makes the shots of the advanced fever cases so difficult for us to endure is the sense they convey, rendered inescapable by the frontal framing, that suffering the camera's scrutiny is one more cross for them to bear. In *Nanook of the North*, Flaherty introduces his protagonist/star by framing him frontally, but for whatever reasons Nanook avoids meeting the camera's gaze; our impression is that he has his reasons, only we do not know what they are, they remain private. In the face of the camera Nanook thus appears reserved, guarded, inscrutable – not "pitiful" like the fever cases. If what makes the latter "pitiful human wrecks" in the eyes of the narrator is their passive acceptance of their suffering, this passivity is revealed to the camera, by the camera, in the "stolid silence" with which they submit to being filmed. The camera is merciless in revealing the humanity of the subjects who passively submit to it. The camera recognizes no horrors, but it also shows no pity.

Unlike the "pitiful human wrecks," the "dwarves and morons" do not suffer under the camera's pitiless gaze. As they play a "sort of hide and seek" with the camera, they grin. Their grins not only reveal their unawareness that the narrator views them as horrors, but reveal them to be unaware as well that the camera views them as human beings, that their humanity is being revealed to, by, the camera. The camera's revelation of their humanity is thus a revelation about the camera as well: The camera reveals their humanity without awakening them, steals upon them unawares, as the Angel of Death threatens to do to all human beings ("Awake, awake, lest the Angel of Death steal upon you unawares!").

Thus it is a logical progression from the "stolid silence" of the fever sufferers to the "mirthless grins" of the "dwarves and morons" and then to the dead baby.

The dead baby looks more full of life than any of the camera's living subjects, as if he were sleeping peacefully, ready to be awakened at any moment. But that only reveals that he

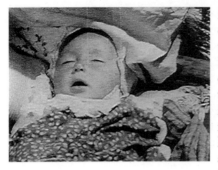 is – of course – completely unaware of his condition, completely unaware that he is dead. Stolen upon unawares by the Angel of Death, dying without ever having awakened, he is the picture of absolute unawareness. Death is not the solution for the Hurdanos, not a way of triumphing over the horror that is their existence. It may appear that these luminously beautiful shots are celebrating this baby's death. But celebrating death rather than life is the ultimate horror.

Lying within the coffin of these artfully composed frames, masterfully embalmed by Buñuel's camera, this baby appears immaculate. But no human being enters the world by "immaculate conception" and none is immaculate in departing from the world. Human beings are creatures of flesh and blood. We are "conceived in sin," and our fate is to die. Revealing the humanity of its subjects, the camera reveals their mortality. Stealing upon them unawares, the camera reveals their unmindfulness of their fate.

Nanook of the North metaphorically equates filming and hunting, as we have seen. *Land without Bread* – and every Buñuel film, it may be added – is quite close to this in allegorically identifying the camera, or the filmmaker behind the camera, with the Angel of Death. (The skulls on the church tower in Alberca, which "seem to preside over the destinies of the village," are another of Buñuel's macabre metaphors for the camera, the most grotesque of which is the "weird tournament of the cock." As many teachers of undergraduate film production classes would perhaps agree, filmmakers *are* akin to the bridegroom/heroes who wrest the heads off living roosters and triumphantly parade the severed heads as trophies.)

Rhetorically, we have said, the narrator is the filmmaker. The prevailing fiction of *Land without Bread* is that the narrator's journey to the land of the Hurdanos is Buñuel's own journey, the one the film "documents." And yet Buñuel also undertakes to expose the narrator's unawareness. He posits his identity with the narrator ironically. (What else should we expect from the director of *Un Chien andalou* and *L'Age d'or* or, for that matter, *Tristana* and *The Discreet Charm of the Bourgeoisie?*)

To the narrator's way of thinking, the horror that is the existence of the Hurdanos is revealed in their unawareness. To Buñuel's way of thinking, the horror is also in the narrator's way of thinking, in the narrator's unawareness. For in simply assuming that he is more aware than these unaware "primitives" ("Note the efforts at interior decorating," he says with barely masked contempt), the narrator reveals that he is no less unaware of his own unawareness than the Hurdanos. Denying their humanity, he denies his human bond with the Hurdanos, denies that the horror that is their existence is the horror that is his existence, too.

Within the film's prevailing fiction, *Land without Bread* "documents" the filmmaker's journey, which is also the narrator's journey. Within this fiction, Buñuel's camera is the narrator's camera. Thus when the camera reveals the humanity of its subjects, when it reveals precisely what the narrator denies, it reveals as well the narrator's failure to acknowledge "his" camera's revelations. Within this fiction, it is the narrator who frames the fever sufferers frontally, for example, subjecting these "pitiful human wrecks" to the camera's pitiless gaze. Within this fiction, it is the narrator who films the "dwarves and morons" without awakening them to the fact that their existence is a horror in his eyes. Within this fiction, it is the narrator who steals upon the baby unawares and encloses it within these luminous, artfully composed frames.

And within the prevailing fiction of *Land without Bread* it is the narrator who, in one of the film's most disquieting passages, comes upon a sick girl lying in a deserted street, directs one of his companions to force her mouth open so as to afford the camera a better view, films her inflamed throat and tonsils in extreme close-up, passively accepts that "unfortunately" he can do nothing to help her, and shows no emotion when he reports that "two days later they told us that the child had died."

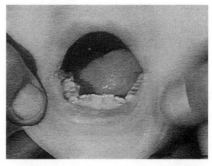

In saying that he posits his identity with the narrator ironically, in part I am suggesting that Buñuel uses the camera the way the narrator would, and that he uses the camera to mimic the narrator in order to reveal the narrator's unawareness (his unawareness of his commonality with "his" camera's subjects, the unawareness that *is* his commonality with them). But however ironic his identification with the narrator, the crucial fact remains that the narrator's camera is really Buñuel's camera. Within the fiction it is the narrator who mercilessly subjects the Hurdanos to the camera's unflinching gaze, but in reality it is Buñuel who steals upon them like the Angel of Death, who films them without awakening them, who reveals their humanity by revealing their mortality. In revealing the Hurdanos, the camera reveals the narrator, but also reveals the filmmaker, Buñuel himself. Buñuel cannot assume he is more aware than the narrator without revealing, ironically, that he and his ironic alter ego are alike. If Buñuel assumes he is superior to the narrator the way the narrator assumes he is superior to the Hurdanos, the filmmaker, like the narrator, would be failing to acknowledge the camera's revelations, would be revealing himself to be unaware of his own unawareness.

The film's "prevailing fiction," as we have called it, is that the narrator is the filmmaker, that the narrator's journey into the heart of the Hurdano region is Buñuel's own journey, and that *Land without Bread* "documents" that journey. To fail to recognize this *as* a fiction is to fail to recognize Buñuel's film as a parody, to fail to recognize that it mocks conventional documentaries that demand uncritical acceptance of their narrators' authority. If we fail to recognize the mocking irony with which Buñuel posits the narrator as a figure for himself, if we simply take the narrator's authority for granted and submit in "stolid silence" to his unrelenting litany of horrors, we subject ourselves to the film's mockery. And we no less bear the brunt of the film's mocking irony if we simply take for granted that our way of thinking is superior to the narrator's. For all Buñuel's irony in identifying this figure with himself, *Land without Bread* also declares that its narrator, like the Hurdanos, is representative of humanity – representative of us, of Buñuel.

To fail to recognize that the prevailing fiction of *Land without Bread* is indeed a fiction is to fail to recognize that the film is a mock documentary. But to recognize its prevailing fiction as a fiction we must recognize that for all we know nothing the narrator claims is really true. At some point in our viewing of *Land without Bread*, or in some viewing of the film, the recognition may strike us like a thunderbolt that the narrator is constantly making assertions about what we are viewing, assertions the camera provides no evidence to support, and that we do not have to believe anything the narrator asserts just because he asserts it.

We view bees swarming around their hives; the narrator tells us that the honey they produce is "poor and bitter." We view a donkey trying to shake

off a swarm of bees and then the head of a donkey, its unblinking eye covered with bees (an image that could be straight out of *Un Chien andalou* or *L'Age d'or*); the narrator tells us that "an hour later the donkey was dead" and that he was told that "a few days before three men and twelve mules had perished in the same way."

We view an encyclopedia page with pictures of different kinds of mosquitos; the narrator tells us that the Hurdanos are plagued with a particularly venomous strain. We view a woman with goiter who looks to be in her fifties; the narrator tells us she is only thirty-two years old. We view a girl's throat and tonsils; the narrator tells us that they are terribly inflamed, that there was nothing he could do, and that the girl died two days later. We view a grinning young man; the narrator tells us he is a "dwarf" or "moron" and that his grin is a horror words cannot express. We view a baby apparently sleeping peacefully; the narrator tells us that this baby is dead.

Again, the camera provides no evidence to support these assertions; we have only the narrator's word for it. And we do not have to believe anything the narrator says just because he says it. Yet for us to believe that the things we are viewing are really horrors, even for us to believe that in the narrator's eyes they are really horrors, it is necessary to accept what the narrator tells us about what we are viewing. There are no horrors in the face of the camera.

In *Land without Bread*, it is a fiction that the narrator's journey to the heart of the Hurdano region is the filmmaker's journey, that the film "documents" the journey that gives rise to it. From the fact that this is a fiction it follows that we do not know that anything the narrator asserts is true. But from this we cannot conclude that *Land without Bread* is a "fiction film," that it is simply a fiction that Buñuel's film is a documentary. For this would be to fail to recognize the allegorical, or mythical, dimension of Buñuel's film.

Allegorically, the filmmaker acknowledges his identity with his ironic alter ego, the narrator. Allegorically, the narrator's journey *is* the filmmaker's journey. Allegorically, the film *is* a "document" of the journey that engendered it. Allegorically, the film's "prevailing fiction" is *not* a fiction, in other words. And this means that it is not simply a fiction that *Land without Bread* is a documentary. For an allegory is not a fiction. Buñuel's film is a documentary in its own way. It is a documentary *allegorically*, we might say.

No doubt, part of the thrust of the film's allegory is to give the lie to the government's "official story" that Spain is a modern nation in which no one lives in dire poverty. But Buñuel's goal is not merely to replace one "official story" with another. Thus he makes a film that calls its narrator's authority into question, calls into question its own "official story." And because rhetorically the narrator is the filmmaker himself, by calling his authority into question *Land without Bread* radically calls into question all claims to authority, including its own.

Then does *Land without Bread* also call into question the camera's claims to authority? But the camera is only a dumb machine; it makes no claims to authority. Indeed, the camera is capable of making no claims, no assertions about the world, at all. Everything revealed by the camera has been revealed to the camera, revealed by its subjects in the camera's presence. And there is no such thing as a revelation that is not true – if it is not true, it is not truly a revelation, not a true revelation. Thus everything revealed by the camera is true. Yet it can hardly be denied that there are obscurities, mysteries, in the truth that everything revealed by the camera is true. (It is obscure, for example, what *counts* as a revelation.)

But if in *Land without Bread* some or all of the narrator's claims about the world may be untrue, if for all we know the narrator's "official story" is a tissue of lies, it may also be that Buñuel uses the camera in ways that implicate it in these untruths. Yet even in that case the camera would be revealing nothing that is not true, as we may observe by attending closely to

the remarkable sequence in which the camera seems to "capture" an unfortunate accident that claims the life of a mountain goat.

The passage begins with a low angle shot of a mountain goat jumping from rock to rock on a craggy mountainside.

In the middle of the narrator's line "The goat is the only animal able to survive in this parched region," there is a cut to an extreme long shot of goats on top of a promontory.

As the narrator begins his next sentence ("Goat milk is saved for the sickest members of the community . . ."), there is a cut back to the previous setup. This is followed by a cut back again to the extreme long shot on the words ". . . A rare treat is a crust of bread moistened with a few precious drops"; by a closer shot in which the camera pans left to follow the movement of one of the goats; then by a closer version of the initial setup.

Within this last frame, we view the goat slowly descending the precarious side of the cliff, evidently taking great care with its footing. On the narrator's words "Goat meat is eaten only when *this* happens. . .," we view the goat taking a leap. With the goat in midair, there is what appears to be a continuity cut to a much longer shot of the side of the cliff, within which we view what we take to be the same goat at the very next moment. Apparently having misjudged its landing, the goat falls crushingly onto a ledge far below.

Upon closer inspection, however, the less-than-perfect match between these shots reveals that the apparent continuity is illusory. (It rarely fails to shock students when this is demonstrated.) Evidently, the second shot was taken at a different time, presumably of a different goat.

The way Buñuel shoots and edits this passage plays as much a part as the narrator's words in leading us to believe we are viewing a real accident. And yet the sequence concludes with a revelation – if we are awake to it – that acknowledges that this "accident" is a fiction. In the final shot of the sequence, before the fade out, we view the goat plummeting all the way to the ground.

Within this shot, the goat falls away from the region occupied by the camera, obviously having been hurled off the cliff by someone in the camera's vicinity – someone too close to

the camera to be visible by the camera. (In fact, it was Buñuel.) This framing not only definitively reveals that this is no accident the filmmaker simply "captured." Expressively, it is as if the camera is revealed, reveals itself, to be implicated in the goat's fall, as if the blood of this scapegoat is on the filmmaker's hands. Allegorically, the shot acknowledges that this sequence was not "conceived without sin."

Nothing appears on film that has not existed in the world. Nothing appears on film that is not subject to nature's cycles of creation and destruction. Because the camera cannot but film everything it is made to film, because it cannot but view the world with an unflinching gaze, the world on film appears before us automatically re-created in its own image, freed from our horror. Because everything that can appear on film has been "conceived in sin," film carries the promise of awakening us to, awakening us from, the unnatural, inhuman ideal of "conception without sin" that in Buñuel's understanding (as in Nietzsche's) is a deep source and expression of the horror of nature that condemns us and our world.

If one comes upon a young girl lying in a deserted street whose throat and tonsils are terribly inflamed, one has a responsibility to try to help. If the child dies, one may well ask oneself in anguish whether one really did all in one's power to try to save her. In *Land without Bread*, the narrator tells us that he came upon such a girl and that "unfortunately" there was nothing he could do to keep her from dying. Merely asserting that he could do nothing does not necessarily absolve the narrator from guilt, of course; her blood may or may not be on his hands. And even if the narrator's story is false, even if the girl he filmed was actually in perfect health, Buñuel did subject her to the camera, did reveal her humanity without awakening her, did reveal her mortality without saving her from the death that is her certain fate. A filmmaker's hands cannot be completely clean, and that, for Buñuel, is the positive side of film, what makes it possible for there to be an art of film that carries the flag of freedom.

And yet in appearing before us without human intervention, the world may seem to be "immaculately *re*-conceived" by being re-created or by re-creating itself in its own image on film. And we may seem to be "immaculately re-conceived" by the world on film, a world that cannot possibly be penetrated. Viewing a film, our hands cannot but feel clean, and that, for Buñuel, is the negative side of film, what the art of film must acknowledge and thereby overcome.

In *The World Viewed*, Stanley Cavell argues that every art has its own way of satisfying our wish for the world re-created in its own image. What is film's way of satisfying this wish? His answer is that film satisfies it "automatically." Then what does it mean ("mythically, as it were") for film to satisfy this wish in this way?

It means satisfying it without *my* having to do anything, satisfying it *by* wishing. In a word, *magically*. I have found myself asking: How could film be art, since all the major arts arise in some way out of religion? Now I can answer: Because movies arise out of magic; from *below* the world. The better a film, the more it makes contact with this source of its inspiration; it never wholly loses touch with the magic lantern behind it.[5]

In *Land without Bread*, the narrator is drawn to what he thinks of as a "hidden and little known" region where "there still exist remnants of the most primitive type of human life." Once in the land of the Hurdanos, he is drawn deeper and deeper into what he thinks of as the horrors he discovers there. The narrator takes his enterprise to be an eminently rational one, yet his belief that his attraction to these "horrors" is a mark of his superior rationality is itself, in Buñuel's estimation, an explanation "of the most primitive type." For no one understands better than Buñuel that no activity – not even the "weird tournament of the cock" – is more "primitive" than making or viewing a film. Our wish for the world re-created in its own image is itself a wish of "the most primitive type." And in satisfying this wish, the camera is not an instrument of science; it is an instrument of magic.

To say that film arises out of magic is to say that films are not created, for example, miraculously, through divine intervention. Film arises "from below the world," as Cavell metaphorically puts it, seconding Buñuel's guiding intuition that it is not possible for films to be "conceived without sin." And Cavell seconds, as well, Buñuel's intuition that it is by arising from "below" that the art of film emerges out of religion, and that from film's perspective religion *is* "below," that in the world on film religion is inseparably linked not with science but with magic. ("Look at this infant literally covered with these silver trinkets," says Buñuel's narrator as a hand reaches into the frame to indicate the jewelry to which he is referring. "Though actually Christian, these trinkets are amazingly like the charms of African natives.")

As Cavell argues, when objects and persons in the world are photographed and projected and screened they are displaced from their natural sequences and locales. And it is this displacement of objects and persons in the world, itself an acknowledgment of their physical reality, that enables film to depict the fantastic as readily as the natural. Film's way of satisfying our wish for the world re-created in its own image is itself so fantastic, so magical, that Cavell is moved to observe, in a provocative footnote,

Dadaists and surrealists found in film a direct confirmation of their ideologies or sensibilities. . . . This confirmation is . . . sometimes taken to mean that dadaist and surrealist films constitute the *avant-garde* of film-making. It might equally be taken to show why film made these movements obsolete, as the world has.[6]

Cavell's remark illuminates the logic of Buñuel's progression from the "surrealist" *Un Chien andalou* and *L'Age d'or* to the documentary – or mock documentary – *Land without Bread*.

Viewed as a social documentary, as it has traditionally been viewed and taught over the years, *Land without Bread* seems a betrayal of the surrealist ideology or sensibility of *Un Chien andalou* and *L'Age d'or*. After all, surrealists are hardly wont to protest that it is a scandal that there exist people in Spain whose lives are so primitive they are deprived of the advantages of bourgeois civilization.

And viewed the way it is now primarily viewed and taught, as a mock documentary that is not really a documentary at all, *Land without Bread* likewise seems to betray surrealism. For the goal of surrealism is liberation, not skepticism – not to deny we can know the truth, but to reveal the truth, however it shocks us.

In these pages, we have viewed *Land without Bread* differently – as a mock documentary, to be sure, yet a mock documentary that nonetheless *is* a documentary, albeit in its own way. It is not a fiction that *Land without Bread* is a documentary; allegorically, it *is* a documentary. It is a documentary *allegorically*, as we put it. Keeping faith with the surrealist goal, it aspires to reveal the truth – to reveal the truth *in* the medium of film, to reveal the truth *about* the medium of film. And the revelation the allegory of *Land without Bread* "documents" is the still shocking Nietzschean – and surrealist – truth that "conception without sin" is an inhuman, unnatural ideal.

Yet in assuming, however ironically, the form of a conventional documentary, *Land without Bread* does abandon the formal techniques and strategies that gave *Un Chien andalou* and *L'Age d'or* their unmistakable surrealist imprimatur. Without denying the truth of surrealism, it acknowledges that the surrealist movement, and the techniques and strategies that movement authorized, have been made obsolete, and that it is both the world and film that made them obsolete, as Cavell suggests.

Cavell writes:

In viewing films, the sense of invisibility is an expression of modern privacy or anonymity. It is as though the world's projection explains our forms of unknownness and of our inability to know. The explanation is not so much that the world is passing us by, as that we are displaced from our natural habitation within it, placed at a distance from it. The screen overcomes our fixed distance; it makes displacement appear as our natural condition.[7]

In *Land without Bread*, as we have seen, what the narrator discovers when he journeys to the heart of the region within which the Hurdanos dwell is that their existence is a sign that we have altered nature against itself, that we have rendered nature – hence ourselves – unnatural, a horror. *Land without Bread* acknowledges that the world has become such, and we have become such, that the specific techniques and strategies of surrealism are no longer needed in order for the world to be revealed to us, to reveal itself to us, on film. The world has become so unnatural to us, we have become so displaced from our natural habitation within the world, that in order to reveal the truths that for surrealism were hard-won artistic achievements a filmmaker need only train his camera on a region of the world and "document" what is to be found there. For the art of film, the difficult task is to acknowledge the camera's revelations. Buñuel never wavers in his commitment to this task.

CHAPTER III

Night and Fog

From a view of a plain, flat landscape the camera tilts down to a barbed wire fence, then holds this framing. A narrator begins to speak: "A peaceful landscape..."

There is a cut to another view of this "peaceful landscape." Again, the camera pulls back to the barbed wire. This time, as the narrator continues, the camera keeps pulling back to reveal an observation tower. "An ordinary field with crows flying over it..." There is a new shot of the landscape, the camera sustaining its smooth, silent motion across the cut. "...An ordinary road, an ordinary village....This is the way to a concentration camp." On these last words the camera crosses the fence that separates the camp from the surrounding countryside. And this is "the way to a concentration camp" in Alain Resnais's *Night and Fog*, widely acclaimed as one of the great masterpieces of documentary film.

In *Land without Bread*, the narrator – within the film's "fiction," he is the filmmaker himself – departs from Alberca and crosses a range of high mountains into the land of the Hurdanos. Once there, he penetrates deeper and deeper into this impoverished region until the horror that is the existence of the Hurdanos reveals itself in its purest form. *Night and Fog* traces a comparable trajectory. It, too, is an allegorical journey into the heart of a region in which unspeakable horrors are to be discovered. Resnais's region of "night and fog," like Buñuel's "land without bread," is at once a geographical and spiritual place. But to enter this region, one must cross only to the other side of a fence, not traverse high mountains.

And to reach its heart one must journey through time, not space.

Before the death camps were built, "Struthol, Oranenburg, Auschwitz, Neuengamme, Belsen, Ravensbruck, and Dachau were names like any others on maps and in guide-books," the narrator reminds us. And now – Resnais's film was made in 1955 – "the blood has dried, the tongues are silent. Only the camera goes the round of the blocks. Weeds have grown where the prisoners used to walk. No footstep is heard but our own."

As the camera glides through the deserted grounds, it almost imperceptibly picks up speed. On the words "No footstep is heard but our own" there is a sudden cut to a black-and-white shot – film students may recognize it from Leni Riefenstahl's *Triumph of the Will* – of a line of soldiers goose-stepping right to left across the screen.

As if to suggest at once the continuity and the gap between past and present, the soldiers' movement, filmed by a stationary camera, both matches and clashes with the movement in the preceding shots, in full (if now faded) color, in which the camera moved left to right, making the landscape move right to left across the screen.

"1933: The machine gets under way," the narrator announces, and with this transition to the first of a series of what in effect are flashbacks, *Night and Fog*, too, "gets under way," begins its chronicle of the creation, operation and liberation of the death camps.

These "flashbacks" are made up of skillfully edited black-and-white archival film footage originally taken by the Germans (later in the film, by the Allied liberators) combined with still photographs – also black-and-white and from the same sources – that Resnais artfully films, sometimes "animating" them (by panning across the still image, for example, or by moving in to a close-up of a detail). Becoming progressively more horrific, the flashbacks work their way forward, chronologically, from 1933 to 1945, this linear progression interrupted only when the film returns to the present (always filmed in color, hence always recognizable *as* such).

First, the camps are constructed. "A concentration camp is built like a grand hotel," the narrator remarks, his observation illustrated by a series of black-and-white stills. "You need contractors, estimates, competitive offers. And no doubt friends in high places."

The analogy between the building of a concentration camp and a grand hotel exemplifies one of the recurring themes of the narration. As Jay Cantor eloquently puts it in "Death and the Image," his remarkable essay on *Night and Fog, Shoah,* and *Hotel Terminus: The Life and Times of Klaus Barbie*:

Resnais makes the horrible ordinary, so we might believe it; and then he makes the ordinary horrible, so that we might fear it. "An ordinary road," his film begins, "an ordinary village. . . names like any other on maps and in guide books". . . . The ordinary becomes horrible – the tracks from our city of the living lead to the camp. The horrible becomes ordinary. The camp becomes a city. Not our city? Perhaps, but not, anymore, *not* our city, either.[8]

The analogy exemplifies another of the narrator's recurring themes as well. To build a hotel or a death camp one also needs architects and craftsmen. "Leisurely architects plan the gates no one will enter more than once," he goes on. "Any style will do," he adds, and his ensuing words are accompanied with an almost comic series of illustrations: "The Swiss style. The garage style. A Japanese model. No style at all."

Building a death camp is a matter of artistry and craftsmanship, in other words. And there is artistry and craftsmanship in the way the camps carry out their murderous work. On this point, too, Cantor writes with great insight:

Whereas for Claude Lanzmann, the director of *Shoah*, the Final Solution is a matter of methodical, step by step, engineering..., for Resnais, the most formally elegant, the most artful and elegiac of...filmmakers, the camp is made by art and by craft....Within those crafted gates, some prisoners are classified as "Night and Fog," a piece of Hitler's poetry; the Jews were to disappear into the night and fog, their fate forever unknown...Poetry – art and craft – made the camp...Poetry is complicit with death.[9]

Even as the camps are being built, the narrator tells us,

Burger, Stern from Amsterdam, Schmulski from Cracow...go on living their everyday lives, ignorant that there's a place for them six hundred miles from home. The day comes when their blocks are finished. All they have to do is arrive. Rounded up in Warsaw. Deported from Lodz, from Prague, Brussels or Athens, from Zagreb, Odessa or Rome.

There is a series of archival shots of "deportees" – we see the Stars of

David they are wearing, but the narrator does not identify them as Jews – being herded into boxcars as indifferent soldiers look on.[10] In one

shot, the anonymous cameraman, not so indifferent, follows the movement of a wheelbarrow-turned-wheelchair, taking an interest in this odd contraption.

In another shot, the camera frames a child staring out from behind the almost closed door of a boxcar, then reframes a bit as if to create a more effective composition, that is, to create a more compelling sense that this child is looking on this scene, looking on the camera that is filming, without understanding what is happening.

The shot does not reveal what the child is thinking or feeling, only that the child is thinking and feeling something, has private thoughts and feelings about this disturbing situation. (This shot, whose framing and reframing perhaps unwittingly testifies to its subject's humanity, is not the last in the

film that may well make us wonder who can be filming this, for whose eyes, for what purpose, and to what effect.)

As the train pulls away, the narrator speaks poetically. "Anonymous trains, their doors well-locked, a hundred deportees to every car. Neither night nor day, only hunger, thirst, asphyxia and madness. . . . Death makes his first pick. . . in the night and fog."

And with this, Resnais brings us back to the present, the movement of the train almost perfectly matched by the camera's movement along the track – now overgrown with weeds and tall grass – that is, by the movement of the track through the frame. "Today, on the same track," the narrator says, "the sun shines. Go slowly along it. . . looking for what? Traces of the bodies that fell to the ground? Or the footmarks of those first arrivals. . . ." As the camera moves, it tilts up to reveal an entrance gate – well-crafted, of course – in the distance. ". . . While the dogs barked and searchlights wheeled. . ." The camera comes to a stop. ". . . And the incinerator flamed in the lurid decor so dear to the Nazis."

The narrator speaks as if from a vivid memory. His words evoke a scene of which, for a camera in the present, no tangible sign remains. Throughout *Night and Fog*, the narration remains in the third person, but we always have the impression that its author has to be a concentration camp survivor. This is, in fact, the case. Although the voice-over is read by Michel Bouquet, a professional actor, the text was written by Jean Cayrol, a Catholic poet who had been imprisoned by the Nazis.[11]

We might think that the narrator's point, in suggesting that it may be impossible for the camera in the present to discover any tangible signs of scenes like those he is describing, those he is remembering, is to deny that it is possible for this film – any film – to restore the reality, the true dimension, of such scenes. Yet from the shot

of the entrance gate Resnais cuts to a luridly lit shot, taken at night, of the same gate, and then suddenly plunges us into a second flashback by a startling cut to a still photograph of a young man, the frame filled by his wide-open, terror-struck eyes. "First sight of the camp," the narrator says, and it is as if these terrified eyes are the narrator's own, as if he is witnessing now, experiencing now, precisely the scene his words have described.

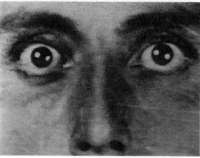

And this compelling evocation of the point of view of a deportee entering the gate intensifies the impact of the succeeding images Resnais gives us of "the individual, humiliated," being "surrendered to the camp."

The new arrival, "classed sometimes as '*Nacht und Nebel*,' 'Night and Fog,'" is introduced to the camp hierarchy. Lowest above him are the "common criminals, masters among the underlings."

Above them is the Kapo, again a common criminal as often as not. Still higher come the S.S., the untouchables addressed at a distance of three yards. Highest of all is the Commandant. He pretends to know nothing of the camp.

Resnais cuts from the face of this Commandant to a shot taken in the present, the camera gliding silently across the abandoned grounds. "Who doesn't, besides?" The unspoken question behind this rhetorical question is whether we, too, are to be numbered among those who "pretend to know nothing of the camp." Then the narrator formulates another rhetorical question central to *Night and Fog*: "How discover what remains of the reality of these camps when it was despised by those who made them and eluded those who suffered there?"

For a filmmaker aspiring to discover the reality of these camps, one problem is that no tangible sign of that reality seems to remain. It is no less a problem that the true dimension of the camps was denied, repressed, even when the camps were in operation. The horror that is the existence of the Hurdanos is plainly visible for the camera to see. But the denial of the reality of the death camps was always part of their reality, part of what the camera must discover a way to discover.

As the camera glides along an endless row of empty bunk beds, the narrator continues to evoke scenes not given to us to view, scenes of which no tangible sign remains:

These wooden blocks, these beds where three people slept, these burrows where people hid, where they furtively ate and sleep itself was a danger – no description, no shot, can restore their true dimension, endless, uninterrupted fear. We should need the very mattress at once meat safe and strong-box, the blanket that was fought over, the denunciations and oaths, the orders repeated in every tongue, the sudden appearance of the S.S., zealous in their check-ups and persecutions. Only the husk and shade remains of this brick dormitory.

Finally, the camera comes to the end of the row. Smoothly turning so that for a long moment it frames nothing but a featureless wall, it completes a half-revolution and then starts retracing its steps, as if it were its immutable fate to keep endlessly traversing this long row of empty beds.

Momentarily, however, Resnais cuts to the exterior of the barracks, the camera continuing its movement from the preceding shot. "Here is the setting. Buildings that might be stables, garages, workshops, a piece of land that has become a waste-land, an autumn sky indifferent to everything . . ."

The camera comes to a stop (as it did when it framed the entrance gate, signaling the cut to staring eyes that suddenly plunged us into the second flashback). " . . . Evoke a night . . . " Resnais cuts to a shot of the night sky,

the moon barely visible through heavy mist (a perfect evocation, it might be noted, of the "night and fog" of the film's title). ". . . Shrill with cries, busy with fleas. A night of chattering teeth. . . Get to sleep quickly."

And suddenly, again, Resnais plunges us into a flashback, this time by cutting to a still photograph of a row of bunk beds crowded with men staring fearfully at the camera.

The words the narrator goes on to speak form a disjointed, impressionistic monologue, as if he were at the mercy of a jumble of all-too-vivid memories.

Wakening at dawn and people falling over one another. Muster on the parade. . . The night's dead throw the figures out. A band plays a march from some operetta, while they leave for the quarries or factory. Work in snow that is soon frozen mud. Work in the August sun. . . Thirst and dysentery. . . Three thousand Spaniards died building this stair that leads to the Mauthausen quarry. Work in the underground factories. Month after month they dig deeper down. . . But these strange workmen who weigh five stone are unreliable. The S.S. watches them. . . . The Kapo has only to count the day's victims. . . The deportee returns to the obsession of his life and dreams – food. Soup. . . A spoon less is a day off your life. . . Many are too weary to defend their ration against thieves and blows. They wait for the mud or the snow.

Resnais accompanies this monologue with stills and archival footage that relate obliquely to the scenes being evoked, as if to underscore what the narrator has already acknowledged, that "no description, no shot" can restore to these settings their "true dimension" of "endless, uninterrupted fear."

And yet, surely, the narrator is evoking these scenes for us, Resnais is presenting these images to us, so we can know something – the crucial thing – about these camps, or can no longer deny to ourselves that we know nothing about them. That is, the task *Night and Fog* sets for itself is precisely to restore the reality of these "buildings that might be stables, garages, workshops," this "brick dormitory" whose "husk and shade" alone remains," these "wooden blocks, these beds where three people slept, these burrows where people hid, where they furtively ate and sleep itself was a danger," this "piece of land that has become a waste-land," this "autumn sky indifferent to everything." And Resnais's film undertakes this task so that we may no longer "pretend to know nothing about" the "endless, uninterrupted fear" that was – is – the "true dimension" of these settings.

The task *Night and Fog* sets for itself is an (all but) impossible one, Resnais's film acknowledges. And yet the film succeeds in accomplishing this (all but) impossible task – at least, it succeeds if we take it upon ourselves to imagine the (all but) unimaginable scenes the narrator is evoking, scenes that once took place here on an everyday basis.

On the narrator's words "They wait for the mud or the snow...," the camera begins panning across a photograph of the camp in winter, the rows of barracks standing out starkly against the snow. As he adds "...To lie down somewhere, anywhere, and die one's own death," we are returned to the present, the camera now gliding along an endless row of latrines. Despite his invocation of the deportee's dream – his own dream – of lying down to await a peaceful death, without a pause the narrator continues in his breathless litany of horrors ("The latrines and their approaches. Skeletons with baby-flesh came here seven or eight times a night.... They watched one another in fear, on the look-out for the familiar symptoms. To 'pass blood' was a sign of death..."). The implication is that even those who died here did not "die their own deaths." Those who died, as surely as those who survived, still haunt these settings, are still haunted by their dream of dying their own deaths. The task of Resnais's film is also to allow these tortured souls to rest in peace.

As the narrator says, "You called on your friends, exchanged rumors and news," the camera, having come to the end of the row of latrines, tilts up to frame the walls. "Gradually, a society developed, its form the image of terror...Less mad, though, than that of the S.S., whose precepts ran 'Cleanliness is Health,' 'Work is Freedom,' 'To Each His Due,' 'A Louse Means Death.'"

There is a brief flashback: We view these slogans, one by one, emblazoned on gates, then stills and archival shots that illustrate the narrator's ensuing words ("Each camp has its surprises. A symphony orchestra. A zoo. Hothouses where Himmler cultivated rare blooms. Goethe's oak at Buchenwald. The camp was built around it. An orphanage short-lived but constantly restarted. An invalid bay.").

Resnais returns us yet again to the present. "Then the real world, the world of the past, seems far yet not so far." Strikingly, the camera is unmoving as the narrator speaks these words. Except for the opening shot of the film, a stationary camera has mainly marked the world of the past. That

the film's opening is being echoed here is confirmed by the shot that follows, in which the camera moves past the double barbed-wire fence separating the camp from the landscape that surrounds it as the narrator speaks the words "For the deportee, it was an image. He belonged only to the self-contained universe hemmed in by observation posts...where soldiers spied on the deportees, killing them on occasion."

With this remark, the camera stops, signaling another sudden cut to a still photograph of a man whose eyes are fixed in a terrified stare. This man, however, is dead. Evidently, he was killed trying to climb the barbed-wire fence to reach the "real world" in plain view on the other side.

This is a privileged moment. Although death has been repeatedly invoked in the film, this is the first image of literal death Resnais gives us. This man did not lie down in the snow or the mud, did not peacefully welcome his death. Neither did death steal upon him unawares. He died with his eyes wide open. His death was sudden, violent, terrible, but when it came he saw it coming. And yet the death he saw coming was a far cry from his dream – the narrator's dream, the human dream – of "dying one's own death."

Perhaps he was shot by a soldier spying on him from an observation post. Perhaps he was electrocuted by the fence, and his death was only viewed, not caused, by such a viewer. Perhaps no one was viewing when he died, and no one viewed him other than the anonymous photographer who later took this shot (as if, to the dead, there is a difference between now and later). However we imagine the scene of this man's death, this photograph reveals – its reality *means* – that his death was not private, that he could not – cannot – call his death his own. Concentration camps are designed and built not merely to kill, but to deny their victims the possibility of "dying their own deaths." To this end, gun and camera work hand in hand.

There is a cut to another still of the same man, then to a photograph of other men killed trying to cross the barbed-wire fence, all killed – and photographed – the same way. In the camps, death is off the rack, not made to order, this shot forcefully brings home. Concentration camps are designed to deny their victims the possibility of "dying their own deaths" not only by depriving them of privacy, but also by denying their individuality. And to this end, too, gun and camera work hand in hand.

"Everything is a pretext for. . . punishments, humiliation. The roll call lasts two hours. . .," the narrator goes on, as we view a lineup of naked men, all skin and bones, some pathetically trying to cover their genitals from the unflinching gaze of the camera. We view a "yard in Block XI, quite out of sight," which has been "specially arranged for executions." We view "coaches with smoked windows. . . 'Black Transport,' which leaves at night." The narrator adds, "We shall never know anything about it," as we view an ominous-looking truck slowly disappearing into a lingering cloud of dust. (This is another of the film's poetic invocations of the "night and fog" of the title.)

Then the image gradually fades out – this is the first fade-out in the film – to bring this part of *Night and Fog* to an end.

The millions who lived and died in the camps were forcefully separated from their ordinary lives. Before they entered the gates of the camps, the present was the "real world" to them – the ordinary world of home, family, friends, jobs. Once they came to "belong" to the "self-contained universe" of the camp, the real world remained in plain view, "far yet not so far" on the other side of the fence. But the "real world" on the other side of the fence was only an image – as real yet impossible to reach as the world on film, "far yet not so far" on the "other side" of the movie screen.

It meant death not to recognize that this fence could not be crossed, that even dying did not get one to the other side. But it meant madness not to recognize that what was on the other side was real. To mistake the self-contained universe of the camp for the real world was to deny the reality of the fence – and its meaning (for its reality was its meaning). The fence that was built to contain the camp, to make it a self-contained universe, meant that the camp was not, could not be, the real world. For the real world encompasses everything that exists. The real world cannot be contained; it has – can have – no fence around it.

To belong to the camp – to struggle to survive, sane, in this self-contained universe – meant denying that the present was the real world. (This is what the narrator means, I take it, when he speaks of the reality of the camps as "eluding" those who suffered there.) Like a movie screen upon which the real world is projected, the fence that made the camp a self-contained universe made the real world an image, made the real world present the way the world of the past once was present to the deportees (before they came to belong to the camp, when the present was still the real world to them).

Night and Fog, we have said, undertakes to restore to these settings their "true dimension," to restore the reality of the world of the past (to make this past as present as it ever was, or to call upon us to acknowledge that it never stopped being present). The world of the past that *Night and Fog* undertakes to restore, of course, is the world in which these self-contained universes were built and operated, the world in which their "true dimension" was denied. It is the world in which the real world *became* the world of the past, *became* present only as an image. In undertaking to restore the reality of the world of the past, then, *Night and Fog* undertakes to restore the reality of the present, too, to enable the present to become the real world again.

There is another aspect, as well, to the idea that the fence that made the camp a self-contained universe made the real world an image. The fence was built to contain the camp, to separate it from the real world, to enable those outside to deny the reality of what was inside. But if the reality of the fence meant that the self-contained universe of the camp could not be the real world, it meant that the world outside the camp – the world that excluded the camp, that denied its reality – could not be the real world either, that it, too, was a self-contained universe. If what was inside the fence was "the semblance of a real city," as the narrator suggests, it was the semblance of a semblance, the facade of a facade. For what was outside the fence was only an image of the real world, was no less a semblance, no less a mere facade.

The camp was only the facade of the real world, but, the narrator goes on, "man has incredible powers of resistance." For those who came to belong to its self-contained universe,

The mind works on. They make spoons, marionettes, which they carefully hide. Monsters. Boxes. They manage to write. . ., train the memory with dreams. They think of God. They even dispute with the common criminals their right to control the camp life. They look after friends worse off than themselves. They share their food with them. . . As a last recourse they take the dying to the hospital.

As the narrator speaks these last words, the camera, in the present, tracks in on the door of a building. "Approach this door and you could hope for a real bed. And there was the risk of death by syringe."

The hospital, of course, was a facade. "The medicines were make believe, the dressing mere paper. . .Sometimes the starving ate their dressings." Accompanying these words, Resnais presents us with three shots that we take to represent still photographs of patients (that is, victims). But a barely perceptible movement of a terrified eye reveals that these "stills" are really motion pictures. They are only semblances of still photographs, we might say.

Cantor writes tellingly about this passage:

The camera. . .pans across black and white stills of patients. Or so one thinks, until an eye blinks. One thinks (forced to a telling misapprehension): so it wasn't a photo (though, of course, it is). If motion pictures-become-snapshots describe nostalgic images, then here nostalgia is defeated by momentarily making the moving picture seem like a still, and then the slight motion of the patient's eye makes a mournful scene horrifying. Death enters because we had felt protected, because we had thought we were looking at a still, at history that had already happened. Outside history's narrative, we did not have to participate in its forward motion. But because this man will die, because he has been returned for a moment to life, we try to grasp him at the edge of the precipice; and feel our failure, and await death, again, with him.[12]

As Cantor suggests, we "await death" with this frightened man who reveals himself to the camera to be still holding on to life. But we might also note the possibility that revealing that he is alive may be precisely what this man fears, as if he believes he can hold death at bay as long as he appears already dead. These shots thus chillingly bring home the fact that the camera is integral to the operation of the death camp – integral to the way the camp brings death, the way it creates "endless, uninterrupted fear." To be sure, we are sympathetic viewers prepared to imagine ourselves suffering and dying in this man's place. But the camera "belongs" to his torturers and executioners. We "await death, again, with him." We also await killing, again, with them.

On the narrator's words "In the long run all the deportees conform to a

model that has no age but dies with its eyes open," there is a one-shot flashback.

In the world of *Land without Bread*, death is not brought by art and craft (except when it "happens" that Buñuel, unviewed by the camera, hurls a goat from the top of a cliff to obtain a shot he needs for his film). In Buñuel's film, death is brought by an angel, as it were. Allegorically, the camera – or the filmmaker – is the exterminating angel that steals upon its victims without awakening them. The horror of the existence of the Hurdanos is their unawareness. The donkey, attacked by a swarm of bees, dies with its eyes open. But the Hurdanos die as they lived, with their eyes closed.

Those who suffered in the camps, and those who built and operated them, may have wished to be unaware of the "true dimension" of these self-contained universes – unawareness would have been a blessing to them, not a horror – but their eyes were open. Nor were their ears closed to what the narrator will come to call the "endless cry."

"Useless to describe what went on in these cells," the narrator says as the camera, in the present, moves in toward a building, its brick wall pock-marked with small openings. "In cages so designed they could neither stand nor lie, men and women were conscientiously punished for days on end. The air holes were not sound-proof."

For a long moment, the camera holds on one of these air holes, all but compelling us to hear the terrified cries that once emanated from this unseen "cage," cries that still echo through the present silence. And we are all but compelled to hear, as well, the cries that emanate in the present from the torture chambers that are still in use all over the world.

Again, death camps were built by art and craft, and there was art and craft in the way they carried out their murderous work. "There was a surgical block," the narrator notes. "It almost looks like a nursing home. An S.S. doctor. A disquieting nurse. What's behind the set-up and scenes? Useless operations, amputations, experimental mutilations. A few of these guinea pigs survive. Castrated. Burned with phosphorous. The flesh of some will be marked for life."

Cantor writes:

"The hospital," the narrator says, "is set-up and scenes."...Set-up and scenes, as in a film. And a crematorium, too, can be a set – a work of art that is a lie. "An incinerator can be made to look like a picture postcard. Later – today – tourists have themselves photographed in them." Beware, then, of settings and set. Beware of picture postcards, backdrops,...snapshots. Beware, this artist says, of art...it might help you forget; and it might help you to commit murder.[13]

Buñuel's faith, as an artist, is that the art and craft that go into the making of *Land without Bread* may enable his film to free us, and him, from the unawareness to which the Hurdanos are condemned. To awaken us to – awaken us from – the horror that is the Hurdanos' existence, Buñuel's film attains an ironic perspective on the world it "documents" – a perspective possessed by no one within that world.

In *Land without Bread*, as we have seen, Buñuel ironically identifies himself with an obtuse narrator whose unawareness of his commonality with the Hurdanos implicates him in the horror. Underscoring Buñuel's ironic identification with the narrator is the filmmaker's strategy of using the camera the way this obtuse figure would so as to expose the narrator's failures to acknowledge "his" camera's revelations. Buñuel's task, in attempting to free his film from the horror it "documents," is to acknowledge these revelations of the camera, revelations the narrator is too unaware to recognize. For the camera *is* free from the horror that condemns the Hurdanos and their world; its gaze is unflinching as it steals upon its subjects unawares, as it reveals the unawareness that at once makes them human and keeps them from becoming fully human. In filming the Hurdanos without awakening them, Buñuel's camera reveals them to be condemned. But his camera also condemns them, makes scapegoats of them. Allegorically, we might even say, the making of *Land without Bread* is this artist's final solution to the Hurdano problem.

Nothing within the world of Buñuel's film manifests the art and craft with which the filmmaker represents the world of the Hurdanos. And that is a fundamental difference between *Land without Bread* and *Night and Fog*. Death is everywhere in the Hurdano region, but Buñuel's "land without bread" is not a death camp. Again, the existence of the Hurdanos is a horror, but the horror is their unawareness. The horror in *Night and Fog* is a creation of art and craft.

In *Land without Bread*, the horror that is the existence of the Hurdanos reveals that humanity, in its attempts to wall out nature, has altered nature against itself, has rendered nature itself a horror. But this horror has stolen upon humanity unawares. Humanity has become estranged from nature, nature has become estranged from itself, naturally, as it were, as an inevitable consequence of humanity's attempts – bred by horror of nature – to protect itself from nature, to keep nature at bay.

Buñuel's faith is that art can awaken humanity to – from – the horror of nature that has rendered nature unnatural, a horror. Art is to save us from the horror, to reconcile us with nature. But in the world of *Night and Fog*, the reality of the death camps means that a further estrangement has taken place: Humanity has altered art against its own nature, has rendered art unnatural, a horror. Death camps were built with fences around them not to try to contain nature, but to try to contain art, to try to protect nature from art, to try to keep art itself at bay. If a death camp is a work of art, how can art save us?

Buñuel asserts an ironic distance, we have said, between his own perspective and that of his obtuse narrator. And he uses the camera ironically, uses it the way the narrator would in order to reveal the narrator's unawareness. In *Night and Fog*, Resnais asserts no ironic distance between himself and his narrator, a concentration camp survivor who is anything but unaware or obtuse. But Resnais carries a crucial step further Buñuel's strategy of using the camera ironically. Most of what is on view in *Night and Fog* is "found" footage or still photographs originally shot by the Nazis themselves. In *Night and Fog*, the camera most often belongs not to Resnais at all, but to the builders and operators of the camps. Insofar as these shots were originally taken in the service of the Nazis' project of denying the humanity of their victims, Resnais uses them precisely to undo their original purpose, to acknowledge the humanity they reveal but were meant to deny.

Yet underlying Buñuel's irony in identifying the narrator with himself is his film's acknowledgment that the narrator's camera is really the filmmaker's own camera. Similarly, it is a central thrust of Resnais's film to acknowledge that there is an affinity as well as a difference between the Nazis' use of the camera and his own, between their project and his. *Night and Fog* acknowledges that there is an affinity in general between guns and cameras, between murder and the art of film (as Renoir's and Hitchcock's films, for example, insistently declare). Beyond this, Resnais's film acknowledges that the particular artistic sensibility it exemplifies, its way of representing the death camps, has a particular affinity with the way the camps were built and operated.

It is one of Jay Cantor's deepest insights that *Night and Fog* understands these cities of death to have been made by art and craft, and in this respect to be akin not only to our ordinary cities, but to ordinary works of art. And that the building and operation of the death camps are not only congruent with ordinary acts of artistic creation (and with ordinary acts of filmmaking, we might add), but have a special link with the creation of Resnais's film, with its particular way of representing the camps. As Cantor puts it, "Poetry – art and craft – made the camps; poetry – art and craft – makes Resnais's response to the camps, its representation."[14]

As we have suggested, *Night and Fog*'s way of representing the death camps is by undertaking to restore their reality. To restore the reality of the camps means to create these cities of death all over again, to create them symbolically, we might say (with our discussion of *Land without Bread* in mind, were might also say "mythically" or "allegorically").

Art and craft are in complicity with the way literal murder is carried out in – by – the camps. And art and craft are in complicity with the way *Night and Fog* symbolically re-creates the death camps, with the way death is represented in – by – Resnais's film. And this must be so, as Cantor observes, for "if Resnais's art did not openly display this complicity it would distance him and us from the camp, turn us into spectators, and the camp into spectacle."[15] Re-creating the death camps in – by – the medium of film, Resnais acknowledges that his artistic sensibility is capable of making the camps, that his art is capable of creating the "endless, uninterrupted fear" that is their "true dimension," is capable of bringing death, at least symbolically.

"In the Talmud it is asked," Cantor writes,

How, now that the Temple is destroyed, are we to make sacrifices? And why, now that the Temple is destroyed, do we study in such detail how sacrifices were made there? The sages answer that our way of making a sacrifice at the Temple is, of course, *to study* how the sacrifice had been made, to sacrifice our lives briefly through study, in remembering the sacrifice, remembering it meticulously, step by step. In this way we symbolically enact sacrifice; our own detailed delineation, which calls upon all our powers of imagination and interpretation, both describes and is symbol for the sacrifice. . . Such symbolic sacrifices are not bloodless, not without scars; . . . death . . . truly operates in the symbolic sacrifice as well as in the . . . literal one.[16]

In studying, now that the Temple is destroyed, how sacrifices were made in the Temple, the act of representation itself is a symbolic equivalent for the action to be represented. Cantor's point is that the making of *Night and Fog*, too, is an act of representation of this kind. The way Resnais makes his film is equivalent, symbolically, to the way the death camps were made. The way the film represents the operation of the death camps is equivalent, symbolically, to the way "endless, uninterrupted fear" was created, the way death was brought, in – by – the camps.

This is why, as Cantor observes, death is

. . . most felt not in still photos or documentary footage from the camps, not in the silence of nature, but in all these things only when the artist has found a way to making himself and us participate in the *building* of these images of the destruction of the Jews, and so, in that limited, symbolic, so necessary way, in what the images show. We can participate, then, *symbolically* in the destruction of the Jews, and in our own destruction; for to imagine properly is also, symbolically, to perform and to suffer.[17]

■

"Nothing distinguishes the gas chamber from an ordinary block," the narrator says, as the camera, in the present, traverses first the exterior and then

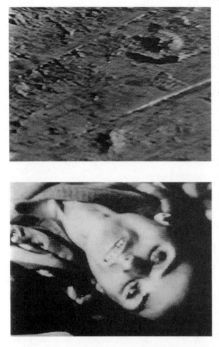

the interior of a faceless brick building. "What looked like a shower-room welcomed the arrivals. The doors were closed. A watch was kept." The camera stops. There is an ominous cut to a barred window. Then the camera, pulling out, "climbs" the stone wall until it reaches the ceiling. "The only sign – but you have to know – is this ceiling scored by fingernails. Even the concrete was torn." The camera pans and tracks slowly across the length of the ceiling. Then Resnais cuts to a photograph of a wide-eyed face, and to a horrifying still of a pile of corpses.

These marks in the ceiling are the only tangible signs that Resnais's camera, in the present, ever discovers that reveal the "endless, uninterrupted fear" that was the "true dimension" of these settings. But to recognize what these marks reveal, to comprehend the significance of these signs, even to recognize them *as* signs, "You have to know," as the narrator puts it. You have to know what the narrator tells us. You have to know what Resnais's film enables us to know, assures that we cannot but know, allows us no longer to pretend to ourselves not to know.

"Hands scraping stone," Cantor observes, "is an image that will recur in [Resnais's] *Hiroshima, mon amour*. . . The image must have spoken precisely *to him*, to his sense of himself and his project."[18] Cantor goes on to convey that he "felt almost" about this passage, that in this image Resnais is "defining himself," as an artist, by responding to an image in Rilke's essay, "In Regard to Art."

"The artist is a dancer whose movements are broken by the constraints of his cell. That which finds no expression in his steps and limited swing of his arms comes in exhaustion from his lips, or else he has to scratch the unlived lines of his body into the walls with his wounded fingers." Art, for Rilke, is eros, sensuousness not yet able to be born, blocked by the recalcitrant unreadiness of history. But art, too, built these camps as well as their sensuous representation. Is there art then in the marks the victims' fingers made in *these* walls? Is this the end of art, or its grim mockery, or what defeats it – its hidden residue? Are these markings ugly? beautiful? sublime? Here are the dangers; the unlived lines; the wounded fingers. "...but you have to know."[19]

I, too, "feel almost" that in this passage in *Night and Fog* (and its counterpart in *Hiroshima, mon amour*) Resnais is defining himself as an artist by responding to the passage in Rilke that Cantor quotes. But there is something else, too, I "feel almost" about this image of marks painfully scraped in stone, namely, that Resnais is defining himself specifically as a filmmaker, defining his artistic project as one cut to the particular measure of the medium of film. For in every film image, the subject's "mark" ("the unlived lines of his body") is "scratched," is scratched by the subject's own flesh and blood (his "wounded fingers").

Further, I "feel almost" that in defining himself as an artist in the medium of film, the creator of *Night and Fog* is responding to an image in *Grand Illusion*, Jean Renoir's masterpiece about prisoner camps during the First World War (a film that, along with *The Rules of the Game*, marks Renoir's artistic project as a central source and inspiration for Resnais's own). I am thinking of the passage in which Maréchal, the Jean Gabin character, on the verge of madness from solitary confinement, digs furrows with a spoon into the stone wall of his cell before he makes his hopelessly abortive attempt to escape.

Like *Land without Bread*, *Grand Illusion* was made before the death camps were built, of course. And it is set in a world that was already past when the film was made. In *Grand Illusion*, to "belong" to a prisoner-of-war camp means to be deprived of the company of women, a condition not easy to bear for any character played by Jean Gabin. But in the world of *Grand Illusion*, the prison camp is not a self-contained universe that makes the real world only an image. Inside and outside the camp, in Renoir's film, the present is still the real world. That is why solitary confinement – being cut off from a world whose reality he does not doubt – is a fate worse than death for Maréchal. (In a death camp, solitary confinement is a blessing.)

In Renoir's film, everyone – Frenchman and German alike – has sympathy for Maréchal. No one wishes to deny his humanity. Yet the machinery is already in place to fence such a man off from the world, even to kill him.

Acknowledging that it represents a world already past, *Grand Illusion* represents a moment at which the present is still the real world, but is on its way to becoming only a facade. The image of Maréchal digging marks in the stone, on the verge of madness, is the one sign in Renoir's film – but it only takes one – that the present may be threatened with horrors that are unimagined, unimaginable, in the world of *Grand Illusion*.

In the world of *Night and Fog*, innocent-looking ovens "coped with thousands of bodies per day," the narrator notes, as the camera moves along the row of ovens, finally stops on an oven door. Resnais cuts to a still of a heap of sunglasses as the narrator says, "Nothing is lost. Here are the reserves of the Nazis at war. Here are their stores."

The camera moves along a mound of hair, then tilts up to emphasize the height of the mound. "Women's hair." The camera pans across rolls of cloth. "At fifteen pfennigs the kilo, it's used for making cloth." The oven door opens, revealing to the camera the remains of cremated bodies. "Bones." The camera pans a mountain of bones. "They're intended for manure."

We view men opening an oven door. "Bodies." We view a charred body with a hand heartbreakingly trying to cover what remains of a face. "There's nothing left to say."

We view heads and headless bodies; motion picture footage of a huge vat; two stills of bars of soap. "The bodies were meant for soap."

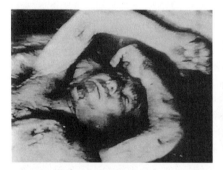

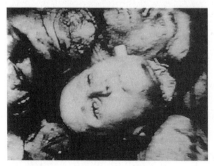

"As for skin. . . ." There is a motion picture shot that pans across pictures painted on human skin.

This last image, however innocent-looking, is so horrifying in its implications that the narrator does not or cannot finish his sentence ("There's nothing left to say").

"The film shows images painted on skin," Cantor writes of this passage. "That is to say: *we watch images of images painted on skin*."[20] If it is an unspeakable horror to use the skin of murdered human beings as a canvas on which to paint images in the name of art, Cantor's use of italics suggests, what makes it less a horror for Resnais to make art out of images of these images-painted-on-skin?

Complementing Cantor's point, we might add that these are no mere representations of images-painted-on-skin that Resnais presents to us. Through the "magic" of photography, we are given to view and contemplate the images-painted-on-skin themselves, as it were, which have "scratched their mark" on these frames. These images of images-painted-on-skin are not painted on skin; film images are not painted at all. In the medium of film, the image *is* the skin, the surface, of the subject. If we may say that film images, symbolically, are "scratched" by their subjects' "bleeding fingers," we may also say that the camera does not paint its subjects; symbolically, it skins them alive. In the face of the camera, there are no horrors. Yet there is something horrific about every film image, not just these images of images-painted-on-skin.

And after this culminating image of images-painted-on-skin, Resnais effects a transition to the last part of his film. "1945," the narrator announces.

The camps are full and spreading. . . . The Nazis may win the war. . . . But they lose. There is no coal for the incinerators. No bread for the men. The camp streets are strewn with corpses. Typhus. When the Allies open the doors, all the doors . . .

We view a series of stills – heartbreaking, grotesque, strangely beautiful – of bodies strewn on the ground; corpses in piles; mounds of severed legs, heads, feet; a woman's dead, sightless eye.

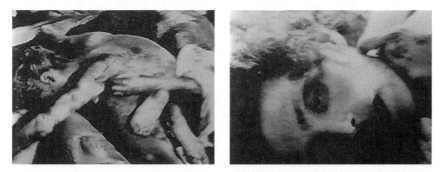

Then we view a series of motion picture images – if anything, even more heartbreaking, grotesque, strangely beautiful – of bodies and body parts being plowed into a ditch, the bulldozers "animating" the lifeless flesh,

causing these corpses to take on a succession of expressive contortions; of uniformed Kapos and officers being led into custody; of Allied soldiers carrying bodies on their backs, tossing them into the ditch, carrying severed heads and adding them to a pile of heads on the ground.

Then there is a still photograph, followed by motion picture footage, of survivors staring blankly across the barbed-wire fence at the camera – in their denial of these subjects' individuality as well as their privacy, these shots are counterparts to the shots of the victims impaled on the barbed wire who died trying to reach the real world in plain view on the other side of the fence – as the narrator speaks the haunting words, "The deportees look on without understanding. Are they free? Will life know them again?"

In this passage, the camera belongs, not to the Nazis who were responsible for building and operating this city of death, but to the Allied soldiers charged with opening the doors (". . . all the doors . . .") of the camp. As we have seen, the camera played an integral role in the murderous operation of the camps. And the camera played an integral role as well in their "liberation" by the Allies. But what is that role? In the face of *this* camera, are these survivors really free? Does life really know them again?

The way these survivors "look on without understanding" at the camera on the other side of the barbed-wire fence is uncannily reminiscent of the way, in *Land without Bread*, the fever sufferers submit in "stolid silence" to the gaze of Buñuel's camera. The camera of the "liberators" – like Buñuel's camera, like the cameras of the Nazis – recognizes no horrors, but also shows no pity. But if *Land without Bread* condemns its "pitiful human wrecks" for not awakening to the reality of their condition, Resnais's film does not condemn these survivors who "look on without understanding." According to the narrator of *Night and Fog*, himself a camp survivor reliving his experience as he speaks, what the survivors do not "understand," specifically, are the answers to two questions: whether they are free, and (in the narrator's peculiar phrase) whether "life" will "know them again" (not "Will they know life again?").

The fact that they cannot answer these questions does not mean that the survivors, like the suffering Hurdanos, are pathetically, horribly, unaware of the reality of their condition. On the contrary, that it is not within their power to answer these questions *is* the reality of their condition. Whether they are free, whether life will know them again, are not questions it is possible for them to answer because these are not questions about them alone, not questions for them alone. They are no less questions about the world, questions for the world. They are questions about, questions for, us. And they are questions about, questions for, the camera.

In *Grand Illusion*, when Maréchal is finally released from solitary confinement, he shows up at the room he is once again to share with his friends. He appears just as the aristocratic de Boeldieu is saying that it is painful for him ("rather embarrassing, in fact"), as it is for the others, that it seems their comrade will not be able to join them in their planned escape.

"But after all it's war, not a matter of sentiment," de Boeldieu says. Then his eyes light up – he is as sentimental as the next man – and Renoir cuts to the doorway through which Maréchal, accompanied by a young German guard, has just entered. Maréchal and the guard step forward, in the direction of the camera, so for a moment they are framed in a tight two shot. The guard studies  Maréchal's face with concern, as we do, for the Frenchman's eyes are fixed in an expressionless stare; he is "looking on without understanding" like the survivors at the concentration camp fence.

Maréchal, too, does not understand whether he is really free, whether life will know him again. And in his case, too, these are questions he cannot answer on his own, because these questions are not about him alone, not  for him alone. Yet in *Grand Illusion* the camera and the world of the film join with Maréchal to provide definitive – and wonderfully satisfying – answers to these questions. First, the camera tactfully pulls back as if to respect his privacy at this difficult moment, but also as if to create room within the frame for Maréchal's friends to join him. And so they do, as the guard nods his permission, or,

rather, his approval. Embraced by his world, acknowledged by the camera, Maréchal is welcomed back to life.

In *Night and Fog*, however, these questions remain unanswered. Within the "fiction" created by Resnais's editing, what the survivors are "looking on without understanding" are the activities of the Allied soldiers, dutifully going about their horrendous work (piling up body parts, plowing corpses into ditches, and so on). Within this "fiction," the survivors are viewing scenes like those we have just viewed, in other words. This sequence casts them as viewers, links them with us, as if our fates were joined. And yet, these shots also remind us, these survivors belonged, as we did not, to the self-contained universe of the camp. Even in these frames, the barbed-wire fence still separates them from the camera, from us.

Of course, what these subjects of the camera are really "looking on without understanding" are the Allied soldiers who are filming them without embracing them, without welcoming them back to life. In using the camera to "document" the status of these subjects as victims of the inhuman Nazis, the "liberators" are denying their privacy and their individuality just as the Nazis did. If in these shots they are still separated from us by the barbed wire fence, the movie screen separates them from us, too. Once they belonged – we did not – to the camp. Now they belong – we do not – to the world on film.

Resnais's film, we have said repeatedly, undertakes to restore the reality of the world of the past – to make this past present, or to acknowledge that it never stopped being present. To restore the reality of the world in which these camps were built and operated, the world in which the real world became present only as an image, means to acknowledge the reality of the fence that made the camp a self-contained universe. It also means to tear that fence down, symbolically, to deny that it is a real barrier. That is the only way to restore the reality of the present, to enable the present to become the real world once again.

And that is why, I take it, Resnais ends this passage – the film's final flashback – the way he does.

First, Resnais cuts from the survivors staring across the fence to film footage of the trials of a Kapo and a Nazi officer. Lending his voice to their words, the narrator says, "I am not responsible. . . I am not responsible. . . " Then Resnais cuts to a still photograph of a man – presumably, he is a survivor of the camps – looking toward the camera, but with his eyes in shadow, as the narrator poses a question we take to be this man's as well as the narrator's own: "Who is responsible, then?" (The shadow covering his eyes does not suggest that the horror he has witnessed has left him unable to see, like the woman with the bloody eye at the climax of the Odessa Steps sequence in Eisenstein's *Potemkin*. It suggests, rather, that in the face of the camera he retains his privacy, keeps his own counsel, is committed to the pursuit of justice. He is blind the way justice is blind. His gaze has the power to pierce facades. His judgment cannot be swayed.)

The passage ends with two unspeakably horrible shots of mutilated bodies that sum up the horror that he – this man, the narrator – has witnessed.

This man is a survivor of the camps, a stand-in for the narrator. But in this privileged frame there is no fence between him and the camera, no sign that he once belonged, as we did not, to the self-contained universe of the camp. He is in our world, and we are in his. Nothing in this frame distinguishes his place from ours, in other words. The only thing that separates us is the utterly contingent fact that he happens to be a subject of the camera at this moment, and we are not. Whether he is free, whether life will know him again, remain unanswered questions about him, unanswered questions for him. This means that they remain unanswered questions about us, unanswered questions for us, as well.

Throughout *Night and Fog*, the fence that made the camp a self-contained universe is identified, symbolically, with the movie screen. By this means, Resnais's film identifies its world – present and past – with its image of the world of the past, with the self-contained universe of the camp, with the "endless fear" that was – is – the "true dimension" of these settings. To acknowledge the presentness of this world of the past is to acknowledge that for us, too, the present is a self-contained universe, not the real world, that the real world is present to us, too, only as an image. Only by acknowledging this can we transform the present from a self-contained universe into the real world once again.

This survivor cannot be free, this passage is saying, life cannot know him again – and *we* cannot be free, life cannot know *us* – unless we acknowledge this past as present, unless we acknowledge that – like the Kapo and the Nazi officer – this man belongs to our world, that we belong to his, unless we acknowledge the world of the film as our world. And to do this means at once to acknowledge the movie screen that separates us from him, and to stop pretending that this screen is a real barrier.

What this passage is saying – what all of *Night and Fog* is saying – is that the Kapo and the officer are responsible – as this victim is not, as we are not – for building and operating these cities of death, for the "endless fear" that was their "true dimension." But responsibility for liberating the camps – condemning the executioners, laying the dead to rest, welcoming the survivors into our midst, freeing ourselves and our world – is in our hands, the hands of all us survivors.

And so Resnais's film returns us, for the last time, to the present. The camera glides along the ground, overgrown with weeds, to a stagnant pond as the narrator intones, "As I speak to you now, the icy water of the ponds and ruins lies in the hollows of the charnel-house. A water as sluggish as our own bad memories. War nods, but has one eye open." The camera now moves across a field of grass, the movement continuing across the cut. "Faithful as ever, the grass flourishes on the muster ground round the blocks. An abandoned village, still heavy with threats." The camera passes the remains of a furnace. "The furnace is no longer in use."

"The skill of the Nazis is child's play today," the narrator goes on, alluding to the awesome fact that one thermonuclear bomb can incinerate millions of human beings in a flash. "Nine million dead haunt this landscape."

And then the narrator, like the old woman at the end of *Land without Bread*, speaks a warning to those who may be listening. "Who is on the lookout," he asks, "to warn us of our new executioners' arrival? Are their faces really different from ours? Somewhere in our midst lucky Kapos survive, reinstated officers and anonymous informers."

On these words, the camera begins pulling out, reprising its movement from the film's opening. "There are those reluctant to believe, or believing from time to time. There are those who look at these ruins today as though the monster were dead and buried beneath them. Those who take hope again as the image fades, as though there were a cure for the scourge of these camps. Those who pretend all this happened only once . . ." The camera abruptly stops. ". . . At a certain time and in a certain place. Those who refuse to look around them, deaf to the endless cry." The music cadences and ends, and the narrator, too, falls silent – this is the only time in the film that there is complete silence. Finally, our view of the present gives way to a blank screen – not blackness but blinding whiteness (an invocation of the nuclear apocalypse that now threatens to come without warning?). And this is the way Resnais's film ends.

The ending of *Land without Bread* is strikingly akin to the ending of *Nanook of the North*, as we observed. And the ending of *Night and Fog* even more strikingly echoes the last moments of Buñuel's film, especially in the original Spanish version, in which the narrator falls silent (for the only time in the film) and we hear the voice of the old woman crying out her warning ("Awake, awake, lest the Angel of Death steal upon you unawares! Awaken and say an 'Ave Maria' that his soul may rest in peace!").

In *Land without Bread*, the narrator's silence is an acknowledgment – the narrator's? Buñuel's? – of his commonality with this Nietzschean herald warning those who are listening to awaken to the horror of their existence. And the silence of Buñuel's narrator is also an acknowledgment – the narrator's? Buñuel's? – of his commonality with the Hurdanos in their homes, who may be listening but who also may be sleeping, heedless of the warning.

Resnais's narrator warns us not to be "deaf to the endless cry" that is all around us (and within us). The silence with which *Night and Fog* ends may be understood as invoking this deafness, as if to acknowledge the possibility that even viewers of this film may remain "deaf to the endless cry." But this silence may also be understood as creating the condition most conducive for us to hear the cry, or to stop pretending we do not hear it. The "endless cry" is also to be heard within the silence.

As we began this chapter by observing, *Night and Fog*, like *Land without Bread*, is an allegorical journey into the heart of a region – at once geographical and spiritual – where unspeakable horror is to be discovered. Both films end with an appeal to acknowledge the horror. In *Land without Bread*, the horror is the unawareness of the Hurdanos, which is our unawareness, too. In *Night and Fog*, neither those who built and operated the camps nor the victims who died there were unaware of the "endless fear" that was – is – the "true dimension" of these cities of death. If we fail to look around us – fail to punish the guilty, fail to free the survivors, fail to lay the dead to rest, fail to recognize the executioners and victims that are everywhere in our world, fail to recognize the executioners and victims that we, ourselves, are – that does not mean we are unaware of the horror, that our unawareness is the horror. It means we are masters of the art of pretending not to know what we cannot help knowing. If we remain deaf to the "endless cry," it means we are pretending not to hear.

■

Readers of *Hitchcock – The Murderous Gaze* and *The "I" of the Camera* may recognize that it is a recurring idea in my writing that a number of the greatest and most influential films that have ever been made have meditated on the mysterious barrier-that-is-no-real-barrier of the movie screen, and that their meditations have led them to envision this "barrier" as magically transcended or transgressed, as *Night and Fog* does in its privileged vision of the death-camp survivor no longer separated from us by the fence that made the camp a self-contained universe. (Evidently, this is an idea that speaks precisely to me, is as definitive for my sense of myself and my project as is the image of "hands scraping stone" for Resnais.)

In the ending of D. W. Griffith's *True Heart Susie*, for example, as I characterized it in *The "I" of the Camera*, "When William appears before Susie as a ghostly apparition and then enters the frame in the flesh, it is as if a dead man comes to life before her eyes, a shadow assumes substance. It is also as if William steps into, or out of, the world of a film, crossing the 'barrier' of the screen."[21] This ending anticipates the ending of Chaplin's *City*

Lights, which provided deep inspiration to films such as *It Happened One Night* and *Stella Dallas* and through them the genres of romantic comedy and melodrama central to the "classical" American cinema of the thirties and forties.

When the Little Tramp finally finds himself face-to-face with the woman he loves, her sight now restored, the glass window of the flower store, which had served as a symbolic stand-in for the movie screen, no longer separates them. Chaplin calls upon us to imagine that he has stepped out of the world of the film and into our presence, that no "window," no screen, separates us. To follow this shot with the woman's reaction would be to speak for her on the subject of what is in her heart about him. Chaplin refrains from doing this because he cannot say what the camera reveals about him, whether he is worthy of this woman's love – or ours. (Chaplin is the Little Tramp, but the Tramp is a mask as well. Chaplin is also the director in control. And even the Tramp is not as innocent as he seems. Chaplin's films come to dwell more and more on this split in his self. Hence *The Great Dictator*, in which Chaplin plays two roles, a Tramp-like Jewish barber and Adolf Hitler himself.) Showing the woman's reaction would also be to cue us as to what we are to feel. Chaplin chooses, rather, to allow us no way to know the woman's feeling, or our own, other than by imagining how we would feel in her place. That is, in the same gesture by which he calls upon us to imagine that he has stepped out of the world of the film, Chaplin also calls upon us to imagine that we find ourselves within his world, not outside and safely fenced off from it. By calling upon us to imagine that the movie screen is a real barrier that has magically been breached, Chaplin steps forward without his mask, and calls upon us to acknowledge him – and love him.

In *The River*, Jean Renoir takes up and literalizes the fantasy (which goes back to Griffith and Chaplin and to Renoir's own earlier work) that the movie screen is a barrier that has magically been breached. And, as I wrote in *The "I" of the Camera*, "it broadens that fantasy into an all-encompassing metaphysical vision – a vision that is indigenous to India, but which has always been at the heart of Renoir's own world-view. 'Reality' is illusion, 'illusion' is real, and to suppose otherwise is 'the grand illusion.'"[22]

Like *True Heart Susie*, *The River* begins with a claim that its story "really happened." But

. . .in *The River*'s meditation, as in classical Indian philosophy, what "really happens" cannot be separated from what is dreamed, fantasized, remembered, acted on stage, or, for that matter, projected on a movie screen. "Reality" itself is theater, a spectacle through which alone the truth reveals itself to human beings, a spectacle whose creator and audience are, ultimately, one, even as they are separated by a boundary. The boundary between imagination and reality, like the boundary between India and the West, is itself a creation of the human imagination. Paradoxically, this means that nothing is or could be more real to human beings.[23]

Chaplin understands film to be a medium whose conditions must be overcome or transcended if he is to fulfill his desperate longing for acknowledgment and love. This is not Renoir's understanding. For Renoir, the way the real world appears on the movie screen is exemplary of the conditions under which alone reality can ever appear to us. For Renoir, "so-called reality," as it is dubbed in *The Golden Coach*, is neither more nor less real, neither more nor less unreal, than the world on film. And it is at once the reality and the unreality of the real world – the fact that nature itself is spectacle, is theater, is a creation of the human imagination; and the fact that imagination, art itself, is natural for human creatures like us – that *The River* undertakes to acknowledge – and to embrace. In *The River*, film is the medium in which Renoir gives his consent to these conditions. At the same time, the medium of film stands in for the conditions he consents to.

However Resnais may respect and admire Renoir's achievement as a filmmaker, the creator of *Night and Fog* cannot bring himself to consent to these conditions. In the self-contained universe of the death camp, the real world *is* only spectacle, only theater, only art. If *Night and Fog* is no different from a death camp, it completely fails in its undertaking. Resnais's project is not to consent to the world that built and operated the death camps, the world that still denies their "true dimension." Resnais's project is not simply to "document" but to transform the world of the past, to restore its reality. And he undertakes this project in order that the present, too, may be transformed, may be made worthy of consent. Death camps, too, are "creations of the human imagination." To restore their reality is to acknowledge that art no longer "naturally" reveals the truth; art lies, and art kills. To make the present the real world, art has to be overcome. Overcoming art is the new end for art.

Night and Fog acknowledges the reality of the fence that made the camp a self-contained universe, and tears that fence down, symbolically. Resnais's film takes upon itself the task of creating these cities of death all over again. It also takes upon itself the task of opening the doors (". . .all the doors. . . "). Resnais understands that the liberation of the camps is not something his film can simply "document." In the world of the past, the doors of the camp were opened. But the reality of this past stands in need of being restored. Otherwise, the opening of the doors is only an image, a mere facade. Symbolically, *Night and Fog* calls upon us to participate in liberating the camps, liberating the world that built and operated them, by acknowledging the movie screen that makes the world on film appear a self-contained universe, and by tearing that fence down, no longer pretending there is a real barrier separating us from the world on film. Overcoming the art of film is the new end for the art of film.

"Part of *Psycho*'s myth," I wrote in *Hitchcock – The Murderous Gaze*, "is that there is no world outside its own, that we are fated to be born, live our alienated lives, and die in the very world in which Norman Bates also dwells."[24] When we first view Norman/mother, wrapped in a blanket, the bottom of the frame is masked (this is, after all, the point of view of the disgusted guard looking into the prison cell through the peephole in the door). Hitchcock cuts away to the fly on Norman's/mother's hand, then back to what might seem to be a reprise of the previous setup. However, the mask at the bottom of the frame is now gone. We are now inside the cell, in the presence of Norman/mother, not separated from this being by a window, a screen. Symbolically, the "barrier" of the movie screen has been breached.

The famous shower murder sequence, too, envisions the breaching of the "barrier" of the movie screen. When the frame-within-the-frame of the shower curtain comes to engulf the frame, it is as if nothing separates this curtain from the screen on which this view is projected. In this shower curtain, the camera's gesture declares, our world and the world of *Psycho* magically come together. Or this gesture declares that there has never been a real barrier separating them. Thus when Marion Crane's killer theatrically pulls the shower curtain open, it is as if the torn curtain reveals that we – like Marion, like the wide-eyed victims who died attempting to climb over the concentration camp fence – are confronting the imminent prospect of our own murder.

To view the world on film as a "private island" (to use Marion's term) wherein we can escape the real conditions of our existence is to make the world on film a self-contained universe. This is to make the real world – the world into which we have been born, the world in which we are fated to die – only an image, not the real world at all. It is to be condemned to a condition of death-in-life, as if we, too, were shadows on a screen, not human beings of flesh and blood.

Psycho is an allegory about the death of the art of film as Hitchcock has known and mastered it – the art of creating self-contained universes on film, "private islands," to which viewers can imagine themselves escaping from the real conditions of their existence. "Marion Crane's dead eye and Norman/mother's final grin prophesy the end of the era of film whose achievement *Psycho* also sums up, and the death of the Hitchcock film," I wrote in *Hitchcock – The Murderous Gaze*. "In *Psycho*, Hitchcock's camera singles out a human subject *as if for the last time*, then presides over her murder. Marion Crane's death in the shower, mythically, is also our death – the death of the movie viewer – and Hitchcock's death."[25]

When Chaplin steps forward in the final frames of *City Lights*, this human being of flesh and blood stops pretending that his desperate longing for love can be fulfilled within the world of the film, stops pretending that the world on film is a self-contained universe, stops pretending that he is separated from us, that his world is separated from our world, by a real barrier.

In *Psycho*, Hitchcock, too, steps forward. His desperate longing to make connection with the world moves him, too, to envision, in the medium of film, that the movie screen "barrier" has magically been breached. Unlike

Chaplin, but like Norman Bates, Hitchcock envisions no possibility of liberation. For Chaplin, the breaching of the "barrier" means the possibility of freedom, the promise that life may know him again. In *Psycho*, it means death. That is, it changes nothing, for we are already fated to die. In Hitchcock's dark vision, we *are* condemned to a condition of death-in-life. We are born and die in our "private traps," as Norman puts it. We scratch and claw, but never budge an inch.

Viewed from the perspective of *Night and Fog*, *Psycho* offers a precise diagnosis of the horror of our present condition, the horror of the unhinging of the present from the real world. But Hitchcock's film, scratched and clawed from within its author's "private trap," is also profoundly symptomatic of the present horror. Hitchcock is not a "special case"; he is representative. In Resnais's understanding, as in Hitchcock's, we *are* all clamped in our "private traps," unable to free ourselves for all we scratch and claw.

Unlike *Psycho*, however, Resnais's film undertakes, at least symbolically, to liberate us and our world. But from what "place" is it possible for Resnais to discover a way to freedom? And how has it been possible for Resnais to have arrived at this place? In *Psycho*, the author's "self" – his sense of himself as a human being, as a filmmaker, which also means his sense of the "private trap" he is desperate to escape – is endlessly present; it is trapped within every shot, every gesture of the camera. Where, in *Night and Fog*, is Resnais's "self" to be located? Where does it locate itself?

The narrator, reliving his own experience as he speaks, clearly locates himself in the world of the past. For the reality of the world of the past to be restored is for life to know him again, for him to be freed from his "private trap." But in *Night and Fog*, Resnais does not speak in his own voice, the way the narrator does. Nor does he reveal himself through the camera, the way Hitchcock does. In *Night and Fog*, the camera most often belongs to the Nazis, sometimes to the "liberators," only occasionally to Resnais himself. True, there is footage taken by Resnais's camera, not simply "found" by him. Yet in these shots the world appears unpeopled, devoid even of signs that human beings still walk the face of the earth. (This is the way the world appears in *Psycho* in the immediate aftermath of the shower murder sequence.) Again, where are we to discover Resnais, where is Resnais to discover himself, in this "peaceful landscape"?

To discover in the frames of *Night and Fog* a tangible sign of Resnais's "self" is a problem of the same kind, and the same magnitude, as the problem Resnais's camera encounters in discovering, in the present, a tangible sign of the "true dimension" of the world of the past.

As we have seen, Jay Cantor discovers a sign of Resnais's "self" – perhaps the only one in the film, but it only takes one – in the image Cantor calls "hand scraping stone," the eloquent shot in which the camera tracks the length of the ceiling scratched and clawed by the fingernails of victims who knew this "shower" was only a facade, who knew they were being murdered, that their dream of dying their own death was being denied.

And in these telltale marks scratched and clawed in the stone as if by the artist's bleeding fingers, the camera, in the present, also discovers a tangible sign – perhaps the only one it discovers, but, again, it only takes one – of the "true dimension" of the "world of the past."

In these marks in the medium of stone – and in the marks of these marks in the medium of film – the "world of the past" is tangible, is present to Resnais's camera. In these marks – and in the marks of these marks – the past is present, is present *as* past, which is the only way the past can be present in the real world. And in these marks in the medium of stone – and in the marks of these marks in the medium of film – the reality of the world of the past is restored. The present becomes the real world again, is no longer a mere image.

But, again, as the narrator puts it, "You have to know." You have to know what *Night and Fog* enables us to know, makes it impossible for us not to know, impossible to keep pretending to ourselves that we do not know.

CHAPTER IV

Chronicle of a Summer

The one thing which we seek with insatiable desire is to forget ourselves, to be surprised out of our propriety, to lose our sempiternal memory, and to do something without knowing how or why; in short, to draw a new circle. Nothing great was ever achieved without enthusiasm. The way of life is wonderful; it is by abandonment.

– Ralph Waldo Emerson, "Circles"

I.

In the concluding sequence of *Chronicle of a Summer*, the pioneering experiment in "cinéma-vérité" they filmed in 1960 and released the following year, Jean Rouch and Edgar Morin walk the corridors of the *Musée de l'Homme* in Paris conducting a postmortem of the event that has just taken place. They have screened rough-cut sequences from their work-in-progress to the ordinary men and women of various walks of life who are in it, whose everyday lives are what the film is about, and presided over a discussion, at times heated, of the film's strengths and weaknesses.

A chagrined Morin sums this discussion up by saying, "They either criticized our characters as not being true to life or else they found them too true." That is, they complained that the people in the film came across as actors who masked their true selves, or else as exhibitionists who stripped their souls bare to the point of indecency. Morin laments the audience's unwillingness or inability to recognize sincerity when it is, as he puts it, "a bit more than life-size." As for himself, he declares himself certain that the people in the film were not acting, and that there is nothing indecent about the way they behaved in the presence of the camera.

Rouch points out that people do not always know whether they are acting. He cites Marceline, who plays a central role in the film. In the discussion following the screening, she maintained that she was acting when she strolled through the Place de la Concorde, followed at a distance by the hand-held camera, and, in a monologue to her dead father, mused about the day the Nazis rounded up the Jews in her neighborhood and she and her family were separated.

No matter what she may think, Marceline did not act this scene, Rouch argues. By this he means that she was not merely pretending to be speaking to her dead father, but was really addressing him, and that when she spoke in her childhood voice her present self was abandoned to the past, possessed by it. When Morin adds "Or if she did [act that scene], it was her most authentic side," Rouch accepts this point, for all its apparent ambiguity (is her "most authentic side" the role she was playing, or is it the actress capable of making that role her own?).

In an interview some years after the making of *Chronicle of a Summer*, Rouch reaffirmed his conviction that film has the power "to reveal, with doubts, a fictional part of all of us, which for me is the most real part of an individual."[26] The camera is capable of provoking people to reveal aspects of themselves that are fictional, to reveal themselves as the creatures of imagination, fantasy, and myth they are: This is a touchstone of the practice Rouch calls "cinéma-vérité."

In Rouch's view, *Chronicle* is not simply a documentary, because the people in the film are provoked to manifest fictional parts of themselves. And it is not simply a fiction film, because the fictions it reveals are real. Yet a fiction is also a lie. As Rouch remarks about the film in the same interview,

There is a whole series of intermediaries and these are lying intermediaries. We contract time, we extend it, we choose an angle for the shot, we deform the people we're shooting, we speed things up and follow one movement to the detriment of another movement. So there is a whole work of lies. But, for me and Edgar Morin at the time we made that film, this lie was more real than the truth.

There is a brief passage toward the end of *Chronicle* that I view as an explicit declaration of the film's practice of revealing reality by "lying." It occurs during the group discussion following the screening.

This whole section of *Chronicle* is initiated by a transition, magical in effect, from a family at a picnic spontaneously singing a folk song – the film's privileged celebration of community – to a blinding projector beam piercing a swirling haze of cigarette smoke (this is Paris, after all). The

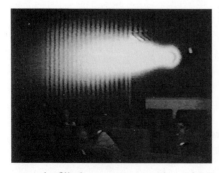

haunting singing continues over this shot transition, linking the beam of light onscreen with the projector beam now carrying this image to our gaze. (Within the film's prevailing fiction, these two beams, these two moments, past and present, are one.)

The voices fall silent, the beam is extinguished (the projected beam, not the projecting one), the house lights go on, the camera tilts down to frame a sparsely filled screening room, and Morin, in the front, turns to face the audience, a big bear of a man ready to take charge. But it is Rouch's voice, gentle and rueful, that breaks the silence, acknowledging that the vision of community the film enabled the audience to share – and to share with us – has vanished. "Now that you've seen yourself on the screen," he says, "Edgar and I want your views. First the children. Did you like what you saw?"

A little girl – one of Morin's daughters – gives a truthful – and true – answer that lightens the mood and provokes general laughter: "Charlie Chaplin is better."

At this relaxed moment, there is a cut to three people in the audience: Jean-Pierre, Marceline, and Marilou.

Jean-Pierre, much younger than Marceline, is a philosophy student who has been her lover, although they seem to have broken off their affair or come to the recognition that they should, because they cannot make each other happy.

Marilou is a dramatically beautiful, or at least beautifully dramatic, Italian woman who has been living in Paris for some time. When Morin first interviewed her, she revealed herself to be lonely and depressed. But when he interviewed her again later in the film, he found her miraculously transformed. Then she announced – to Morin? to the camera? – that she had found love, had made the connection with reality that had so long eluded her. As she made this announcement, her hand, anxiously caressing the charm around her neck, and her proud yet trembling smile testified to the reality of her happiness and to its fragility, her awareness that happiness can be lost as mysteriously as it is found.

The transfiguring power of love is a mystery movies ordinarily make no claim to resolve. But in *Chronicle of a Summer* there is also a mystery of a lesser kind, a kind movies ordinarily do resolve, namely, Who is Marilou's new lover? (Late in the film, there are two shots in which we view the couple holding hands, but not the man's face. Why is his identity not revealed?)

But back to the moment in question.

Within this frame, Marilou passes a cigarette case to Jean-Pierre as Marceline looks on, uneasy. Offscreen, Morin asks, "What was your impression?" His daughter replies, "You tell me," at once besting her father and inviting him to assert his authority.

By now, we know Morin well enough to realize that this is an invitation he will ungrudgingly accept. He does, saying "Some say it's not true; others, it is," and thereby setting the agenda for the discussion. But immediately following this line, there is a medium close-up of Marilou. She is languidly leaning back in her seat, her gaze directed to someone offscreen.

There is a cut to Jean-Pierre. According to the conventions of "classical" editing, which *Chronicle* follows almost as consistently as any Hollywood movie, his eyeline confirms that Marilou is staring at *him*, and that he is meeting her unflinching gaze. Marceline, sitting beside him, seems disturbed by this silent exchange. As if trying to distract herself from a disagreeable thought, she lights a cigarette, even as we hear a woman say, "What's not true? Cameras can't lie."

Read in accordance with classical conventions, this series of shots implies that there is hanky-panky going on between Jean-Pierre and Marilou, at least that Marceline imagines this. But by conspicuously synchronizing the series of shots with the words "Cameras can't lie" (an effect of simultaneity created in the editing room, it might be noted), *Chronicle* brackets this ostensible assertion, suggests that it may be a "lie." Movies do not reveal reality by acquainting us with the literal truth, this series of shots reminds us, but by awakening us to worlds of possibilities. Nothing revealed to or by the camera in any of these shots "documents" that a tense scene of romantic intrigue was really taking place here. It is the way they are edited together, and the context in which they are placed, that create this (probable) "lie." And it is the way they are edited together, and the context in which they are placed, that accord them the status I attribute to them, that of a revelation that the traditional conventions of editing on which *Chronicle* relies are capable of lying, perhaps incapable of not lying. The sequence reveals this the old-fashioned way, by lying.

A good place to turn in reflecting on what Rouch understands to be *Chronicle*'s practice of telling the truth by lying is the powerful passage – it immediately precedes her walk through the Place de la Concorde – in which, in Jean-Pierre's embarrassed presence, Marceline confesses that she feels responsible for the painful failure of their relationship. Before turning to this sequence, however, we will examine the passage immediately preceding it, the first of Morin's two interviews with Marilou.

Marilou

Marilou, not previously introduced to us, walks through a corridor into the foreground, the lighting and composition and echo of footsteps all expressing a sense of isolation. The camera twists as Marilou turns the corner, walks into the depths of the frame, then disappears around another corner into a blinding pool of light. In a series of shots, we view Marilou descending the stairs, walking in the street, typing in her office. She pulls a page from a typewriter, sits at a table, begins writing. Morin's offscreen voice says, "Marilou..." There is a cut to a nearly frontal medium close-up of her, as his voice goes on, "...You're twenty-seven, an Italian living in Paris..."

Synchronized with Morin's words, but seemingly not in direct response to them, Marilou looks up. Her face backlit, her eyes lustrous, she seems not so much viewing something as absorbed in a reverie. Her self-absorption is underscored by a continuity cut to an extreme close-up in which she is gazing in the same direction, her head still in the clouds, as it were. In a Hollywood movie, such a shot – a study in rapt absorption – might well be used to nominate her as a woman with whom we are to fall in love. Within this close-up, Marilou looks down, troubled, as if Morin's words (". . . These three years are in total contrast. . . ") were finally impinging on her reverie.

The cut between these two shots – like every shot transition in the sequence – gives the impression that there is no interval between the end of the first and the beginning of the second. In giving this impression, the film "lies." (Only one camera was used; every cut elides a stretch of time.)

There is a cut to Morin, who looks exceptionally unromantic. That he appears to be reading from notes, or is in any case looking down at the table, averting his gaze from Marilou, makes his delivery seem all the more ponderous (". . . To your life in Cremona in a middle-class home. Here you live in a maid's room. You're a foreigner. . . "). As Morin's voice continues offscreen (". . . You know men. . . "), there is a cut to Marilou.

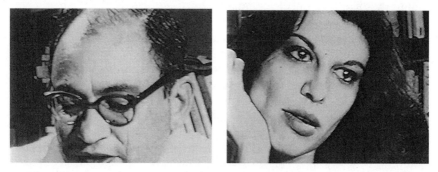

Thus is initiated a series of alternations between these two matched setups. In the shots making up this series, the camera is on a tripod; there is no camera movement. The compositions of these static frames, as well as

73

the pattern of editing, emulate the form of the classical shot/reverse shot dialogue sequence. The alternations respect the "180 degree" rule, for example. The shots of Morin, which locate Marilou offscreen to the left, are alternated with shots of Marilou in which we understand Morin to be located offscreen to the right. Screen direction is preserved: Marilou is always screen left; Morin is always screen right. We always know the direction she needs to look in order to look at him, and vice versa. Thus the sequence is able to make us aware that Marilou is looking away from Morin (except on the occasions she punctuates her words by looking right at him), and that he is looking away from her (also except for specific occasions).

In a conventional shot/reverse shot dialogue, the prevailing fiction is that no camera is present. In the sequence we are considering, we understand the camera to be a real presence, if one invisible within the frame. We understand these shots to be documenting not only an encounter between Marilou and Morin, but also an encounter between Marilou and the camera, whose invisible presence represents not only Rouch (who was really present), but also viewers like us (who were – are – absent). By emulating the shot/reverse shot form within a "documentary" mode, the sequence makes us aware that Marilou is not only avoiding eye contact with Morin, but is also averting her gaze from the camera.

Indeed, the two "romantic" shots of Marilou looking offscreen precede the first shot of Morin, who to that point is manifest only as a disembodied voice. The camera stakes out its spatial relation to Marilou prior to locating Morin; we are aware that Marilou is averting her gaze from the camera *before* we become aware that she is averting her gaze from him. Not until Marilou looks down, apparently reacting to Morin's words, is there a visible indication that they are in the same space. Even at that moment, we do not know where he is located in relation to her; visually, she is relating to the camera, not to him.

In this medium close-up, Marilou's eyes are closed and her face bears an enigmatic smile. By withholding her gaze from Morin, she is acknowledging that she is, indeed, a woman who "knows men," who has what Morin refers to as "affairs." This acknowledgment is not addressed to Morin, who is not even looking at her, but to the camera, which is. She is acknowledging to the camera that she is withholding her gaze from Morin, and it is by withholding her gaze from the camera, too, that she performs this acknowledgment. By not looking at the camera, she acknowledges that she is the object of its gaze. She is presenting herself to the camera as an object to be gazed upon. Paradoxically, in thus presenting herself, she is revealed by the camera, reveals herself to the camera, as an active subject after all. She is not a mere object; she is a human being whose individuality and privacy call for acknowledgment.

For the first time, Marilou speaks for herself, rather than letting Morin speak for her. Her eyes downcast, she begins, ". . . My maid's room has had its uses. There was no heating. I'd never been cold or gone without. It was a sop to my conscience. . ." She opens her eyes and looks at Morin, as if to imply that submitting to this interview is a "sop to her conscience," too. ". . .I was glad to have a hard time. It was the first time I'd ever worked. I'd wake up at seven, exhausted, almost glad of the rush hour crowd. . ." She gestures sweepingly with her hand (she is Italian, after all). ". . .I think I really felt I belonged. But. . .that didn't last. . ." Again she looks up, this time in the general direction of the camera, but without addressing it; it is as if the camera were not there. (As emerged in our discussion of *Nanook of the North*, denying the camera's presence can be a way of acknowledging its presence.) ". . .Now I'm sick of my room and the cold. . .I find human contact. . .I dislike it. . .It's pointless."

Marilou has been speaking very deliberately. Having said that she has come to "dislike" human contact, to find it "pointless," she stops speaking. Having had her say, her face expresses distaste (for what she has said? for herself for saying it? for Morin? for the situation? for the whole nauseating human condition?). Her silence creates a mood that threatens – or promises – to terminate the conversation.

When Morin asks his next question, we hear his voice even before the cut to him. This sound overlap, created in the editing room, conveys the impression that he feels a sense of urgency, that he is anxious to disrupt this mood – anxious to deny that he feels drawn to it, perhaps – before it engulfs the entire scene. "But you've some aim. . .a hope?" he asks, evidently torn between wanting to convince this woman that she is not a hopeless case and wanting to observe in fascination a woman utterly devoid of hope, beyond rescue.

"To be honest, I don't know. . .," Marilou answers, looking directly at Morin, smoke curling from her ciga-rette as if she were Dietrich in a von Sternberg film. Her gaze momentarily locks with the camera's – at this moment, she shows no expression – before it again seeks Morin out.

". . .When I first came here I felt stranded. . .," Marilou goes on. ". . .I was shut up in myself, isolated. When I was in Italy. . ." Her voice has become rhythmic, and she has begun bobbing her head, leaning her whole body forward and backward, in rhythm to her words, as her eyes lower and half close. ". . .I'd exhausted my inner resources. I wanted to come up against reality. . ."

Flicking her cigarette against the ashtray below the frame line, she lowers her gaze before she looks back in Morin's general direction. ". . .I wonder if this was the right way. For example, I drink, you see. . ." Finally, on her words ". . .I wanted to get rid of alibis when I came to France. . .," her eyes lock with Morin's. She gives a trace of a smile. ". . .I wanted to live on my own terms. I've destroyed the false reasoning, only to find it again in drink, men. To put it baldly, in trash. . ." She clears her throat, raises her eyebrows, purses her lips as if to speak – but no sound comes out. This time, Marilou is not silent because she has had her say, but because she is unable or unwilling to go on. The anguish in her silence is marked by a cut

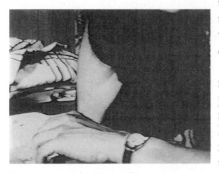

to her hand, tapping anxiously on the table. Again, it is Morin's offscreen voice that breaks the silence. "What do you mean by reality?"

The cut to Marilou's hand – the first break with the shot/reverse shot pattern – masks an ellipsis. This is made clear by the transcription published the year after *Chronicle* was released, which includes exchanges that were deleted from the film at a late stage of editing.[27] In a passage that was deleted, Morin breaks the silence not by asking what she means by reality, but by reminding her that there are people who care about her (Morin, for one?), hence that if she feels isolated she must be denying reality.[28] Marilou in turn explains to Morin that it is not enough for her to *know* she is in the world with others, but that she needs "in a given situation" – the present one, for example? – to "feel like I am in the real world, whereas I constantly feel like I am in the imaginary."

In any case, Morin's "What do you mean by reality?" occasions a new setup. He is in the foreground, staring into the frame at Marilou, who is leaning forward, intently listening (". . .Is it a job that interests you? Doing what you like? Or is it to live with a man you love, not have affairs?").

This cut marks a definitive break with the shot/reverse shot pattern. No longer is there an alternation between "his" and "her" frames; there is only this one setup. And within this frame, Morin is no longer averting his gaze from Marilou, but is staring at her. The framing so favors Marilou that the transcription refers to it as "a close-up of Marilou from Morin's profile point of view."[29] But it is crucial to the expressive effect that he is not in profile, that he is looking into the frame, much as the camera is; he is an object to the camera, but is also viewing what it is viewing. This setup links Morin with the camera (with Rouch, with us), even as it emphasizes their separateness (Morin is visible, the camera is not). He is turned away enough so that we cannot see whatever reaction he may be expressing, so our impression is that he is impassively taking everything in. In this frame, we might say, Morin becomes the camera's stand-in. Or its scapegoat.

"I want a job that doesn't scare me . . .," Marilou begins. Meeting the camera's gaze for an instant, she glances toward Morin, then, looking back down, says with a shrug, " . . . To live with someone for an hour. Two hours, a month, two weeks even. Just to be with him . . ." As she describes the relationship she dreams of having, she looks right into his eyes for a moment, as if citing their present encounter as an example of the relationships she is stuck with, which fail to make her feel connected with reality. It is as if her eyes are saying, not to Morin but to the camera, "I know this man feels connected with me, but to me this connection feels imaginary, not real."

Again looking down, Marilou adds, " . . . Without any ghosts to stop me loving him . . .," almost bangs on the table for emphasis, and, with a trace of a smile, levels the camera with her gaze.

This is not the first time Marilou has looked at the camera, but it is the first time she acknowledges that it is a deliberate gesture on her part. Looking at the camera at this moment bears directly on her case (a case she is making to the camera, not to Morin). It identifies the camera as a "ghost" that even now is keeping her from loving, from living, from feeling connected with reality, from being real. Almost immediately, Marilou looks down and resumes speaking, but she has made her point. Morin has failed to make her feel connected with reality. And the camera at once witnesses this failure and is implicated in it.

Visibly agitated, Marilou goes on. " . . . To get outside myself. To die even, provided I'm in touch with something . . ." In a state of great anxiety, she meets the camera's gaze, but again only for a moment. Her anxiety reveals that even now she does not feel she is "in touch with something," that the camera represents to her something imaginary, not something real.

For the first time, Marilou's voice breaks as she adds, " . . . instead of being forced back on myself. I've not even the right to kill myself. It would be an act . . ." She searches Morin's gaze, then lowers her eyes. She opens her lips as if to speak, closes her mouth, opens it again, this time as if gasping for breath. As if speaking now seems not only difficult but pointless (what is left to say?), she bites her lip and chokes back tears. As if enacting a fantasy of dying her

own death, or imagining she had never been born, she tilts her head, rests it on the table, slowly shuts her eyes, and seems to drift into a trance.

This time letting the mood cast by her silence sink in, Morin waits a long moment before he finally asks, in a melodramatic hush, "Why are you forced back on yourself?" Taken aback, she says, "What?" Her tone is petulant, even contemptuous, as if astonished that this man cannot recognize that pulling her out of her fantasy only to ask such a question *is* the kind of thing that forces her back on herself.

Yet when Morin repeats his question, Marilou answers, "If only I knew," her smile suggesting that she does know, but is not telling. Breathing in deeply, she allows herself to be engulfed by her silence. (What she knows, she will not try to explain to this man. What she wishes to know, she cannot learn from him.) Forgoing further questions, Morin views her in silence.

The published transcription describes Marilou here as "silent again, edgy, anguished."[30] But this does not acknowledge the ecstatic aspect of the moment. It does not acknowledge the anticipation of pleasure expressed by her secret smile, nor the pleasure she is evidently taking now in offering herself unresistingly to be viewed. It denies the pleasure she is taking in being transformed, in transforming herself, from an anguished subject into an object to be gazed upon, a mere image. And it denies the pleasure to be taken in viewing this image.

To speak of this as a moment Marilou is "forced back on herself," as I wish to do, suggests that in her trancelike state she imagines herself as having no audience for which she feels she now has to perform. To speak of her as "offering herself to be viewed," as I also wish to do, suggests, apparently to the contrary, that she imagines herself as having an audience. Is her imaginary audience, the camera, one for which she does not have to perform, to act, in order to satisfy?

It may strike us throughout this scene, and never more than at this moment, that Marilou is being theatrical, that she is playing the role – she is certainly costumed and made up for it – of a woman in the throes of Sartrean nausea who longs for a connection to reality uncorrupted by role playing. The deep point is that it is not possible to be such a woman without playing such a woman. And in the kind of film *Chronicle* aspires to be, it is not possible to play such a woman without being such a woman.

When Marilou presents herself to the camera as an image to be viewed, she turns her face into a mask. This is an act, a "lie" – a denial that she really is a subject, that she has, that she is, a self. It culminates a series of moments in which she acknowledges the camera by withholding her gaze. By presenting herself as an object, she reveals herself to the camera, is revealed by the camera, as a subject (it takes a self to act, it takes a self to mask itself). In playing this part, she is "telling the truth by lying."

In presenting Marilou as an object, the camera reveals itself to be implicated in her self-denial, her "lie." In revealing her to be forced back on herself, the camera reveals itself to be *forcing* her back on herself. The camera is "telling the truth by lying," too, for it reveals that to Marilou it is not something in the real world, something outside her self, but something in the "imaginary." We may say that in forcing her back on herself, the camera, or Rouch behind the camera, is forced back on her, possessed by her face-turned-mask. We may also say that she is possessed by the camera, but that is another way of saying that in its presence she feels alone, that what lies behind her face-turned-mask is nothingness.

In the prints in regular distribution, the sequence ends with this silent tableau. But the transcription includes here another passage deleted in the final version of the film, which begins with what is described as the "intervention of Rouch, who, after baiting this Morin-Marilou dialogue, remained silent and out of the conversation."[31]

This language seems apt: We may well sense that Rouch, silent behind the camera, has somehow baited this exchange. Yet it is problematic: Morin asked the questions, Marilou answered them, and Rouch said and did nothing to bait anyone – nothing, that is, apart from filming. Evidently, it is the presence of the camera, the reality of the act of filming – it is also the absence the camera represents, its unreality – that baited Marilou into revealing herself, provoked her into enacting her fantasy of dying her own death, or returning to the womb.

Rouch begins his intervention by saying to Morin, "Ask a question now, anything, about the Pope..." Perhaps it is out of human concern for Marilou that Rouch, sensing Morin has abdicated his task as interviewer, urges him to ask a question in the hope of "snapping her out of it." Or is Rouch (also?) manifesting a filmmaker's concern to jump-start a stalled scene?

When Rouch adds "...Ask the question now, and don't get too close to her...," perhaps he senses she is so upset Morin had better not crowd her. But again, his concern may (also?) be for the film: If Morin moved closer he might block the camera's view of Marilou, or alter the expressive framing that has served the passage so effectively. If Rouch's sole concern were for Marilou's well-being, would he not say something to her himself, perhaps even stop filming to go over to comfort her, rather than directing Morin to ask a question?

Obliging Rouch, Morin begins, "Okay, now listen, Marilou..." Rouch interrupts. "No, you're moving closer, Morin. Stay back. Morin, move back. Start the question over." As long as he is giving directions, of course, Rouch can, if he wishes, tell Morin to move farther away so as to isolate Marilou in the frame. Evidently, Rouch wants Morin to stay where he is, to keep the frame composed as it has been. Evidently, too, Rouch wants to stay where *he* is, to remain behind the camera, to continue filming.

Morin finally asks the question Rouch urged on him: "What do you think of the Pope?" This gives rise to a mostly pointless exchange. But Morin's final question is not pointless: "Do you think this film could help you say something?" Nor is Marilou's answer: "You are all very nice, that's all I can say."

If there is gratitude in Marilou's words, there is also rebuke. Morin believes that France has become a country of alienated individuals who long for community even as they are "forced back on themselves." To him, Marilou is an extreme case. Yet Morin makes no secret of his hope, and expectation, that by interviewing this woman in the camera's presence, he will tear down the walls of her "self-enclosed universe." This he fails to do.

In the camera's presence, Marilou has, indeed, "said something," has revealed a profound side of her self. But our recognition of this profound side of Marilou does not enable her to feel connected with reality. For we are not in her presence; in her world, we are invisible phantoms, ghosts. From his place behind the camera, Rouch, too, may recognize the profound side of Marilou that has been revealed. But as long as he is filming, his recognition no more than ours enables her to feel real. For when Rouch is filming Marilou, she imagines him, he imagines himself, to be no longer in the real world, to be absorbed within her imaginary world.

Marilou "lies" when she presents herself to be filmed as an object, for she is really a subject, a self. Rouch "lies," too, when he absorbs himself in filming her, for he is not a phantom or a ghost; he is a human being of flesh and blood. It is not possible for us to make connection with Marilou, but for Rouch, who is really in her presence, making connection with her is not in the same way impossible. It requires, however, that he step forward from his place behind the camera, forsake his cloak of invisibility, declare his presentness. Failing this, his intervention inevitably fails. Hence Marilou's rebuke extends to Rouch, too.

Then what provokes Rouch to intervene at all? Why does he break the spell of his silent communion with Marilou by urging Morin to ask a pointless question that inevitably ends up on the cutting-room floor? I have raised the possibility that he may wish to jump-start a stalled scene. But when Marilou falls silent and Morin watches her in silence, forgoing any further attempt to reach her, the scene is not stalled; it has ended. Why does Rouch not recognize that the scene is complete, that he can now stop filming? Evidently, Rouch cannot bear the endless cry that echoes through this silence. Evidently, he feels a desperate urgency to deny what the silence reveals about Marilou, about himself, about his act of filming her, which she imagines as her death to the world, or as a return to the womb. Evidently, he feels a desperate urgency to deny the pleasure of filming her enchanting face-turned-mask. Evidently, too, he cannot bear simply to stop filming, to forgo that pleasure.

Marceline

The scene of Marceline's "confessions" begins with a cut from the silent Marilou to a medium shot of Jean-Pierre looking down from the balcony of his apartment. In a series of shots, the hand-held camera follows him inside, where he sits at a table and lights a cigarette. Offscreen Morin says, "Jean-

Pierre, you're twenty and a student. How do you make out in life?"

A cut to a tight close-up masks a change of location to another room. Jean-Pierre answers, "I manage perhaps better than most students. But only by horrible compromises. . ." There is a close-up of Morin looking off-screen, presumably toward Jean-Pierre, followed by a cut to Jean-Pierre, who looks neither at Morin nor at the camera. ". . . Once I accept that I can't change things I've no problems. . ." The camera tilts down to Jean-Pierre's hands, nervous-ly playing with an empty glass, giving the lie to his claim he has "no prob-lems." He adds, ". . . I don't think my generation, or any other, can get along until this impotence is accept-ed." There is a cut to a troubled-look-ing Marceline, puffing a cigarette. Before this cut, we did not know she was present. Even now we do not know why.

Marceline listens intently as Jean-Pierre's monologue continues (". . . For example, I failed my exam. I tried to live with a woman. We tried to make each other happy, but it went wrong. It was futile. The same with politics. . .").

There is a cut to Jean-Pierre (". . . I wouldn't take any positive action. I can justify myself intellectually. . ."), then to Morin as Jean-Pierre says, offscreen, ". . . I've seen what commitment does. I've seen so many practi-cally reduced to tears by it. Left shattered. . . Helpless. . . It applies to almost all of you. . ." On this last remark, there is a cut back to Jean-Pierre, who looks right at Morin, implying that Morin is among the impo-tent, helpless, shattered ones. ". . . It's my intellectual justification to keep out. . . ." Then Jean-Pierre contra-dicts himself. ". . . But deep down I know it's false. . ."

At this point we are given a view of Marceline, framed in near profile, eyes almost closed, sad face resting on gracefully curving hands. Jean-Pierre's words seem to pierce her heart.

As Jean-Pierre says, offscreen, ". . . It's a lack of courage. . .,"

Marceline turns almost to the camera. As if she were still troubled, her eyes remain downcast.

There is a cut back to Jean-Pierre as he continues, ". . . One's forced to realize. . . that there's no black and white. Just varying shades of gray." On these last words, he turns to Morin as if to solicit his agreement. Morin nods, then, quite surprisingly, addresses Marceline. "Do you have something to say, Marceline?"

Authorized to speak by Morin's question, Marceline begins by confessing to him, "I feel responsible for it all. . ." Then she shifts to addressing Jean-Pierre (". . . I introduced you to people broken by political experiences. . ."). There is no change in Marceline's voice or expression or even in the direction of her gaze when she shifts from addressing Morin to addressing Jean-Pierre. This creates the impression – an impression underscored when she adds ". . . Not excluding myself. . ." – that no matter whom she may ostensibly be addressing, her "confessions" are a monologue, as if she were really talking to someone absent (the way she does when she walks across the Place de la Concorde, that most public of Parisian spaces, completely absorbed in speaking to her dead father).

Caressing her neck in a manner worthy of a Method actress, Marceline drops what for us is a bombshell (it is the film's first disclosure of the fact, already known to Morin and Rouch, that she and Jean-Pierre are lovers): ". . . When you talk of making a woman happy, I know you mean me. So I feel responsible because, in a way, I took you out of your own world. . ."

Morin takes this occasion to intervene (or, in the editing, this is taken to be an appropriate place to insert this intervention). "When Jean-Pierre says 'impotence,'" he intones, "Marceline thinks of the word 'failure.'"

When we cut back to Marceline, her face is a picture of sadness as she confesses, with a bitter laugh, "I've felt a failure for a long time. . ." Once more referring to Jean-Pierre in the third person – again, without a perceptible shift in her voice or the direction of her gaze – she adds, ". . . When I met Jean-

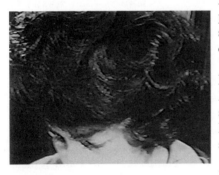

Pierre. . ." There is a long, painful pause, as if she is fighting back tears, struggling to keep from being overcome by the feeling she is invoking. ". . . I did so want to avoid it for him. I didn't want him to feel like me. . ." Marceline lowers her head, as if in shame at having failed to keep Jean-Pierre from feeling the sense of failure she wanted to keep him from feeling.

The moment Marceline raises her head again to speak (". . . I thought. . . I would make him happy. . ."), the camera begins slowly tilting down, apparently with a purpose, but one we cannot surmise. As if this framing disclosed its purpose, the camera holds on Marceline's hands, which are anxiously clenching and unclenching, eloquent testimony to her feeling of failure.

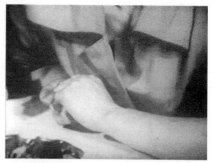

But on Marceline's charged words ". . . In spite of everything, I loved him so much. I still do . . . ," the camera moves again. It pans slightly to the right along her arm, then tilts down a bit, first revealing, then dramatically displaying, the concentration camp number on her arm. This is a privileged moment in the film; prior to this dramatic disclosure, we had no way of knowing that the sad-eyed Marceline was a death-camp survivor. The camera holds this framing a long time, letting its significance sink in.

Finally, as Marceline goes on (". . . But it was another failure. And not only a failure for me, but a painful experience for him. . . "), there is a cut to Jean-Pierre; back to Marceline, who once again bows her head; then lastly to Jean-Pierre, who

turns away from Marceline as we hear her whisper, ". . . Because I think he still loves me." Remarkably, the sequence ends with this vision of Jean-Pierre in the act of turning away from Marceline.

When the camera first tilts down to Marceline's hands, its calm deliberateness conveys a sense that it knows what to look for, where to find it, and what finding it would mean. Yet this movement also appears to be a spontaneous response to Marceline's lowering of her head, as if the camera is not acting on its own but following the cue of her lowered gaze, which leads it to her clenching and unclenching hands. When it momentarily holds on Marceline's eloquently expressive hands, we have no reason to doubt that the camera's gesture, attuned to her feelings, has fulfilled its purpose (especially in its doubling of a similar movement – the camera's tilt down to frame Jean-Pierre's hands – early in the sequence).

When the camera moves again to disclose the number, and when it hastily reframes to display it more dramatically, these movements are roughly executed, and seem like afterthoughts, if inspired ones. It is as if the camera, once it frames Marceline's hands, finds itself so close to the number, which has all along been in plain view ("Far yet not so far," like the world on the other side of the fence in *Night and Fog*), that it is only natural for it to take this small further step. And what better moment for it to do so? What better way for the camera to show it is not deaf to this woman's "endless cry" than to connect her present feeling of failure with the fact that she once looked out from behind a death camp fence, not knowing whether life would know her again?

When it makes this connection between Marceline's present and past, the camera's gesture seems spontaneous. Yet the apparent spontaneity of the camera's movement may also strike us as disingenuous, as if this were a *coup de théâtre* Rouch has been waiting for the perfect opening to spring – a moment that allows the disclosure of the number to appear unpremeditated, yet to have the most dramatic possible impact. And it may also strike us that, although Marceline seems to do nothing to provoke this dramatic disclosure, it may nonetheless be solicited by her (as it may strike us that by lowering her head she solicits the camera to follow her gaze to her clenching and unclenching hands).

To view Marceline as soliciting the camera to disclose the number on her arm, it is necessary to imagine that it is her self-consciousness about this visible mark that motivates her to choose – from all the ways one can express anxiety – to clench and unclench her hands, to draw the camera so close to the number that it can be expected to take that small further step – as, indeed, it goes on to do.

In imagining this gesture as solicited by Marceline, we can imagine that she provokes the camera, without consciously meaning to, to make a connection she believes she wants it not to make. We can also imagine that she deliberately provokes the camera to make the connection she wants it to make. To view her as deliberately provoking the camera to disclose the number is to view this marked woman, who appears so vulnerable to the camera, so easily exposed, as (also?) possessing a cunning, and a power, equal to the camera's own. (To be sure, the camera, or Rouch behind the camera, can in turn be imagined as provoking Marceline to express her feelings by clenching and unclenching her hands, as provoking her to provoke the camera's gesture, as it were. But Marceline can also be imagined as provoking the camera to provoke her.)

When Rouch's camera frames the number on Marceline's arm, it can be viewed as affirming her humanity, as calling upon us to imagine ourselves in her place. (We all have numbers tattooed on our arms, metaphorically, and we are all responsible for tattooing numbers on the arms of others.) But the gesture can also be viewed as saying, emphatically, "It is not possible to imagine being in this woman's place," "Her feelings cannot be imagined," "She cannot be revealed by the medium of film." In identifying Marceline with the mark by which the Nazis denied her humanity, the camera can be viewed as denying her humanity. (Insofar as her anxiously clenching and unclenching hands reveal how Marceline imagines this moment, they reveal a "fictional" part of her self, the "most real" part, in Rouch's view. But the number on her arm is not a "fictional" part of her self. It is no part of her self at all; it is a *denial* of her self.)

That the camera's gesture denies Marceline's feelings seems to follow from its taking the form of a brilliant success, when what Marceline is confessing is her feeling of abject failure. However, what it is that the camera's gesture so brilliantly succeeds in accomplishing is an acknowledgment of its own failure – its failure to "welcome her back to life," to "open all the doors." But if the camera's success is the measure of its failure, its failure is also the measure of its success. We may say that the camera fails to tear down the fence that makes Marceline's world a self-contained universe; we may also say that it succeeds in rebuilding that fence, at least in keeping the fence standing.

The camera's gesture coincides with Marceline's confession of her failure to keep Jean-Pierre from feeling like her. But what does this mean, "feeling like her"? Evidently, it means feeling like a victim. But insofar as Marceline feels responsible for taking Jean-Pierre out of his own world, she feels she has victimized him as the Nazis victimized her. "Feeling like her" also means feeling like a Nazi, or, rather, like a Nazi, failing to feel. When she confesses her failure to keep Jean-Pierre from "feeling like her," she denies his humanity even as she denies her own. Her failure, too, is the measure of her success – her success in consigning Jean-Pierre, as well as herself, to a "self-contained universe."

For years, I viewed the camera's disclosure of the number simply as a denial of Marceline's humanity, as if she were only the camera's victim, not also its accomplice. I have come to view the gesture as also a frightening demonstration – at once Marceline's and Rouch's – of the way she uses this visible mark, with the camera's complicity, to force Jean-Pierre back on himself, to turn him away, to make him turn away, to make him deny her humanity, thereby denying his own. The concentration camp number on her arm is provocative the way the act of filming is provocative. In filming Marceline, Rouch discovers a frightening equivalence between the way she is marked by the visible number on her arm and the way he is marked by the act of filming, by being behind the camera, invisible. When Rouch films Marceline, he consigns her, conspires with her to enable her to consign herself, to a "self-contained universe" that renders the real world an image. Symbolically, he builds a death camp for her, and for himself.

II.

Cinéma-Vérité

In enumerating some of the "intermediaries" that make *Chronicle of a Summer* "a whole work of lies" ("We contract time, we extend it, we choose an angle for the shot, we deform the people we're shooting, we speed things up and follow one movement to the detriment of another movement"),

Rouch primarily has in mind formal devices the film borrows from classical movies (continuity editing, "eyeline" matching, and so on) to weave its views of reality into "fictions" while leaving reality itself – the world off-screen, not the world on-screen – unchanged.

Yet in the process of making *Chronicle*, the filmmakers also alter reality, make it other than it would have been had they not made the film. The filmmakers intervene by interviewing their subjects, for example, and by thrusting them together hoping sparks will fly (as in the "screening" sequence, or the passage in which they introduce Angelo, the Renault worker, to the African, Landry).

Morin, who is never behind the camera, primarily intervenes by interrogating people, sometimes very aggressively (at one point, Rouch half-jokingly refers to him as "the bully"). When Morin is on-screen, he reveals himself to the camera, is revealed by the camera, no less than the people he is interviewing. Rouch is more fugitive and elusive. When he is on-screen, he, too, reveals himself to the camera, is revealed by the camera (not always in a flattering light). But his impact is most strongly felt when he is behind the camera. Ordinarily, when Rouch is filming he does not intervene the way Morin does (or the way he himself does when on camera). This is not to say that then he does not intervene at all, but that the act of filming itself, not some act he performs over and above filming, is his *way* of intervening.

In his useful monograph *Anthropology – Reality – Cinema*, Mick Eaton argues that Rouch's aim in filming is not to make people comfortable so they will reveal themselves honestly and directly to and through his camera. "In the disjunction caused by the very presence of the camera," Eaton observes, "people will act, will lie, be uncomfortable, and it is the manifestation of this side of themselves which is regarded as a more profound revelation than anything a 'candid camera' or 'living cinema' could reveal."[32]

Eaton's language suggests that Rouch, believing his subjects to be less likely to reveal themselves if they are comfortable with the camera, deliberately "shakes them up" so as to cause their comfortably fitting masks to slip, forces them out of their practiced routines of acting and lying so they will act and lie in unpracticed, more revealing, ways. But if it is the very presence of the camera that causes the "disjunction" in which "people will act, will lie, be uncomfortable," why need a filmmaker do anything to "shake up" his subjects, to provoke them into revealing themselves, other than simply filming them?

Sometimes Rouch's subjects are uncomfortable when he films them. When Simone feels left out of her husband's animated conversation with Morin, for example, the camera's presence adds to her discomfort in that she has to decide how she should relate to it, whether to try to hide her discomfort from the camera. Other times, Rouch achieves profound revelations from subjects who are comfortable with the camera, like Landry; who are too comfortable, like Morin himself (he is so trusting – or complacent – he never seems to suspect the way he is being revealed, the way he is revealing himself); or who, like Marilou and Marceline, are comfortable only with the camera.

It is not that people reveal themselves more profoundly when the camera provokes them than when they behave candidly. The point is that in our world people have to be provoked to behave candidly, that candor is not – any longer? – our "natural" mode of being in the world, but must be achieved. Similarly, it is not that the camera achieves more profound revelations when it provokes its subjects than when it is a "candid camera." The point is that the camera cannot truly become a "candid camera" – cannot fulfill its promise of revealing all and only what is revealed to it – without provoking its subjects to be candid.

Rouch's oft-quoted remarks on the need for the camera to provoke its subjects should not be taken as authorizing filmmakers to adopt an "in your face" attitude toward their subjects, to throw their weight around like Morin, rather than to try to become a "fly on the wall." As the sequences we have studied make clear, no one knows better than Rouch that sometimes, perhaps always, filmmakers best provoke their subjects by doing nothing – nothing other than filming them.

Eaton seems to acknowledge this when he speaks of the "disjunction" in which people reveal themselves as being "caused by the very presence of the camera" rather than by anything the camera does over and above its mysterious work of filming. However, to characterize the camera as a "provocateur" or a "catalyst," as Rouch often does, is to envision its presence not as causing a "disjunction" – whatever exactly a "disjunction" is – but as provoking one to become manifest, to manifest itself. (If there were not already a "disjunction," how could the presence of the camera cause one? If people were not already acting and lying, how could the camera's presence cause them discomfort?)

Rouch is fond of saying that he does not film reality as it is but reality as it is provoked by the act of filming. It is this new reality, which would not exist apart from the making of the film, that the filming "documents," revealing a new truth, a cinema truth. Cinéma-vérité.

It has become a critical commonplace to assert a clear-cut distinction, even opposition, between "cinéma-vérité," as Rouch understands and practices it, and what has been dubbed "direct cinema" – what Eaton calls "living cinema" or "candid camera" – as practiced by such filmmakers as Richard Leacock or D. A. Pennebaker. Rouch himself has never subscribed to this view, it may be noted; he has always considered such filmmakers to be fellow practitioners of "cinéma-vérité." The distinction between "cinéma-vérité" – a cinematic practice in which the camera engages in provocation – and "direct cinema" – a cinematic practice in which the camera refrains from being provocative – is rendered moot by the fact that it is the very presence of the camera, when it is doing its mysterious work, that constitutes the kind of "provocation" that most interests Rouch.

In his important recent study *The Cinematic Griot: The Ethnography of Jean Rouch*, Paul Stoller attempts to flesh out this problematic distinction by defining "cinéma-vérité" as cinema that is both "observational" and "participatory" (implicitly opposing it to "direct cinema," which is presumably observational but not participatory).[33] The problem with this definition is that Rouch's practice undermines it. In Rouch's practice, as surely as in Leacock's or Pennebaker's, observation is the camera's way of provoking its subjects to manifest profound sides of themselves, the camera's way of participating.

For Stoller, nonetheless, "participation" is a skeleton key that opens all the doors of Rouch's work. Stoller writes, for example,

Flaherty's most important lesson for Rouch is that of participation. Flaherty's participation went beyond living with the people and understanding their ways. He not only asked Nanook for feedback, but taught him about making films – about the necessity of staging some events. With Flaherty, filming becomes a joint enterprise, narrowing the gulf between filmmakers and the people they film.[34]

But filming, like hunting, is always a joint enterprise, whether or not the resulting film fully acknowledges the participation of the camera's subjects in its making. Even the Hurdanos in *Land without Bread* participate in their own filming when they submit to the condition of being filmed. Nor is the "gulf between filmmakers and the people they film" really any narrower in Flaherty's film than in Buñuel's. When Nanook, consuming the flesh of the walrus he has killed, pauses to confront the camera's gaze, the gulf between Flaherty and his protagonist/star is as wide as the gulf between Buñuel and the Hurdanos, as wide as the gulf between Rouch and Marilou or Marceline, as wide as the gulf between two people can be. As the penultimate passage of *Night and Fog* declares, the goal of the art of film is not to create a gulf between filmmakers and subjects, but neither is it to deny the real gulf between them, the reality of their separateness. All the filmmakers whose works are discussed in this volume aspire to acknowledge the humanity – the individuality, the privacy – of the people they film, the particular individuals who are their cameras' subjects. All of these filmmakers recognize that such acknowledgments cannot be achieved without acknowledging the subjects' participation in the filming, participation that emerges from their privacy – their unknownness – and from their individuality, which is an expression of their privacy. These filmmakers all recognize, as well, that there is no "method" that automatically guarantees such an acknowledgment.

When Stoller characterizes Rouch's filmmaking practice as "participatory as well as observational," he is making a number of claims we might usefully distinguish. One is that in the act of filming Rouch participates in the events being filmed rather than simply observing. Another is that Rouch's subjects participate in the filming rather than simply being observed. Because filming is Rouch's primary way of participating in the events he is filming, as we have argued, and because filming is always a joint enterprise, which we have also argued, these are distinctions without a difference. Yet another claim is that not only do Rouch and his subjects participate jointly in the filming, but that the resulting film, rather than being an end in itself like a traditional work of art, participates in a larger enterprise that may be called "shared anthropology." This is a distinction *with* a difference. We will return to it.

One Take/One Sequence

When Rouch wrote, long after the making of *Chronicle of a Summer*, that "at the time" its "work of lies" was "more real than the truth" to him, he was acknowledging that in the ensuing years his understanding had changed.

Rouch was already a veteran of over a decade of filmmaking among the Songhay and Dogon peoples of West Africa at the time his sociologist friend Morin asked him to collaborate on a film about the way Parisians live their everyday lives. Subsequent to the making of *Chronicle*, Rouch returned to his practice of filming the Songhay and Dogon rituals that have been his abiding subjects for almost half a century. The new lightweight synch-sound equipment with which he experimented in *Chronicle* became an indispensable tool in this lifelong cinematic enterprise.

Formally, Rouch's post-*Chronicle* films are very different from his pre-*Chronicle* films. In this respect, *Chronicle* is a pivotal work. As he incorporated the use of portable synch-sound equipment into his films among the Songhay and Dogon, and no doubt partly as a response to his experience making *Chronicle*, he developed a new method of filming (it is also a new method of editing, or, rather, of avoiding editing). What he calls the "one take/one sequence" method enabled him increasingly to forgo the classical conventions that made *Chronicle* a "work of lies."

Paradigmatic of the "one take/one sequence" method is *Les Tambours d'avant: Turu et Bitti* (*The Drums of Yore: Turu and Bitti*) (1971). In this remarkable ten-minute film, not just one "sequence" but the entire film consists of a single continuous take that lasts the duration of the camera magazine. Within the single shot that constitutes the film, Rouch walks with the camera on his shoulder into a Songhay village in which a possession ritual is underway. Rouch focuses his camera on the dancers who have been waiting for many hours without yet being possessed by invisible spirits, then on the musicians. Just as it appears that nothing is going to happen, he again turns his camera on the listless dancers, whose demeanor suddenly changes, this transformation seemingly precipitated by the attention of the camera. (No moment better epitomizes the camera's ability to undermine the distinction between "participation" and "observation," to provoke revelations by its very presence.)

In classical cinema, there are conventional categories of shots – close-up, two shot, point-of-view shot, and so on – and conventions for their use. Even in the forties, when the "long take" style flourished as an alternative or complement to the analytical editing of the thirties, the long takes tended to take the form of stable framings – each virtually a separate shot, conventional in format – linked by reframings instead of cuts.

Unlike *Chronicle*, which emulates classical conventions, *Turu et Bitti* is shot in one continuous take, as we have said. Everything is viewed from the perspective of a fixed focal-length lens; there are no zooms that create an illusion of movement through space. As fully as possible, the camera becomes an extension of Rouch's own body – a closer view means the filmmaker/camera has moved closer, a more distant view means the filmmaker/camera has moved further away. Except for the narration – a crucial exception, to be sure – in which Rouch explains the "one take/one sequence" method and speculates that the act of filming precipitated the possessions he was filming, nothing is added after the fact, nothing edited out, no effects are created on the editing table, no "lies" told of the kind *Chronicle* tells.

In a "one take/one sequence" film like *Turu et Bitti*, the frame is never stable or fixed. The camera is never completely motionless, but most of its movements have no significance apart from their status as indicators of two conditions, which are linked. First, the incessant movements of the camera indicate that the camera *is* hand-held, that it is an extension of the filmmaker's body. Second, these movements, with their accidental jostlings, hesitations, revisions of focus and framing, indicate that this is not a scripted film, that the filmmaker is an embodied human being, not an omniscient "author."

The camera's normal state of incessant motion in a "one take/one sequence" film contrasts strikingly with the motionlessness that is the camera's normal state in classical "fiction films" or in the sequences in *Chronicle* that emulate classical conventions. At any given moment, the classical camera's fixity of position has no particular significance apart from sustaining the prevailing fiction that no camera is present (in "fiction films") or apart from simply marking the camera's presence (in *Chronicle*). The classical camera's motionlessness is broken only when it is moved to declare itself in self-possessed gestures that call for acknowledgment. In *Turu et Bitti*, the camera's incessant motion binds it to a human hand and eye, a human body this motion continuously manifests.

Convinced it was his act of filming that precipitated the possession trances of the dancers, Rouch was moved to write "On the Vicissitudes of the Self: The Possessed Dancer, the Magician, The Sorcerer, the Filmmaker and the Ethnographer," an essay that attempted to explain how this was possible.[35] How could the camera's presence have had this effect, not only on the mediums (who were possessed when the camera was filming them), but also the spirits (who possessed the mediums precisely then)?

We may well believe that these "spirits" are imaginary, not real, or even that these mediums were not really possessed at all, but only acting. But then it still requires explanation how invisible spirits can be so much as *imagined* to be capable of being provoked by a camera into manifesting themselves. What do the mediums believe the camera to be that they understand its presence to be capable of provoking them to fall into a trance, to abandon themselves, so as to enable, as they imagine it, invisible spirits to possess their bodies?

According to Rouch's essay, the Songhay believe that when a medium is possessed he or she is approached by an invisible spirit carrying the bloody skin of a freshly slaughtered animal. The spirit wraps the skin around the medium's head, at the same time capturing and protecting the "self" of the medium, who is now in a deep trance. Then the spirit enters the medium's body. When it is time to leave, the spirit lifts off the bloody animal skin, liberating the medium's displaced "self."

When filming *Turu et Bitti*, Rouch suggests, he fell into a trance – a "ciné-trance" – comparable to the trances that enabled the mediums to be possessed. Walking with the camera on his shoulder, he became other than the person he ordinarily is; he became the being that Stoller, in his eloquent account of the film, calls "Rouch-the-camera." Filming *Turu et Bitti*, Rouch-the-camera walked among the villagers gathered for the ceremony, and also among invisible spirits, who recognized him as belonging to their realm as well as to the realm of the visible. Evidently, invisible spirits and human mediums alike wanted Rouch-the-camera to be present – observing, filming – at the moment of possession.

"While shooting a ritual," Rouch wrote some years after writing "On the Vicissitudes of the Self," the filmmaker "discovers a complex and spontaneous set-up." To record it, he

. . .only has to "record reality," improvise his frames and movements. . .If, by chance, while shooting a. . .trance dance, I happen to accomplish such a performance, I can still remember the acute challenge of not wobbling, not missing focus nor exposure, in which case the whole sequence would have to be resumed, therefore be lost altogether. And when, tired out by such a tension, the soundman drops his microphone and I abandon my camera, we feel as if a tense crowd, musicians and even vulnerable gods who got hold of trembling dancers were all aware and stimulated by our venture.[36]

As Rouch here describes it, he became so distracted filming *Turu et Bitti*, so absorbed in the technical details of pulling off this performance, that he fell into a "ciné-trance." It is this state that made it possible for his "self" to become displaced, his body to be possessed.

This is as far as Rouch takes his analysis in his published writings. Keeping in mind our discussion of the images-painted-on-skin in *Night and Fog*, however, perhaps we might venture a further speculation. The camera, symbolically, skins its subjects alive. Then perhaps, in Rouch's terms, it is the camera/machine that, capturing and protecting the filmmaker's "self" within the bloody skin of the world, possesses his body, becomes fused with it, enabling the camera's subjects, each a medium capable of being possessed, or the spirits that possess them, to possess the entranced filmmaker. (Perhaps we might also venture to speculate, in this spirit, that if Marceline was acting in the Place de la Concorde sequence of *Chronicle*, the only difference between her "real" self and the character she was playing is that the latter has no need to perform an act, to deny the present, in order to feel connected with the world of the past, the only world real to her. The only difference between Marceline's "real" and "fictional" selves is that one is an actress and the other a medium through whom her past self was capable of speaking. But if Marceline was acting, was consciously absorbed in the mechanics of pulling off her virtuoso performance, perhaps she was so distracted, so entranced, in effect, that the "fictional" Marceline was able to steal upon her, possess her, even as she remained unaware she was doing anything but acting. Once she abandoned herself to the role she believed she was only acting, the difference between her "real" and "fictional" selves dropped away.)

"Whatever the mechanism, the paramount fact of possession is that the medium's [self] is displaced," Stoller writes. And the paramount fact of the filming of *Turu et Bitti*, he goes on, endorsing Rouch's own formulation, is that "Rouch literally attached himself to the ritual and entered a 'ciné-trance of one filming the trance of another.'"[37] But it is quite without support from Rouch's words that Stoller adds, "Ciné-trance, however, is entered only by filmmakers who practice cinéma-vérité, who hunt for images in the real world."[38]

Rouch's profound insight, gleaned from his investigation of the way the Songhay understand these matters, is that filming and being filmed are akin to phenomena of possession, that filmmakers as well as the people they are filming are capable of becoming possessed, or, at least, capable of undergoing a metamorphosis so profound as to be meaningfully compared to possession. In truth, this insight is capable of illuminating a wide range of films, perhaps all films, not only films we might associate with the term "cinéma-vérité," much less films shot by the "one take/one sequence" method. All filmmakers "hunt for images in the real world," after all. (Where else are they to find them?) Can we not say that Resnais is possessed by those who scratched and clawed their marks in the ceiling of the gas chamber? that Hitchcock is possessed by Norman Bates (as Norman is possessed by his mother)? that Chaplin is possessed by the Tramp, who is also his own image? that Rouch is possessed by Marilou and Marceline, even though he does not use the "one take/one sequence" method to film them?

The centrality of the "one take/one sequence" method to his later work, along with the central roles concepts like "self," "trance," "possession," "authenticity," and "revelation" have played throughout his career, suggest that it would be wise to take with a grain of salt Rouch's repeated claims that Vertov, along with Flaherty, is one of his "cinematic ancestors." Without denying Vertov's importance as a role model for Rouch (who borrows his term "cinéma-vérité" from "*Kino-Pravda,*" after all), it is important to keep in mind the ways Rouch's theory and practice of cinema are antithetical to Vertov's.

Following Eaton, Stephen Feld, and others, Stoller takes Rouch's remarks about Vertov at face value. Stoller writes:

Whereas Flaherty's creative influence on Rouch is fundamentally methodological, Dziga Vertov's cinematic contributions lead to the heart of Rouch's cinematic art, to Rouch's practice of cinéma-vérité, in which one edits film as one shoots it – in which the camera becomes an extension of the filmmaker's body. . . . Vertov's aim was to plunge the cinema into the stimulating depths of real life, a construction of the real prompted by the camera.[39]

But Vertov's practice is at a far remove from "editing in the camera." For Vertov, montage is almost everything, and the function of montage is not to enable the camera to become an extension of the filmmaker's body (the way it increasingly does for Rouch, who comes to forgo montage all but completely); rather, the filmmaker's body becomes an extension of the camera/machine, which liberates the body, allows it to assume more than human powers.

As Feld notes, Rouch is fond of citing Vertov's passage,

I am the kino-eye, I am the mechanical eye, I am the machine that shows you the world as only a machine can see it. From now on I will be liberated from immobility. I am in perpetual movement. I draw near to things, I move myself away from them, I enter into them, I travel toward the snout of a racing horse, I move through crowds at top speed, I precede soldiers on attack, I take off with airplanes, I flip over on my back, I fall down and stand back up as bodies fall down and stand back up.[40]

Rather than follow Vertov's flight of fancy, Rouch brings the camera down to earth, grounds its powers in the finite limits of his human body. He never ceases to be inspired by the simple fact that it is possible for a human being to *walk* with the camera. (Rouch brought Michel Brault from Canada to shoot part of *Chronicle* so he could learn from him how to "walk the camera.")

Vertov is a Constructivist. Like Buñuel, Rouch is a filmmaker whose artistic roots are in surrealism. (The "one take/one sequence" method is designed to enable filmmakers to achieve what may be thought of as a kind of "automatic writing.") Rouch's project, like Buñuel's, also has a Nietzschean aspect to it. Rouch's goal is for us to become more fully human by acknowledging our humanity, by discovering – or rediscovering – the possibility of freedom within the limits of our condition as human. Vertov's goal is to deny the constraints of being human. For Vertov, a film like *Man with the Movie Camera* is a simulacrum of a revolutionary new society; what matters most is the revolutionary reality being constructed. For Rouch, reality needs to be provoked to manifest its full profundity, but reality as it is counts for everything.

Shared Anthropology

Stoller writes of *Turu et Bitti*:

In ten minutes of footage it indexes a radical method, that of a shared, participatory anthropology. In a sense the subtext of "shared anthropology" runs through most if not all of Rouch's films. "Shared anthropology" is the story of Rouch's films. It is a story in which Rouch has used the medium of film to share with the "other" the results of his work.[41]

Inspired by Flaherty's practice, Rouch regularly screens his footage to his subjects, asks them questions about events he has filmed whose meaning he does not already fully understand, receives answers that help him to film in ways that will enable him to ask further questions, to receive further answers. Films like *Turu et Bitti* are at once fruits of his commitment to "shared anthropology" – without his long-term immersion in studying Songhay society, he would not have known how to film this possession ritual – and fruitful sources for asking further questions, receiving further answers, and making further films that advance the enterprise of "shared anthropology."

In the "shared anthropology" Rouch champions, film occupies the central place that writing has occupied in traditional anthropology. By making films that beget films (as Vertov also envisioned himself as doing), Rouch aspires to usher in a revolutionary anthropological practice that acknowledges rather than denies the medium of film, that transforms traditional anthropology into a discipline no less rigorous for acknowledging the magical, the strange, the fantastic, the fabulous.

That Rouch aspires to transform traditional anthropology from within means that he must establish his credentials by publishing writings meant to be read by other anthropologists. That Rouch's writings do, indeed, establish his legitimacy as an anthropologist is a leading claim of Stoller's book. (This is one of the many things that make Stoller's writing such a major contribution to the critical literature on Rouch's work.)

In transforming traditional anthropology from within, Rouch's goal is to make anthropology accessible to people from preliterate cultures – to enable them not only to have access to the results of research, but to participate in the research in ways going far beyond the traditional role of "informant." We might say that Rouch's goal is to enable "ethnographic others," the objects of anthropological study, also to become subjects who make this study their own.

94

Rouch understands that the "ethnographic others" change through participating in this new "shared anthropology."

The field changes the simple observer. When he works, he is no longer one who greeted the oldtimers on the edge of the village; to take up. . . Vertovian terminology, he "ethno-looks," he "ethno-observes," he "ethno-thinks," and once they are sure of this strange regular visitor, those who come in contact with him go through a parallel change, they "ethno-show," they "ethno-speak," and ultimately, they "ethno-think". . . . Knowledge is no longer a stolen secret, which is later devoured in western temples of knowledge. . . [It] is the result of an endless quest in which ethnographers and others walk a path which some of us call "shared anthropology."[42]

For almost a half-century, Rouch has developed his theory and practice of "shared anthropology" by extensively filming two West African peoples: the Dogon of the Bandiagara cliffs of Mali, the people studied by his mentor Marcel Griaule, whose rituals are spectacular achievements of *mise-en-scène*, of staging; and the Songhay of Niger, whose rituals of possession have been the subject of Rouch's own ethnographic publications.

Rouch's many years of filmmaking among the Dogon culminates in a series of films (1967–74) about the epic "Sigui" ritual, staged once every sixty years to commemorate the invention of death, and in two feature-length films that may be his artistic masterpieces, *Funeral at Bongo: The Death of Old Anai* (1972) and *Ambara Dama* (1974). (The last of these works closes a circle: Rouch films the mask dance ritual first filmed by Griaule, and in the narration Rouch speaks his teacher's own words.)

In filming a Dogon ritual, Rouch's primary interests are its theatricality (inherent drama, value as spectacle) and its texture of meaningfulness (in every step of every dancer, a system of cosmology is inscribed). Rouch's interest is in the esoteric knowledge inscribed in the ritual (rather than, say, the personal thoughts or feelings of the individual performers).

At one level, Rouch films Dogon rituals in order to vindicate Griaule's claim, rejected during his lifetime by the French anthropological establishment, that this African people has kept alive the knowledge of what its ancient rituals mean. But Rouch also films these rituals in order to vindicate his own practice of "shared anthropology." It is because Griaule's claim is true, Rouch believes, that it is possible for him to show the Dogon the footage he has shot, ask questions, and receive answers that will enable him to know better how to film – how to create new films that enable him to ask new questions and receive new answers, furthering the quest for anthropological knowledge.

The Death of Old Anai opens with a glimpse of Anai Dolo, filmed two years before his death in 1971 at the age of 122, protected and warm within his little hut. In his poetic narration, Rouch speaks of the old man's condition as a return to the womb (Anai lived through three Sigui rituals, Rouch tells us; during the first, he was literally in his mother's womb). Deaf and blind and unable to walk, he is no longer an actor on the world's stage, no longer even a spectator, but he remains a valued member of a community that acknowledges and appreciates the life he has led, a life that began in 1849 and spans so much of the history of the Dogon people.

This history comes alive in the funeral that follows, which takes several days to play out. The story of Anai's life, the story of the Dogon people and the story of the Creation of the universe are reenacted in a spectacular piece of theater, staged without author or director, in which all the inhabitants of Bongo and the surrounding countryside have roles to perform.

We know only those meanings that Rouch's narration explains to us. This is what makes *Anai* a work of anthropology: The way of thinking it "documents" belongs to "others," not to ourselves; we cannot search within ourselves to discover the meaning of what we are viewing. Yet in our lack of knowledge, we share the condition of most of the performers, only a few of whom are initiates. The ritual's power as theater does not depend on the esoteric knowledge possessed by the Dogon elders, perhaps none of whom possesses it in full. Rouch possesses this knowledge to a limited degree, and communicates some of what he knows to us, but it is not his aspiration to provide answers to all questions we may have about the meaning of what we are viewing. He does not have all the answers; he makes this film hoping to learn things he does not already know.

Anai presents us with a spectacle at once strange and uncannily familiar. This ritual is familiar because it is only a funeral, after all, and we have funerals, too. But Rouch's film brings home to us something we have forgotten about what a funeral is (what it once was to us, perhaps what it can once again be). That our rituals have become degraded is hardly news. But Rouch makes it news by allowing us to view a ritual more alive than any we had imagined. *Anai* is meant to expand our capacity to imagine, not to "document" a dying way of life.

Rouch's dream is that the human race may one day cherish its diversity and value its oldest traditions most of all. For Rouch, the Dogon are an ideal society; without written laws or central government, they sustain ancient beliefs and rituals – they antedate Judaeo-Christian civilization – which create an authentic sense of community we have lost. It is a mystery that the Dogon know how to stage spectacles that help free their society from the alienation and fear of death that haunt our own. Rouch communicates to us above all his wonder at what these people know, that we do not, about how human lives may be lived.

What the Dogon know is something about theater, about conquering the fear of death. What the Songhay know is something about possession, about accepting the limits of self-control, about abandonment, about overcoming the fear of enchantment. Songhay rituals are not staged spectacles. The Songhay do not don masks and play gods and mythical beings; they *become* those beings. Songhay rituals are not reenactments of history, mythical or otherwise; they enable the invisible deities always in their midst to make themselves manifest so they can answer questions, here and now, about matters of life and death.

The Songhay and Dogon to whom Rouch shows his films-in-progress have their own ways of understanding what films are, what becomes of Rouch when he goes into a "ciné-trance" and films their rituals. Because his acts of filming are capable of playing profoundly meaningful roles within these rituals, Rouch cannot fully comprehend the systems of thoughts that underlie the rituals without comprehending how the camera appears, how his acts of filming appear, when viewed from within those systems. As we have seen, one Songhay idea that strikes Rouch as profoundly revelatory is that in the act of filming he straddles the realm of the visible, of the living, and the realm of the invisible, of spirits, deities, ghosts. Equally revelatory to Rouch is the Dogon idea that film has an intimate connection with masks, with spectacle, with theater.

In *Anai*, the ritual Rouch is filming fuses with his own act of filming. This occurs, for example, during the reenactment of the Dogon battle against the French in 1895, a battle in which Anai was wounded by a French bullet, when some participants aim their old flintlock rifles directly at the camera, or at Rouch behind the camera. However sincere he may be in making this film to share with the Dogon his quest for anthropological knowledge, Rouch remains a Frenchman. He is implicated in the history of the Dogon people, and this fact is not lost on them, nor on him.

But if the shooting at the camera acknowledges that Rouch is a Frenchman, not a Dogon, it also acknowledges something else. The point in reenacting the battle, its function within the funeral as a whole, is to help provoke Anai's soul to leave the village and begin its long journey to the land of the dead. A soul separated from its body is very vulnerable, the Dogon believe, and also very dangerous. However much it wants to stay in the village that was its home, Anai's soul must be made to leave, even if this requires frightening it away. Shooting their rifles at the camera not only reveals that the Dogon place Rouch on the French side of the colonial war they are reenacting, it also reveals that they connect the camera, or Rouch behind the camera, with the ghost of Anai, a spirit haunting the world in which it can no longer dwell, longing to die its own death yet reluctant to sever its ties with the living.

In *Ambara Dama*, too, the ritual Rouch is filming and his own practice of filming are profoundly linked. The performers in their spectacular masks dance for the villagers in the audience, and also for the souls of the dead that may be lingering around the village. The dancers hope not to frighten these souls, but to enchant them so they may safely be led to the land of the dead. The masks and dances are so seductive, however, that there is a danger that the living may be enchanted, and may die. Rouch's camera is at once in the position of the living, for whom enchantment is dangerous, and the dead, for whom it promises release from their attachment to the living. The "veracity" of the Dogon beliefs cannot be separated from the question of whether these masks projected on the screen enchant *us*.

Rouch is not the author of what such films show us, although his acts of filming play a role in what he is filming. What makes it possible for us to view what we are viewing is a mystery linked to the mysteries on view. In the climactic sequence of *Anai*, Rouch invokes this mystery directly.

I am thinking of the remarkable passage in which a Dogon elder, in a cave whose darkness is penetrated only by the flashlight Rouch has strapped to his camera hoping it would provide enough light to film, recites the sayings that recount the history of the universe from the Creation to Anai Dolo's death. As if under the spell of the myth being chanted, the film suddenly avails itself of the powers of montage, which Rouch developed the "one take/one sequence" method of filming in order to forgo. Liberated from its connection with the filmmaker's body, we magically depart this claustrophobic setting to encompass a series of visions of the world outside, each vision serving to illustrate an aspect of the Dogon myth. The series culminates in an awesome vision of heaps of bones of animals killed by uncounted generations of Dogon hunters, a vision that takes us back to the beginning of time.

At one level, this passage distills the intellectual charge of the film. Rouch means *Anai* to be a critique of Claude Lévi-Srauss's view that myths are structures of oppositions. A structuralist account forgets that a myth is a tale told by human beings to human beings on particular occasions for reasons that are matters of life and death to them. What Lévi-Strauss omits – the scene of the telling – is what Rouch wishes this passage to invoke.

The passage is also an explicit declaration of the power of film – a power film shares with theater as the Dogon practice it – to transcend the bounds of space and time. As if by magic, film is capable of connecting the visible and the invisible, the living Anai, 122 years old, and the soul of the dead Anai, whose funeral is itself capable of connecting one man's life, the historical struggle between the Dogon people and their French colonizers, and the Creation of the universe.

This passage links the mystery of film's power to connect the living and the dead, the visible and the invisible, with the universal mysteries of Creation, death, and rebirth meditated upon by the ancient Dogon sayings. At the same time, the passage is an intensely personal one in which Rouch finds poetic words for the feelings this sublime spectacle arouses in him. The Dogon account of the Creation illuminates the creation of this film, too, for the words Rouch speaks in French to express his own feelings are literal translations of the words the elder chants in his people's ancient ritual language, words that inscribe the knowledge the Dogon hold sacred.

Rouch's Dogon films revolve around the quest for knowledge. His Songhay films are about something else, call it the limits of knowledge. In *Turu et Bitti*, it is not film's utility as an instrument of science that is demonstrated, but film's power as a medium of possession. This is why it seems strange to single out *Turu et Bitti* from among all of Rouch's films as "indexing" the method of "shared anthropology." The Songhay villagers who are participating in this event seem hardly to be "ethno-thinking," hardly to be motivated by a quest for anthropological knowledge. What they want to know – the prospects for the next harvest, for example – only the invisible spirits can tell them. (Stoller is perhaps being a bit sentimental when he suggests that the spirits possess the mediums in the camera's presence because they honor Rouch, and that they honor him because he has honored them. The moment the first possession occurs, the spirit announces – who is to doubt him? – that what he wants is *meat*.)

It is not to further the goals of "shared anthropology" that the mediums allow themselves to be possessed, and the deities choose to possess them, precisely when Rouch-the-camera is present. Rouch describes their motivations more plausibly, and reveals something about his own, when he writes that the trembling dancers and vulnerable gods were "stimulated" by his virtuoso feat of filming, and characterizes himself as so absorbed in pulling off a technically difficult performance that his conscious mind abandoned itself to a trance-like state.

What *Turu et Bitti* "indexes" is less a joint quest for anthropological knowledge than an acknowledgment of the limits of knowledge, of the value of abandoning oneself, overcoming the fear of enchantment, becoming possessed. If Rouch's films are in pursuit of knowledge, they also acknowledge the value of the transcendental, the unknowable, the unsayable. Rouch is a poet as surely as he is an anthropologist. Like Buñuel, he is also a Nietzschean prophet, as we have said. The new world Rouch heralds is also an ancient world, a world older than our Western civilization. To arrive at this new/old world is to create or re-create a human form of life in which the invisible is at every moment manifest, a form of life in which every event, however "ordinary," at once expresses what we know, and acknowledges what we cannot know, about being human.

This visionary aspiration of Rouch's project separates him from other major "ethnographic" filmmakers, who stand apart from him, respecting but not following him – from the late Timothy Asch, for example, and others who retain their faith in rational analysis; from the skeptical Mac-Dougalls, who envision their subjects as playing out an all too familiar human comedy unaltered by being set in exotic landscapes and acted by so-called primitives; from Robert Gardner and John Marshall, who view human existence in poetic, yet tragic, terms.

For both Gardner and Marshall, who worked together on *The Hunters* before they went their separate ways, the tragedy is the failure of all human society to fulfil the human longing for acknowledgment and love; society is the mask by which we veil from ourselves the truth that we live inhuman lives.

For Gardner, culture is the system of masks and lies humans create to deny the truth of our condition, a truth that nonetheless can be recognized by anyone with eyes to see. It is the system by which we hide our cruelty, and our tenderness, from each other and from ourselves. Films like *Dead Birds, Rivers of Sand, Deep Hearts,* and *Forest of Bliss* are sublime and beautiful poems in which each society Gardner films becomes a metaphor for the tenderness and cruelty of all human existence, the tenderness and cruelty we all are capable of recognizing when we look deep into our own hearts. Gardner's "ethnographic" films are about people he does not claim especially to love. The human need for love, which is the other face of the human resistance to loving and being loved, is the subject of his films.

Marshall's subject is the powerlessness of love in the face of forces that are transforming the world into a place unfit for human habitation. His "ethnographic" films are about a people – the Bushmen of the Kalihari Desert – and a person – N!ai, whom he first filmed when she was a precocious eight-year-old – he loves but is powerless to save. Marshall's own story (son of the anthropologist Lorna Marshall, he lived among the Bushmen from his childhood) is inseparable from the story of this people and this person. And this story is a tragedy: This nomadic people is being herded into "camps," dying out *as* a people, and what he loves about N!ai is dying out, too.

The words "dying out" suggest that this is occurring naturally, that no one is responsible, that what is happening is not murder or genocide. Marshall's films point no accusing finger, but their premise and conclusion is that this is a tragedy for which no one is completely exempt from guilt – including Marshall himself, whose films inscribe his knowledge that his fate is to tell this tragic story, hence that he plays a role within this tragedy, that he, too, is a figure of tragedy, a tragic figure. His powerlessness to avert this people's fate cannot be separated from the tragedy that is their fate, and his.

Gardner's and Marshall's films bear an intimate relationship to one another. Gardner turns to a particular people to make a film that speaks an unspeakable truth about humanity, then moves on. (That humans are nomads is one of these unspeakable truths.) Gardner films others to formulate statements that are really about himself, that unburden his own heart by creating cruel and tender poetry capable of moving us beyond words. But Marshall's films, too, are implicated in the cruelty, as well as the tenderness, that is an alienable part of being human.

As far as the MacDougalls are concerned, we are to be skeptical of the very idea of change; we are what we are, we have always been that way; we are not really all that bad, but we should be under no illusions that what is merely economically determined is "sacred." In a film like *The Wedding Camels*, the MacDougalls accept the absence of the sacred with good humor, as if it never amounted to much in the first place. Gardner and Marshall are inconsolable in mourning the loss of the sacred. Christians in despair, they, too, are skeptical of the possibility of change. Rouch is not skeptical, and he is not in despair. But neither is he a Christian, even a lapsed one.

As we have observed, when Rouch films Dogon rituals, he is not concerned with the realm of the private, the everyday, which is the primary focus of *Chronicle of a Summer*; he is concerned with everything that bears on the esoteric meaning of the ritual, that reveals its underlying cosmology, and with nothing that does not. Rouch is especially attached to the Dogon cosmology, first, because he believes it has enabled the Dogon people to sustain a way of life not haunted by alienation and fear of death, as *Chronicle* reveals ours to be. Second, because Rouch is attracted to the Dogon vision of a cosmos not eternally in the throes of a terrible war between good and evil, as Christianity envisions, but animated by the joyful give and take between a God who stands for order and the mischievous Pale Fox who takes pleasure in sowing disorder, in subverting God's script. To see the gleam in Rouch's eye when he talks about the Pale Fox, whose antics provoke God to manifest profoundly revealing sides of himself, is to recognize that this is a figure he aspires to emulate (when he is behind the camera, and when he is not).

In *Land without Bread*, the impoverishment of the Hurdanos – it is our impoverishment, too – is a sign that in its attempts to wall out nature, humanity has altered nature against itself, has rendered nature – hence human nature – unnatural, a horror. The Dogon are not the Hurdanos. They have never built walls to try to keep nature out. Worshipers of the Pale Fox, they have always been "beyond good and evil" in Nietzsche's sense. Even today, their rituals reveal that they have kept alive their ancient way of thinking, a way of thinking that predates Christianity, predates the birth of Western civilization itself, which in Nietzsche's vision coincides with the birth of tragedy. Nor are the Songhay the Hurdanos. In the presence of Rouch's camera, they do not suffer in stolid silence; like Dionysian revelers, they abandon themselves, overcome their fear of enchantment, become possessed.

No less than Buñuel, Rouch believes that our way of life must change, that our way of life cannot change unless we change, and that we cannot change unless our way of thinking changes. We must awaken to, awaken from, the horror to which we have condemned ourselves and our world. We must tear down the fences we have built, the fences we continue to build, to deny that nature exists within us as we exist within nature. But Rouch does not share Buñuel's faith that art is capable of awakening us, capable of reconciling us with nature, with our own nature, from which we have become estranged.

In the world of *Night and Fog*, as we have seen, the reality of the death camps reveals that a further estrangement has taken place. We have altered art against its own nature, too, have rendered art itself unnatural, a horror. Resnais refuses to consent to the horror of the world that built and operated the death camps and still denies their "true dimension." The present cannot be made the real world again without acknowledging that art lies, and art kills. Death camps were built with fences around them not to contain nature, but to contain art, to keep art at bay. If death camps are works of art, art cannot reconcile us with nature, with our own nature, unless art participates in tearing those fences down. In Resnais's modernist vision, overcoming art is the new end for art; overcoming the art of film is the new end for the art of film.

But Rouch does not share Resnais's modernist faith in art, either. In Rouch's understanding, the fences we build around art, the fences works of art build around themselves, must be torn down, to be sure, but this cannot be achieved by art alone – by objects to be treated as self-contained, as ends in themselves. Rouch treats neither the rituals he films nor his films of those rituals as works of art in this sense. He understands the rituals he films to be of value insofar as they participate in ways of thinking and living that are meaningful to the human beings who think and live these ways. And he understands his films to be of value insofar as they participate in the meaningful way of thinking and living he calls "shared anthropology."

Chronicle of a Summer, made largely in the editing room, assumes the form of a traditional work of art; in editing the film, the filmmakers (at least to the degree that they succeed in reconciling their differences) stake out their authorship of the work, assume responsibility for its composition. *Turu et Bitti*, exemplary of "shared anthropology," is not in the same way a "composition"; it is improvised. The rituals Rouch films likewise have an essential element of improvisation. This is obviously true of the ritual *Turu et Bitti* "documents," in which the Songhay must be responsive to the whims of invisible spirits if the possessions are to take place at all, and in which those spirits, once they manifest themselves, speak words that are not scripted in advance (otherwise there would be no point in going through this rigmarole). But it is no less true of the elaborate rituals the Dogon stage, in which everything appears to follow an age-old script. When the participants in the mock battle that is the centerpiece of Anai's funeral point their flintlock rifles at the camera, at Rouch, they are not following a script; these are improvisations provoked by the act of filming.

In the "one take/one sequence" method of filming Rouch develops after *Chronicle of a Summer*, and partly in response to his experience of making that film, the camera becomes an extension of his bodily presence. Sequences edited according to the conventions of classical movies give way to continuous "long takes." In his post-*Chronicle* films, Rouch does not treat editing as a way of asserting authorship. *Turu et Bitti*, which consists of one shot, is not edited at all. The editing of a longer film like *The Death of Old Anai* is simply a matter of splicing together a series of "one take" sequences. (The climactic montage is the exception that proves this rule.)

A film created by the "one take/one sequence" method respects the spatiotemporal integrity of the filmed event in the way championed by Bazin. It does something else, as well: It invokes an "original" scene in which the filmmaker was present as the "first viewer." When Rouch completes such a film by recording a narration, he does not treat the voice-over (any more than the editing) as a way to assert authorship. A Rouch narration, essentially improvised, is his response to the film, spoken by one viewer to other viewers. By virtue of the narration, the film also invokes a second scene of Rouch's presence: He speaks to us as if he were now in our presence, viewing with us. The figure who silently filmed these events in the past is the bearer of the voice that speaks to us in the present: This is the mysterious reality the narration declares, both by the words spoken and the hushed, poetic tone of the voice that speaks them, a tone that bespeaks the sacredness of the ritual we are viewing (and the ritual of our viewing).

When Stoller suggests that Rouch's films participate in the enterprise of shared anthropology, he primarily has in mind the filmmaker's practice of screening the footage to his Songhay and Dogon subjects, asking questions and soliciting answers that instruct him how he should make further films, films he can screen to his subjects in order to ask further questions and receive further answers. However, in such scenes of instruction, his own and his subjects', it makes little difference (to him, to them) whether the footage screened was filmed by the "one take/one sequence" method.

But there is another scene of instruction in which Rouch's films are meant to participate. And in this "other" scene of instruction, the "one take/one sequence" method makes a crucial difference. I am thinking of the innumerable occasions in which Rouch has presented his films to students in schools, museums, and libraries all over the world. Those who have had the experience of viewing a Rouch film on an occasion in which the filmmaker introduced it and presided over the subsequent discussion, much less those who have taken part in one of the many intensive seminars he has conducted all over the world, know that this is how most of his films are meant to be viewed. To some degree, Rouch's narrations create the illusion that he is in the room with us, but that is a pale substitute for his presence in the flesh, which completes the experience of his films, or, rather, enables us to experience them in a way that transcends experiencing them as self-contained works of art. Unlike Flaherty, Buñuel or Resnais, Rouch makes his films *to be* transcended this way.

If Rouch makes his films to beget films, part of what this means is that he uses them to win converts to the enterprise of "shared anthropology" to which he has dedicated his life, to inspire others to emulate his practice. This does not mean he wishes for others to join him in filming Songhay or Dogon rituals – those are *his* subjects, not theirs. It means he wishes as many people as possible to discover subjects they might film and be instructed by in this way that has freed him from the alienation, the despair, the joylessness, to which our society would otherwise have consigned him, to which he would otherwise have consigned himself. Rouch wants his audience to emulate his way of thinking, which is also his way of living, a way that taps into sources of ecstasy that have become lost to our society. Above all, I take it, it is to facilitate his films' usefulness as exemplars of "shared anthropology" that Rouch considers it a "must" to use the "one take/one sequence" method.

As we have said, it makes little or no difference to the Songhay and Dogon whether the footage Rouch shows them was shot in accordance with the "one take/one sequence" method. He is committed to the "one take/one sequence" method because it makes his films not only "documents" of the events he filmed, but of his filming as well. The reality his films "document" is one in which he did not merely witness these fabulous spectacles; in filming from his place behind the camera, he was possessed by the spirits animating them, was able to abandon himself and pull off performances so thrilling that the gods themselves were compelled to take notice.

When Rouch discusses his films, he shares knowledge with the audience, but he also banks on his presence – he is the man who has not only witnessed but participated in these events, the man who has pulled off these performances that reveal him to have been initiated into the mysteries he has filmed, the man whose presence among us is itself a mystery. On such occasions, Rouch unfailingly projects an infectious joyfulness. But his boyish enthusiasm is always tinged with melancholy, as if he were at the same time a young man filled with hopes and dreams and an elder whose life has stripped him of his illusions, perhaps a bit of his once boundless energy, though not his sense of wonder. We might also say that his melancholy acknowledges that his irrepressible enthusiasm is an act, part of a "*shtick*," as it were. Of course, the melancholy may itself be part of his act. Surely, however, if this joyfulness-tinged-with-melancholy is an act, it is one that manifests a profound side of Rouch.

It is part of Rouch's act, if it is an act, always to be friendly and approachable, good-humored and down to earth, but also to be a bit distant, as if part of his self remained among the Songhay and Dogon, or as if, in our presence, he were viewing us from a place behind the camera in which spirits invisible to us are visible to him. And it is part of his act, if it is an act, always to be a bit elusive as well, never to offer revelations unless they are solicited, in the manner of a Songhay or Dogon teacher who forthrightly answers every question but refrains from so much as hinting that there are further questions that remain to be asked. Rouch, the most charismatic of teachers, is the kind of teacher who teaches by example. His way of thinking, of living, *is* the example he teaches his followers to emulate.

Chronicle of a Summer provides glimpses of Rouch's trademark joyfulness-tinged-with-melancholy. I am thinking of the moment, for example, in which he initiates the discussion following the screening. However, there his manner does not have its full effectiveness. First, because the ensuing discussion is hopelessly unfocused, largely because the questions Morin expected the film to answer (how do Parisians live their lives? are Parisians happy?) so obviously remain unanswered, unanswerable, by a film divorced from the rigorous intellectual framework characteristic of Rouch's Songhay and Dogon films. Second, because at this moment of *Chronicle*, Rouch does not step forward as the filmmaker – ostensibly, Morin, who was never behind the camera, is no less this film's "maker" than Rouch, who was sometimes behind the camera, but who even then did not employ the "one take/one sequence" method.

When Rouch, aspiring to further the goals of "shared anthropology," screens his films for the Songhay and Dogon who are in them, there is an asymmetry in their relationship. Although he never explicitly acknowledges this asymmetry, it is reflected in his language when, mimicking Vertovian terminology, he writes that the observer "ethno-looks" and "ethno-observes," but that what the "other" does is "ethno-show" and "ethno-speak." The result, Rouch maintains, is a conversation in which observer and "other" jointly pursue knowledge. But from the point of view of the observer, the "other" remains other; the conversation of "shared anthropology" is about the "other," not about the observer. The observer pursues knowledge about the way the "other" thinks and lives, while the "other" pursues knowledge about his or her own way of thinking and living. What for Rouch is anthropology is not anthropology at all for the Songhay and Dogon participants, but, rather, a pursuit of self-knowledge akin to philosophy. And what is philosophy for them is for him not philosophy at all, but, rather, a pursuit of anthropological knowledge, knowledge of the way "others" think and live. (Rouch has taught his method of filming to Africans. However, insofar as they go on to film their own "others," they become observers, no longer "others." And if they film people who think and live as they do, they are, again, not participating in anthropology.)

Putting a positive face on this asymmetry, we might say that "shared anthropology" effects a marriage between anthropology and philosophy, disciplines that have barely spoken to each other since the time of Kant. We might also say, less positively, that for the Songhay and Dogon, "shared anthropology" entails a denial or avoidance of pursuing knowledge of the way Rouch thinks and lives, and that for Rouch it entails a denial or avoidance of pursuing knowledge of his own way of thinking and living.

And yet when Rouch screens his films to Western students the asymmetry is reversed. It is his way of thinking and living, not theirs, which becomes the object of their study. Insofar as they pursue this study by asking questions about his way of filming, respond to his answers with further questions, and so on, their questions are capable of provoking Rouch to manifest a philosophical perspective of self-reflection, to articulate aspects of his way of thinking and living he may never before have put into words. What for his students is a training in anthropology becomes for him, at least potentially, a pursuit of self-knowledge akin to philosophy. That Rouch must be provoked to manifest a philosophical perspective, however, underscores that "shared anthropology" otherwise resists self-reflection.

In the summer of 1978, my wife, Kitty Morgan, who was Director of the University Film Study Center Summer Institute on the Media Arts, arranged for Rouch to offer a seminar on film and anthropology. I regularly sat in, as I did when she brought him back to the Institute in 1979, and when she coordinated the seminar the following summer at Harvard. During those years, I was writing *Hitchcock – The Murderous Gaze*, and was deeply immersed in philosophical issues intimately related to Rouch's work. Recognizing that I was able to provoke Rouch into addressing questions of philosophy he would otherwise have passed over in silence, and sensing – or imagining – that he appreciated my provoking him to overcome his resistance to speaking about such matters, I took it upon myself to draw him out philosophically. Every page of this book, and not only the present chapter, is profoundly indebted to those memorable seminars.

I do not share Rouch's faith that participating in "shared anthropology" gives his films a value that transcends their value as works of art. Rouch's resistance to treating his films as objects of value in and of themselves has had the regrettable consequence of leading him to neglect the real-life fate of his films, most of which have no distributors, commercial or otherwise, and are thus difficult or impossible even for educational institutions to obtain. No doubt, part of this apparent neglectfulness is a resigned acceptance of the depressing realities of nontheatrical film distribution. Rouch shot some of his greatest films on reversal stock, and it takes money to make negatives, money it is time-consuming to raise. But I cannot doubt that Rouch also takes satisfaction in knowing that he is screening the only print of a film he prizes, that every time he runs it through a projector he risks permanently mutilating or obliterating it. Rouch wants his films to be mortal, to have finite life spans, to be vulnerable to the whims of the Pale Fox.

In the climactic passage of *The Death of Old Anai*, as we have seen, Rouch breaks with his self-imposed "one take/one sequence" discipline, and discovers or rediscovers resources within the medium of film that enable his work to equal in beauty and power the elder's recitation of the Dogon myth of Creation. I take this to be, in part, an acknowledgment that this film's creation did not proceed of its own accord, that this film is a work of art, that the maker of this film is a master of the art of film, that he has made this art his own.

Rouch might deny this by saying that when he edited the sequence he was entranced, possessed (by Anai's spirit? by the spirit of the Pale Fox?). But he can hardly deny that the gesture he was possessed to perform is one that manifests a profound side of himself. And part of what this confirms is that, as I have argued, the applicability of such concepts as "ciné-trance" and "possession" is not limited to films made in conformity with the "one take/one sequence" method. When Rouch avails himself of the powers of montage at this most charged moment of perhaps his greatest film, he is acknowledging that there is a profound side of film – and of himself – that the "one take/one sequence" method is not capable of manifesting. Evidently, Anai's funeral provoked Rouch to make manifest this profound side of film, this profound side of his own art.

Rouch's reluctance to treat his films as works of art may help him to charm audiences for whom he screens them, but there is something about the art of film, something about his own art, his own self, that it denies.

Many Rouch films are enhanced, not diminished, when he uses them to win converts to "shared anthropology." But that is because such films were already diminished by being made to be used for this purpose, diminished by the way they were made. *Anai* is not one of those films capable of enchanting an audience only when Rouch is present to screen it. For Rouch to treat it as if it were would be for him to diminish the film, to deny something about what it is, something about who he is. In truth, it must be admitted, only a few of Rouch's dozens of films are in this category; only a few Rouch films merit comparison, as examples of the art of film, to masterpieces like *Land without Bread* or *Night and Fog*. Viewed as an example of the art of film, even *Chronicle of a Summer* is at times slapdash and incoherent, and not only because Rouch and Morin so often worked at cross-purposes. That is why I chose to write about the film by singling out two perfectly crafted sequences, rather than by addressing its overall form or structure or "message."

Noting that the films that preceded it were very different from the films that followed it, I characterized *Chronicle* as a pivotal work in Rouch's career. It might seem, rather, to be an anomaly, for it differs in crucial ways from all his other films, early or late. No Rouch film before or after *Chronicle* treats the people in it as characters in depth, takes such an interest in them as distinctive individuals worthy of acknowledgment in their own right. No other Rouch film focuses so intimately on the realm of the private – on the ways people quest for love, the ways they pursue happiness, the ways they work, the ways they live and think about their everyday lives. Not coincidentally, no other Rouch film is so passionately involved with the lives and thoughts of women.

Chronicle, for all its distinctiveness, is not really an anomaly, however; mythically, as it were, its making is profoundly meaningful within the context of Rouch's career. In *The Rules of the Game*, André persuades his friend Octave (played by Renoir himself) to stop whatever he is doing in order to initiate – against Octave's better judgment – a chain of events that ultimately leads to André's death and Octave's banishment or self-banishment. On the occasion of the invention of the lightweight synch-sound camera, Morin similarly persuaded his friend Rouch, against Rouch's better judgment, to stop filming Songhay and Dogon rituals long enough to return to his own village to make a film about ordinary Parisians, a film promising to change the way they live and think.

Within *Chronicle*, Rouch may appear the optimist and Morin the pessimist. But it is Morin who expected that their film would spread love, and Rouch who entered into the project believing that the people they were filming – like all of us in Western society – were hopelessly stuck in "private traps." *Chronicle* not only confirmed Rouch in this belief, but revealed something further. In filming Marilou, he was enchanted by her, even as she was being forced back on herself, was being possessed not by a spirit hungering for life but by nothingness. And in filming Marceline, he consigned her, conspired with her to enable her to consign herself, to a "self-contained universe" that renders the real world an image. He built a death camp for her, and for himself. For Rouch to film these human beings in despair, trapped in a society that consigns them to despair, is to deny their humanity. And it is to deny his own humanity, too.

And so after *Chronicle of a Summer* Rouch makes no more films that are "scratched and clawed" from within his "private trap." Like Octave at the end of *The Rules of the Game*, Rouch breaks his attachment to his home. Frightened by filming Marceline, enchanted by filming Marilou, behind whose mask lies nothingness, Rouch departs his village, like the soul of the dead Anai. Never again has he filmed this world in despair – his world, our world.

It may appear that Rouch has given the world up, given up on the world, and that "shared anthropology" is his excuse, that it is, to paraphrase Jean-Pierre, Rouch's intellectual justification to keep out, a justification that deep down he knows to be false, to mask a lack of courage. I prefer to believe that "shared anthropology" is Rouch's faith, not his excuse – that in turning back to filming Songhay and Dogon rituals, in turning away from filming the realm of the private, the everyday, the familiar, he is not giving the world up, not giving up on the world, but, rather, trying to save the world the only way he believes it can be saved – by reclaiming the knowledge our society possessed before we became alienated, alienated ourselves, from nature, from our own nature, from art. I may not share Rouch's faith, but I do respect it.

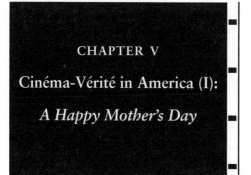

Primary (1960), the first of the Drew Associates productions that are usually considered the earliest examples of cinéma-vérité in America, was made simultaneously with *Chronicle of a Summer* in France. Cinéma-vérité on both sides of the Atlantic – because the distinction between "cinéma-vérité" and "direct cinema" is not a viable one, I have no qualms about using "cinéma-vérité" as a general term to cover a wide range of films – was inspired and influenced by Canadian filmmakers working under the auspices of the National Film Board, who were the first to venture into the "real world" with portable synch-sound equipment to capture unscripted, undirected "reality." (The National Film Board of Canada was founded in the forties by John Grierson, who coined the term "documentary" in the twenties, defining it as the "creative treatment of reality," and presided over the British documentary film movement in the thirties. The National Film Board filmmakers inherited, but also fundamentally revised, Grierson's understanding of documentary as primarily playing a social or political role.) Nonetheless I associate cinéma-vérité primarily with the United States. It is in the United States that the grandest hopes for cinéma-vérité have been harbored. It is in the United States that cinéma-vérité filmmakers have created the most extensive and impressive body of work. And, although it has not ordinarily been thought of in this way, cinéma-vérité in the United States has been perhaps the fullest inheritor of the classical American cinema of the thirties and forties.

Given the early example of *Nanook of the North*, 1960 may well seem a surprisingly late date for cinéma-vérité to have emerged. To be sure, the technology for portable synch-sound shooting became available only at the end of the fifties. Yet in the twenties filmmakers could have made silent films that emulated Flaherty's pioneering work. In the intervening decades, filmmakers could have made such films by shooting them silent and post-dubbing them in the studio, the way postwar Italian directors did in the forties and fifties when (in pursuit of realism and in the absence of practical alternatives) they began shooting their "fiction" films on location using nonprofessional actors in many keys roles. In American films of the fifties, the advent of Method acting likewise reflected a pursuit of realism (an actor like Marlon Brando discovers so deep a connection with the character he is playing that, from the inside as well the outside, nothing appears to separate them). However, not even André Bazin, France's great champion of realism, advocated the decisive further step of dispensing altogether with scripts, actors, and directors to film "real" people going about their lives. Filmmakers evidenced little interest in taking this step until the end of the fifties, when technology became available that made it possible to film people in the world *speaking* – speaking spontaneously, speaking their own words in their own voices.

The role of speaking in the human form of life, hence also the role of silence (and of singing, it might be added) – when and how and why human beings in the world break their silence, the powers and limits of the human voice – has always been a central concern of cinéma-vérité in America. This concern is the other face of cinéma-vérité's forgoing of "authoritarian" voice-over narration. In cinéma-vérité films, no assertions have absolute authority; words are spoken in particular ways by particular people to particular people on particular occasions for particular reasons. "Truth" is to be revealed, not asserted by a narrator whose authority is not to be questioned.

It may thus be said that there is a particular philosophy of language – a particular philosophy of expression, of language *as* expression – that cinéma-vérité embraces. Cinéma-vérité affirms the reality of the one existing world, the world in which language is a condition of the form of life we call "human." The world on film, in cinéma-vérité, is the real world in which our speech acts, like all of our actions, are expressions of our existence as embodied, finite creatures who are fated to be born into the world and to die, having lived out myths whose every moment means more than we know.

It is no accident that cinéma-vérité emerged at a particular moment in the history of technology, a moment equipment became available that made it possible to affirm such a philosophy *by* filming people going about their lives of speaking and silence. Nor is it an accident that cinéma-vérité emerged at a particular moment in the history of Western philosophy, a moment this particular philosophy was itself available to be affirmed, as it were, for example, in the existential phenomenology of Maurice Merleau-Ponty in France or, in America, in the "ordinary language philosophy" associated with the names of Ludwig Wittgenstein and J. L. Austin. (I am not suggesting that the filmmakers who pioneered cinéma-vérité were students of the philosophical writings of Merleau-Ponty, Wittgenstein, or Austin, but, rather, that the understanding of language as a condition of the human form of life in the world that finds philosophical expression in such works as Wittgenstein's *Philosophical Investigations* finds cinematic expression in cinéma-vérité, the way the skeptical problematic that finds philosophical expression in Descartes's *Meditations* finds expression in Shakespearean theater.)

Having said this much, however, it is necessary to add that the particular philosophy that finds expression in cinéma-vérité had already found expression in America's "classical cinema." It had found expression in the popular genres such as the comedy of remarriage and the melodrama of the unknown woman (as Stanley Cavell has named them) that crystallized in Hollywood in the thirties and forties, at the moment in the history of technology when the equipment became available that enabled movies in synch-sound, "talkies," to be made, at least in the studio. (Then what moment was this in the history of philosophy that a way of thinking yet to be articulated by such philosophers as Wittgenstein was already available to the makers and viewers of popular American movies? One way of answering this question would be to suggest that this way of thinking *originated* in the popular American movies to which Wittgenstein was personally devoted. Another way of answering the question, without denying the originality of Hollywood movies, would be to trace their philosophical sources, as Stanley Cavell does when he discovers, for example, the magnitude of classical American cinema's inheritance of the transcendental philosophy of Emerson and Thoreau.)

Cinéma-vérité and classical cinema share a common picture of human existence, a common way of picturing human existence, a common way of expressing the reality of the world on film. What is a cinéma-vérité film but a talkie, after all? When a classical movie is made, a screenplay is first written. The screenplay is a blueprint for a film that does not yet exist in the world; it may also be thought of as a transcription of a film that already exists, but only in the writer's imagination. In imagining in advance this film that is subsequently to be realized in the studio, the writer imagines it as a succession of happenings that unfold of their own accord, unscripted and undirected. It is thus tolerably close to the truth to say that every classical movie is first imagined as a cinéma-vérité film. In turn, every cinéma-vérité film can be imagined as having really been scripted and directed (like *David Holtzman's Diary* or Mitchell Block's *No Lies*), as really being a closet classical movie, in effect. To paraphrase our discussion of *Nanook of the North*, what is fictional about a classical movie resides in its fiction that it is only fiction; what is fictional about a cinéma-vérité film resides in its fiction that it is not fictional at all. Strip away what is fictional, and there is no real difference between them. The difference between a cinéma-vérité film and a classical movie is not a function of particular features that one possesses and the other lacks, in other words. The difference between them amounts only to the difference between what is real and what is imagined.

Viewing *On the Waterfront*, I know it is impossible for me to be – to have been – present with Terry and his brother Charlie when Terry recognizes the lost chances, the betrayals and self-betrayals, that he has allowed to define his life. However, although I was not in fact present with Marlon Brando, Rod Steiger and Elia Kazan when these shots were taken, it is not in the same way an impossibility. I *could* have been there, as I *could* have been in the limousine with Dylan and his entourage (among them D. A. Pennebaker and his sound recordist) after the Albert Hall concert that culminates *Don't Look Back*, when Dylan's manager, Albert Grossman, subversively plants the idea in the head of the young singer/songwriter/poet/prophet that "anarchist" is the word for the kind of rebel he is.

And yet, of course, the past is as it is. Reality is a world of possibilities, but it is never a possibility for the past, for history, to have been, to be, to become, other than what it is. The only real way of changing the past is by attaining a new perspective on it, a perspective that acknowledges that it *is* past, that it cannot otherwise change. In cinéma-vérité, the past is viewed from a new perspective that brings it into alignment with the myths of movies. This means both that cinéma-vérité brings the myths of movies down to earth, reveals them to be played out within our lives in the real world, and at the same time elevates the real world to the status of myth, reveals our lives to have the mythical dimension of movies.

In the thirties and forties, the average American went to the movies more than once a week. By the end of the fifties, the audience for movies, once all of America, had dwindled and fragmented. More and more, it was rock 'n' roll, seductively promising to break down barriers *now*, not film, in which a screen appears to separate us from the world of our fantasies, that fired the imagination of young Americans, although they went to the movies anyway (at least it got them out of the house). More and more, their parents, once the audience for classical Hollywood movies, stayed home and watched television, opting for television's assurance that what was happening now was not really passing them by, that they were monitoring the world, were plugged in after all. How could they not have known in their hearts that their lives in fifties America failed to fulfill the transcendental aspirations expressed by the movies they had once embraced? The younger generation did not "connect" with the classical genres, which seemed to have lost their vitality and relevance to the older generation, too. America seemed to have lost even the memory of the profound and inspiring conversation its movies had once sustained with their culture.

In part, the changed pattern of American moviegoing is a reflection of the rise of suburbia in the period following the Second World War. What remains mysterious is why the generation of Americans that was Hollywood's primary audience in the thirties, the generation that had taken to heart the utopian dreams of classical American movies, embraced these wholesale changes in the American landscape and social and cultural fabric. To be sure, suburbia was aggressively sold; Americans were manipulated and exploited by forces (the automobile lobby, for one) that stood to profit – are still profiting – from its construction. But to say that Americans were sold a bill of goods does not explain why they bought it.

One possible explanation is that Americans simply changed their minds, converted, gave up an old dream in favor of a new one, or – they had been through so much, having lived through the Great Depression and the Second World War – in favor of no dream at all. There is truth in this view, but there is also truth in the view that Americans saw their investment in the suburban way of life as not only consistent with the old dream but mandated by it, as if, having survived the Depression and won the war against the enemies of freedom, Americans were seizing this historic moment to undertake the heroic enterprise of making real the collective dream of their popular movies.

In the thirties and forties, comedies such as *It Happened One Night, The Awful Truth, Bringing Up Baby, His Girl Friday, The Philadelphia Story, The Lady Eve,* and *Adam's Rib* envisioned a new kind of marriage between a man and a woman, one that acknowledges their equality without denying their difference. Such a marriage also marries the realities of the day and the dreams of the night, the realms of public and private, and the worlds of cosmopolitan city and all-American small town. This last point is registered in the films' insistence that, for the man and woman to resolve the conflicts in their relationship, they must at a certain moment find themselves in a place conducive to the attainment of a new perspective. Shakespearean criticism calls such a place the "Green World," and it is typically located, like Thoreau's Walden, just outside a major city. Hollywood movies, as Cavell delights in pointing out, usually call this place "Connecticut."

When America emerged from the Great Depression and the war and undertook to build suburbia, it aspired to make this utopian dream real by making it possible for ordinary Americans (not all Americans, to be sure, but that is another story) to own a house in the real Connecticut or in an equivalent place. This appears to interpret "Connecticut" as a real, not a mythical, location; to interpret America's lack of perspective, its need for renewal, as a material, not a spiritual, condition. But the post-World War II aspiration was also a transcendental one, or, rather, it was the aspiration of transforming the material, the here and now, into the spiritual, the aspiration of transforming the real Connecticut into the mythical Connecticut of the remarriage comedies, of transforming reality into dream, or, rather, marrying them.

If the creation of suburbia heralded the ascendancy of consumerist materialism in America, it also expressed America's continuing wish for spiritual renewal. In this sense it was an extension of the transcendentalism of Hollywood movies of the thirties. Indeed, it precisely articulated an intuition crucial to these films, that happiness is not to be found in some mythical "other" realm in which we might be imagined as living happily ever after, but is to be achieved here on Earth, achieved by living every day and night in a festive spirit, a spirit of adventure. The real suburbia even goes remarriage comedies one better. In *The Awful Truth,* after all, the remarriage comedy that most emphatically insists that spiritual renewal calls for a transformed perspective on the everyday, Cary Grant and Irene Dunne make the liberating move – in this case, to Long Island, rather than Connecticut – only once. If "Connecticut" means the perspective that transfigures the everyday, discovers the mythical within the ordinary, how much better to buy a house in Connecticut and make the commute every day!

113

This would be to participate in the creation of a new America in which renewal was itself to become an everyday occurrence.

In pondering these matters, I think of *It's a Wonderful Life*, surely a profound expression of America's mood immediately after the war. I am struck especially by the Stewart character's depression as he finds his dream of exploring the wide world, his dream of adventure, continually deferred, and by his rage and despair – to the point of mad rage and suicide – when he realizes he is fated never to leave his hometown, that he is condemned to a life split down the middle between domesticity and work. When he dies and is reborn into humanity like the heroine of a remarriage comedy, he comes to understand what his wife (Donna Reed) had always known: His dream of adventure had come true, his everyday life was all the adventure of his dreams. All he needed was to awaken to this reality.

With Stewart's awakening, a powerful resistance an American male might feel to settling in a suburb is symbolically overcome. (To a man who dreams of adventure, moving to a suburb would have seemed less depressing than staying in a town like Bedford Falls, since in a suburb a man can commute to the city, from which only half his life need be divorced.) Renewed, he rededicates his life to his beleaguered savings and loan, to helping the town's "little people" buy their own little houses with yards, their own pieces of suburbia. The film's most prophetic image – in retrospect, perhaps its most horrifying one – is the glimpse it offers of the new suburb, a veritable miniature Levittown, with its neat little streets of identical matchbox houses, each a self-contained universe.

It's a Wonderful Life prophesies the creation of suburbia, envisioning it as a utopian undertaking, the real fulfillment of the dream of classical American movies. Yet for the Stewart character himself, the man who dreams this American dream, accepting life in Bedford Falls – and hardly in a matchbox – is shown to necessitate a cataclysmic spiritual struggle. What is devastatingly honest in the film is its deep acknowledgment that, for the generation that was Hollywood's audience in the thirties, settling for suburbia, trading freedom for a life split down the middle between job and family, felt more like the death of a dream than its fulfillment. What is devastatingly dishonest is the film's assurance that Mr. Potter, the archetypal American capitalist, stands to lose rather than profit from the creation of suburbia; its assurance – or is this ironic? – that, for those who are truly worthy, guardian angels will assure that their dreams will come true, that they will pass safely through the dark night of the soul and regain all they have lost and more; its assurance that "little people" experience no comparable loss when they move into matchboxes; and its assurance that a woman who never doubts for a moment that marrying the right man and being mother to his children will make her a happy, fulfilled human being will, indeed, find happiness and human fulfillment.

This unequal division between man and woman is not what remarriage comedies had in mind, as can be seen by contrasting *It's a Wonderful Life* with the contemporaneous *Adam's Rib*, the latest of the definitive remarriage comedies and something of an anachronism among late-forties Hollywood productions. In *Adam's Rib*, Katharine Hepburn and Spencer Tracy are both successful lawyers, and the film endorses the woman's demand that their equality be acknowledged privately (within the intimacy of their marriage) and also publicly (by society at large). In its assurance that the Donna Reed character is happy without such acknowledgment, *It's a Wonderful Life* negates the conditions of the remarriage comedy genre. Yet in Stewart's desperate wish for a marriage of dream and reality, of romance and the everyday, and in the film's conviction that one never wins one's dream without taking the risk of losing it, the film also keeps faith with the genre's spirit.

Split down the middle though it is, *It's a Wonderful Life* is saying to its postwar audience that we have to risk change, America has to risk it, if we are not to abandon our dreams. Beyond this, it is saying that we must change now or our American dream, our dream of America, will be forever lost. *It's a Wonderful Life* entertains a vision of the death of the dream of classical American movies only to proclaim, however problematically, the dream's rebirth and fulfillment. At the same historical moment, American film noir was claiming to unmask that dream, and to celebrate its destruction. In film noir, a man possessed by the romantic dream of Hollywood films of the thirties undergoes disillusionment, awakens to the fact that he has been the victim of his dream and the cynical men and evil women who exploit it to satisfy their own sordid appetites. With luck, he lives to tell the tale and goes on to live a life stripped of illusions, to marry a nice "girl" and live a safe, normal existence, perhaps even in Connecticut. In film noir's nightmare revision of the myths of classical American movies, suburbia is not the fulfillment of the American dream, it is what remains of America when the dream is mercifully destroyed in a cataclysm that is, despite everything, to be welcomed.

Both film noir, which participates in the destruction of the utopian dream of classical Hollywood movies, and *It's a Wonderful Life*, which reaffirms that dream even as it participates in undermining it, point their audience toward suburbia. On this, there is a consensus. (At this moment also Hollywood stopped making "women's films," a genre that might have resisted endorsing this consensus.) A subtler point is that both an unreconstructed dreamer like the protagonist of *It's a Wonderful Life* and the disillusioned men of film noir share a characteristic prophetic of the fate of Hollywood's American audience of the thirties: Each can readily be imagined as being a regular moviegoer prior to his metamorphosis, but it is difficult to imagine that either man, after his transformation, finds Hollywood movies – old or new – to have anything to offer him. On this, too, there is a consensus.

The concept of "consensus," indeed, is almost unavoidable in thinking about this period in American film, as it is in thinking about this period in American politics. The late forties and early fifties are a period of transition in which consensus (enforced, if need be, by the silencing of opposing voices) gains ascendancy over conversation, conformity gains ascendancy over diversity, in American culture. Consensus is both a condition and an effect, for example, of television's supplanting of film's position of dominance. When *It's a Wonderful Life* gives way to the *Donna Reed Show*, the glorious conversation of classical Hollywood movies, already muted in the postwar environment, is reduced to silence, or, rather, reduced to what television calls "talk."

Rather than facilitating the marriage of urban and rural America, men and women, day and night, reality and fantasy, which was the aspiration of Hollywood films of the thirties and forties, suburbia built a fence between them. Rather than enabling men and women to be joined in marriages that acknowledge their equality without denying their difference, suburbia locked women into the domestic realm while it denied them the public identity it accorded men. And the ideal marriages envisioned in classical remarriage comedies, relationships envisioned as being of absolute value in themselves, decisively gave way, in the American reality as well as the American cinema of the fifties, to the traditional imperative of raising children in the proper environment, as if bringing up babies were the only valid goal of marriage.

This negation of the utopian dream of classical American movies is both a condition and an effect of the consumerism that is the other face of the creation of suburbia. Consumerism was American capitalism's solution, along with the Cold War, to the threat of sliding back into economic depression. Already in the thirties, marketing of consumer goods had begun to exploit the glamour of Hollywood movie stars. By the early forties, the American film industry was acutely conscious of the possibilities of promoting films, especially "women's films," by linking them with product tie-ins. Manifestly, however, in the fifties the primary product of Hollywood remained movies. Hollywood sold theater tickets, not consumer goods. The ascendancy of consumerism over transcendentalism called for the ascendancy of television over movies, called for the repression, or sublimation, of the utopian aspiration of classical American movies, the dream of attaining a new perspective that would enable Americans to acknowledge our equality without denying our differences, the way Katharine Hepburn and Spencer Tracy do in *Adam's Rib*. In the fifties, Hollywood's once profound exploration, and revision, of the concept of marriage tended to degenerate into regressive assertions of the doctrine that happiness necessarily follows from meeting and marrying Mr. or Miss Right, and the cognate doctrine that reality is secondary to the realm of appearances, the realm of images (if love is at first sight, one had better keep one's hair in fighting trim, better dress fashionably and have cool things to say, to assure that one makes the right impression).

Part of the explanation is the sheer power of television in the hands of forces aggressively using the new technology to sell consumer goods, to sell consumerism itself, by exploiting the utopian dreams as well as the material needs of Americans. But another part of the explanation must be internal to the Hollywood films of the thirties, to the dream that underwrote, and was underwritten by, their bond with their audience. The reality of suburbia failed the dream. But in the new suburban reality, the dream, too, failed.

Cavell puts his finger on one source of this failure when he points out that Hollywood remarriage comedies, when they envision ideal marriages that are of value in themselves, represent such marriages as being without children, and when he points out that fathers but not mothers have major roles to play in these movies. Remarriage comedies avoid the subject of motherhood, and in the "women's films" of the thirties and forties that do center on motherhood, a woman's happiness in marriage and her fulfillment in motherhood never turn out to be compatible. The creation of suburbia is simultaneous with the baby boom, the moment at which the generation that was Hollywood's American audience in the thirties stopped putting off having children. A house in Connecticut is one thing for two childless professionals like Spencer Tracy and Katharine Hepburn in *Adam's Rib*. It is something else when the woman has no career and is stuck at home with the kids. Hollywood films of the thirties, which never envision combining children with an ideal marriage, provided no instruction for coping with the poignant and stressful new situation in which their audience, especially their audience of women, found itself in the fifties. So it was up to the children of these women, with no instruction from their parents and no help from Hollywood movies or from television, to create the next stage of feminism, in which motherhood and career, not marriage, became the central issues.

In any case, it is understandable that in the climate of the late fifties the pioneers of American cinéma-vérité, men like Richard Leacock and D. A. Pennebaker, and their audiences, believed that cinéma-vérité owed nothing to classical movies, that cinéma-vérité was, indeed, Hollywood's enemy. In truth, however, cinéma-vérité in America owed more to the classical American cinema than to the tradition of documentary films. Indeed, cinéma-vérité in America inherited, more fully even than most of the Hollywood films that were contemporaneous with them, the philosophical concerns of classical American movies. And cinéma-vérité inherited from classical cinema its picture of – and its way of picturing – human being-in-the-world. In *The "I" of the Camera* I characterized this in terms of a dialectic between the public and the private:

Typically, the camera alternately frames its human subjects within public and private spaces. The frame of an "objective" shot is a stage on which human beings perform, subject to view by others in their world. Within the frame of a reaction shot, a subject views the spectacle of the world, reacts privately to it, and prepares the next venture into the public world. Point-of-view and reaction shots together combine to effect the camera's penetration of the privacy of its human subject, who alternates tensely and hesitantly between acting and viewing as he or she prepares an entrance onto the world's stage, performs, and withdraws again into a privacy to which only the camera has access.[43]

Cinéma-vérité did not follow classical cinema in its use of point-of-view technique. Nonetheless, it inherited classical cinema's stake in the everyday, the ordinary. It inherited, as well, classical cinema's understanding that within this private realm the noncandid – the unspontaneous, the manipulated and the manipulative, the theatrical – is everywhere to be found. And it inherited classical cinema's conviction that our happiness as individuals, and America's as a nation, turns on our ability to overcome or transcend the split between our private and public selves, between our public acts and our private fantasies and dreams.

As we have seen, Jean Rouch's intention in coining the term "cinéma-vérité" was less to distinguish between truthful and untruthful kinds of films than to affirm that cinema has its own ways of being truthful (as it has its own ways of lying). He was suggesting that the world on film is capable of revealing its own reality, its own truth, *cinema* truth. What I am now suggesting is that cinéma-vérité emerged in America at a moment at which this "cinema truth," the reality of the world on film, stood in need of being restored.

By the end of the fifties, amid the ruins of inner cities ringed by spotless new shopping centers, and amid the ruins of the classical Hollywood tradition, the "truth of cinema," the reality of the world on film, was all but lost to American movies. For all their pursuit of realism, in the typical movies Hollywood was making at the time of the emergence of cinéma-vérité, the world on film had become a self-contained universe that was all but unimaginable as real. The promise of cinéma-vérité in America was not that it might free the cinema from its traditional way of lying, but that it might restore its traditional way of being truthful, might reaffirm the reality of the world on film, the "cinema truth" that classical American movies had once underwritten and been underwritten by. (Again, I am not suggesting that Leacock and Pennebaker, much less Robert Drew, consciously thought about their work in such terms.) If it was portable synch-sound equipment that made cinéma-vérité possible, it was a crisis of conviction in the reality of the world on film that made it necessary – necessary, that is, if movies were to continue to be made in America that would seem – would be – as real, as truthful, as Hollywood films of the thirties and forties had been, in their day, to their audience of all Americans (and their audiences worldwide).

The crisis of conviction in the reality of the world on film was not a crisis within the history of film alone, not a crisis for film alone. What was becoming all but unimaginable was the real world itself, a world in which it was becoming all but impossible for Americans to recognize their own dreams. Even as reality was becoming all but unimaginable, hence all but inexpressible by any medium other than film (the medium in which the world automatically reproduces itself in its own image), reality was becoming all but inexpressible, as well, by movies made the traditional way, that is, by being realized only after first being imagined. To be filmed, however, the world does not have to be imagined or even imaginable; all it has to be is real. Hence the possibility of cinéma-vérité. Hence, too, its necessity, at this moment of crisis.

The earliest works of American cinéma-vérité, *Primary* (1960), *Crisis: Behind a Presidential Commitment* (1962), and the other Drew productions, were not made to be shown in movie theaters, with their dwindling and fragmented audiences.[44] They were broadcast with great fanfare on prime-time network television. Like television dramas, soap operas, and situation comedies, and like classical movies before them, the Drew productions were concerned with the realm of the private. But they were also public affairs programs, news.

Ordinarily, what television called "news" was reported by newscasters who addressed the camera directly; the mode was assertion. Even in the kind of investigative reports associated in the fifties with the name of Edward R. Murrow, newscasters told viewers what to make of what they were viewing; the mode was still assertion. Whether the newscaster was a neutral reader or put a personal stamp on the story the way Murrow characteristically did, he or she was always making or relaying assertions as to what was happening. The newscaster was always playing the role of reporter, always wearing a mask, always "on." The format of television news provided no way of calling into question the authority of these assertions, of distinguishing the private person from the role of reporter, no way even of acknowledging that there was a role being performed, a mask being worn. And this was also true for the newsmakers themselves, the people whose public actions and declarations *were* the news as television reported it.

At least up to a point, in the Drew productions the mode was revelation, as it was in classical movies, rather than assertion. The cinéma-vérité camera revealed its human subjects continually putting on masks, taking them off, putting them on again, and so on, as they reacted to the spectacle of the world, prepared their next ventures into the public realm, performed on the world's stage, and withdrew again into a privacy to which the camera grants us access. (To be sure, when television was primarily live, masks had often slipped, or cracked, or inadvertently been put on not quite straight. Already by 1960, however, television was changing from a primarily live medium to one in which there is no longer a perceptible difference between the live and the canned, in which masks are only dropped when other masks are firmly in place beneath them. The effect is not to make the canned seem live, but to make even the live seem canned; it might be said that this is a denial of the uncanny.)

The Philadelphia Story, made in 1940 at the height of the classical era, presented itself as a picture story published in *Spy Magazine*, a sleazy, voyeuristic scandal sheet. The cynical intention of *Spy*'s editor, in sending a reporter and photographer to intrude as unwanted guests at the wedding of socialite Tracy Lord and the social-climbing George Kittredge, was to "open all the doors" of Philadelphia society and thereby to reveal the American reality to be so corrupt that nothing remained of the utopian ideals of the American Revolution. But the wedding it was the editor's intention to expose, to exploit, never took place. Instead, *Spy* found itself revealing the story behind a very different wedding, one that showed American ideals to be alive after all. When *Spy* published *this* picture story, made public *these* revelations of the private realm, it *was* an event of national importance. And, extending the film's allegory, the "publication" of *The Philadelphia Story* was no mere entertainment or cynical expose; its public affirmation of the "truth of cinema" was an event of national importance, too.

The Drew productions were broadcast as news, although they reported little or nothing of journalistic substance. They did not probe beneath the surface; all they did was open doors. Most revolved around public figures, whom they revealed to be ordinary people even as they revealed these ordinary people, on film, to have what it takes to be stars (classical cinema had always made its stars out of ordinary people who happened to "have what it takes"). In them, public events were revealed to be made up of a succession of private moments. Transfigured by being viewed by millions of Americans in the privacy of their separate homes, these private moments were turned back into public events, events that television presented as being of national importance.

And this in itself was an event of national importance. For television had built a fence separating assertions about the public realm, what it called "news," from revelations of the private realm, which it exploited yet hypocritically relegated to the status of mere "entertainment." Television purported to keep us "plugged in," to enable Americans, without leaving their homes, to monitor what was happening in the outside world. And yet it built a fence that was a denial of the true dimension of the realm of the private, a denial of the importance, the reality, of what is not capable of being asserted, only revealed. And it was a denial, as well, of the true dimension of the public realm, one that reduced the public to a self-contained universe that was closed off from us, not the real world itself.

At least up to a point, in the Drew productions, as in classical movies, there is no world apart from the world on film, a world in which the public and the private, like the real and the imaginary, are both encompassed, are dialectically joined, as they are in myths. By broadcasting the Drew productions *as news*, by declaring their revelations of the private realm to be of national importance, network television was promising to tear down the fence it had built to deny the "truth of cinema," the reality of the world on film.

These broadcasts heralded a new era of film, wedded to network television, that promised to reclaim classical cinema's audience of all America, to enable film to resume the profound conversation with its culture that American movies had once enjoyed. They also heralded a new era of television, wedded to the reality of the world on film, that promised to overcome or transcend television's denial of the "truth of cinema."

And yet these much-heralded promises were fated not to be kept. Within a few short years, broadcasts like *Primary* and *Crisis* were exorcised from prime-time network schedules, never to return. The Drew team broke up, and the likes of Leacock and Pennebaker declared their separate identities *as filmmakers* in such works as Leacock's (and Joyce Chopra's) *A Happy Mother's Day* (1963) and Pennebaker's *Don't Look Back* (shot in 1965 and released in 1967) and *Monterey Pop* (shot in 1967 and released in 1968). In these works, dispossessed from network television and thus compelled to discover or create their own audiences *as films*, cinéma-vérité in America was reborn, humbled yet confirmed in its commitment to the "truth of cinema." Indeed, it is this moment when cinéma-vérité "found itself," not its short-lived marriage with network television, that I think of as the true birth of cinéma-vérité in America.

This does not mean, however, that television came to forgo the practice, pioneered by the Drew productions, of presenting (or appearing to present) "real" people in unscripted, undirected situations. Rather, as we might put it, the cinéma-vérité impulse was split. It is an indisputable fact that cinéma-vérité permanently altered American television, where its impact and influence remains everywhere to be found (in the chitchat of Eyewitness News teams; in the anguish of relatives of murder victims who find cameras and microphones thrust into their faces as they are asked how they feel about the death of their loved ones; in "up-close and personal" mini-documentaries that help to "package" celebrity athletes and politicians; in the quasi-spontaneous confrontations that spice up talk shows such as Oprah Winfrey's; in "gavel to gavel" coverage of events such as the O. J. Simpson trial; in the personal testimonials for name-brand products that crop up in commercial after commercial; in music videos in which lip-synching rock stars simulate the conditions of live performance; and so on). Television developed its own uses for the techniques of cinéma-vérité (as well as for techniques that enable cinéma-vérité to be more or less convincingly faked). It might well be argued that television primarily uses these techniques to deny the "truth of cinema" that filmmakers like Leacock and Pennebaker, and the generation of independent filmmakers that have followed them, use those techniques to affirm.

The Drew productions, made before this split they were also instrumental in precipitating, provide glimpses both of what was to become of cinéma-vérité on television, and the devastating critique of television that cinéma-vérité was to become in the work of independent filmmakers.

It is in this context that I understand the significance of the kind of "crisis structure," as Stephen Mamber has called it, that Robert Drew imposed on all the productions he supervised. In *Primary*, for example, the "crisis" is the 1960 Wisconsin presidential primary itself: Will Hubert Humphrey, the picture of a traditional politician, hold off his telegenic young challenger, John F. Kennedy? In *Crisis: Behind a Presidential Commitment*, the "crisis" revolves around Governor George Wallace's threat to stand in the doorway to block two African-American students from entering the University of Alabama: Will the Kennedy administration succeed in stopping him?

By imposing a "crisis structure," Drew was attempting to make these productions conform to journalistic conventions; well-written news stories put their dramatic conflicts in the lead, after all. He was also attempting to invest them with the dramatic qualities of classical movies. In classical movies, however, the kinds of crises around which the Drew productions were made to revolve, like the plot devices Hitchcock liked to call "MacGuffins," are not of significance in themselves, but only insofar as they facilitate the dramatic revelations (and transformations) of character that students of screenwriting are taught to call "character arcs."

That human character is not fixed, that human beings are spontaneous creatures, that we are thus capable of change, that we are incapable of not changing, that we are changing at every moment of our lives, is an aspect of the "truth of cinema" that classical cinema underwrote and was underwritten by. Every moment of our lives has its "arc," every moment is a moment of decision, every moment is fateful, every moment means more than we know, every moment has a mythical dimension: This is classical cinema's picture of our human form of life. We might sum this picture up by saying that every moment of human existence is a crisis, as long as we keep in mind that to say that every moment is a crisis is also to say that no moment really is, that crisis is our *ordinary* condition, hence not, in itself, a crisis. To impose a "crisis structure" in the belief that this is the only way to render cinéma-vérité footage dramatic is to deny this condition, to deny the true dimension of the ordinary, to deny the mythical in the typical, to deny the utopian aspiration of classical American movies, to deny the reality of the world on film. And it is this denial of the "truth of cinema" that constitutes the real crisis to which cinéma-vérité in America is responding.

In *Crisis: Behind a Presidential Commitment*, there is never a doubt that President Kennedy and his brother, the attorney general, will prevail in enforcing the court-ordered integration of the University of Alabama. The only question is whether Governor Wallace will succeed in forcing the Kennedys, with the whole world watching on television, into a brief but embarrassing delay. Apart from the question of how these events will play out on television, how the media coverage will affect the president's image, there is no crisis in *Crisis*. Clearly, the "crisis structure" that is imposed in this case at once reveals and masks the real crisis, which is television's new-found efficacy – only in times of crisis, but television makes every time a time of crisis – in reducing the reality of presidential politics to a realm of mere images. The "crisis structure" imposed on *Crisis* at once reveals and masks this unsettling change in television's relationship to political power, which is documented, but also exemplified, by the broadcast of *Crisis* itself.

Night and Fog, made on the eve of the emergence of cinéma-vérité, undertook to restore the reality of the world of the past, the world that built the death camps and continued to deny their true dimension, in order that

122

the present, too, might become the real world again, not the mere image it had become. To restore, on film, the reality of the world meant to restore the reality of the world on film, to acknowledge that the world on film is not a mere image, not a self-contained universe. To make the present the real world, Resnais's work undertook to acknowledge, in the medium of film, that the past was past, that it was present only as past, the only real way the past can be present. To acknowledge this in the medium of film meant acknowledging that the world on film, too, was past. It meant enabling the world on film to die its own death, as it were. In the modernist project of *Night and Fog*, the end *of* the art of film became the new end *for* the art of film.

Chronicle of a Summer seconded *Night and Fog* in identifying the "truth of cinema" (the reality of the world on film) and also the present threat to that truth (our society's alienation from nature, from human nature, from art) with the unimaginable reality of the death camps (the number branded on Marceline's arm). For all the camera's powers of provocation, however, Rouch found that his acts of filming ordinary Parisians failed to provoke them to free themselves from their private traps, to tear down the fences that enclosed them within self-contained universes. Indeed, when Rouch filmed these subjects, he found himself conspiring with them to keep those fences standing, or to build them all over again, symbolically. Rather than welcoming them back to life, enabling life to know them again, he found himself denying their humanity, and his own, in his acts of filming. So he returned to Africa to resume filming Songhay and Dogon rituals, turned away from filming the realm of the everyday, the familiar, the private.

In the films Leacock and Pennebaker made after the Drew team broke up, no less than in *Night and Fog* or *Chronicle of a Summer*, the "truth of cinema" finds itself under threat in a world that has become all but unimaginable as real. These films, too, are responses to a sense that the reality of the present, like the reality of the world on film, stands in need of being restored. But America is the New World, not the Old. In these very American films, the death camps seem a world away. These films do not undertake to restore the reality of the world by restoring the true dimension of the past, but by embracing the present directly. Without looking back, they find promises of redemption – after all, this is America – in the flashes of humanity spontaneously revealed to, and by, the camera. And they equate the present threat – what it is that is making reality all but unimaginable, reducing the present to a self-contained universe – not with the legacy of European culture, not with the art and craft that built the death camps, but with the virulent new consumerism, the mindless conformity in the guise of pragmatism, the Hurdano-like obliviousness, that in America is signaled above all by the ascendancy of television.

In the aftermath of its traumatic expulsion from network television, American cinéma-vérité undertakes, by filming the world as it is, to discover a way of embracing the adventure of living, not a way of dying one's own death. *Night and Fog* calls upon us to hear the "endless cry" that is all around us and within ourselves. *Chronicle of a Summer* calls upon us to hear this cry reverberating in Marilou's and Marceline's silences. American cinéma-vérité, too, calls upon us to hear the "endless cry," but to hear it – to paraphrase a song Bob Dylan sings in *Don't Look Back* – as that of those who are busy being born (or busy giving birth), not those who are busy dying (or busy killing). What American cinéma-vérité undertakes to acknowledge is not the necessity of death, but the reality of life, the life of reality, the real possibility of spontaneous expression, in the present. Freedom is the "truth of cinema" that television in America was – is – busy denying.

A Happy Mother's Day

In 1963, Mary Ann Fischer of Aberdeen, South Dakota, gave birth to quintuplets. The *Saturday Evening Post*, which paid a substantial sum to the Fischer family for exclusive rights to the story, advanced funding to Richard Leacock, who had been Robert Flaherty's cameraman on *Louisiana Story* (1948) before joining Drew Associates, to cover the event in cinéma-vérité style in the expectation that the ABC network would broadcast the resulting program in prime time and with great fanfare.

In the hour-long program ABC prepared from the footage Leacock shot (with Joyce Chopra taking sound), the "crisis" is a rather uncompelling one: Will Dr. Berbos, who does not approve of mixing medicine and commerce, participate in the parade organized by the business community to celebrate the blessed event that has put Aberdeen on the map? (In the end, he does.) Apparently reflecting a loss of confidence in the Drew format, the program was a hybrid that mixed the modes of revelation and assertion, with the balance tipping toward assertion. Instead of broadcasting the cinéma-vérité material as a single film interrupted only by commercials, ABC divided it into segments, with an "anchor" in the studio introducing and commenting on each segment.

In the end, ABC decided not to broadcast the program. Leacock and Chopra edited the material into their own sixty-minute version. It so appalled the *Saturday Evening Post* that it washed its hands of the project, selling rights to the footage to the company Leacock and Pennebaker had jointly formed. Pennebaker helped edit the version down to the half-hour version that constitutes *A Happy Mother's Day* (1963) as we know it. No longer beholden to ABC's demand that they mask their point of view behind journalistic "objectivity," Leacock and his collaborators were free to think of the work simply as a film. No longer bound by Drew's dictum that they impose a "crisis structure" on their footage, they were free to explore other ways of investing it with the compelling impact of a "real movie." The result is a film that neither the *Saturday Evening Post* nor the ABC network could possibly have endorsed.

A Happy Mother's Day builds to a powerful emotional climax, to be sure. As is the case with great classical movies, however, what makes the film emotionally compelling cannot be separated from the intimacies of the relationship between the camera and its human subjects. In particular, the developing relationship between Mrs. Fischer and Leacock's camera is internal to the drama of *A Happy Mother's Day*. Within the events of the film, this woman's fate is at stake, symbolically or mythically. So is the fate of the filmmaker. So, too, is the fate of cinéma-vérité itself.

■

A Happy Mother's Day opens with the title "Leacock/Pennebaker," followed by the title "Presents," each title superimposed over a logo of two camera-carrying filmmakers walking down a road into the depths of the frame à la Charlie Chaplin, presumably on their way to discover new subjects to film. This is followed by what we take to be a family photograph of five children, each holding a baby. The title "A Happy Mother's Day" appears superimposed over this image.

A moment later, the narration begins, spoken by Ed McCurdy in a tone of voice that here, as throughout the film, positively drips with irony. "On September 23rd, 1963..." The image fades out.

As the narration continues ("...Mrs. Andrew Fischer, already a mother of five, left St. Luke's Hospital in Aberdeen, South Dakota. Mrs. Fischer had just become the mother of quintuplets"), we fade in on footage of Mrs. Fischer being escorted from the hospital.

I use the word "footage" here because at least initially nothing distinguishes this shot from one that might have been shown on a television newscast to document the departure from the hospital of this suddenly famous woman. After the shot has been on the screen for a few moments, however, it may well strike our attention that Mrs. Fischer's "entourage" is made up almost

125

entirely of reporters wielding cameras and microphones. That is, the shot turns out to document not only Mrs. Fischer's departure from the hospital, but also the documenting of this event by the news media.

All these cameras are present to facilitate the reporting of a real event, to transform a private moment into a public spectacle, an image of a real event. Insofar as Leacock's camera has been commissioned by ABC, a major television network, its presence, no less than that of the visible cameras whose presence it documents, is implicated in effecting this transformation of real into media event.

But Leacock's camera is also different from the others. It is the only camera that documents not only Mrs. Fischer's departure from the hospital, but also the presence of all those other cameras that are there to transform reality into images of reality. Then is this camera that provides us access to these events implicated, as all these other cameras are, in transforming, not merely documenting, the reality its presence enables us to view?

Leacock's camera is fated to be disowned by the network that initially authorized its presence. At the time this camera is performing its singular work – when it is shooting Mrs. Fischer leaving the hospital, for example – this fate is as yet unrevealed. And yet it is by virtue of doing its singular work – by shooting what it shoots the singular way it shoots it – that Leacock's camera seals its fate. As we shall see, *A Happy Mother's Day* chronicles the events that at one level culminate in the camera's discovery, and declaration, of its own independence.

Within the interview that ensues, too, nothing at first distinguishes the shot from news footage. Leacock's camera might just as well be a news camera, for example, when it films Mrs. Fischer saying, with a sigh, "I don't have many feelings," laughing, and thanking everyone, or when (in a new setup with Mr. Fischer beside her in the frame) it films her answer ("Wonderful!") to a reporter's question ("How will it feel to see your children at home?").

However, when a newsman asks the apparently innocuous question "What do the kids call you?," Mrs. Fischer becomes so upset she is unwilling or unable to respond. And when her husband then says "You'd better cut it off" to the assembled media people (a remark that leaves it ambiguous whether he is simply reluctant to allow his wife to be filmed when she is so upset, or is also blaming the cameras for upsetting her), we find ourselves viewing a disturbing incident that surely would have been edited out of news broadcasts.

This exchange exposes an underlying conflict, or anxiety, that undermines the image of the Fischers as an all-American family happily anticipating the pending homecoming and equally happily basking in the attention of the media. It is precisely because it undermines this image that this tense, revealing exchange is not edited out of *A Happy Mother's Day*: What television news cameras ordinarily do not reveal, what is ordinarily edited out of news broadcasts, are the revelations Leacock's camera (if not ABC's camera) is seeking.

The narration does not offer an explanation for Mrs. Fischer's momentary little breakdown. It gives us no way of knowing whether she is simply exhausted, for example (as would be understandable for a woman who has so recently labored to give birth five times); whether she is emotionally unstable and such outbursts are typical behavior for her; whether a long-standing private conflict with her husband is surfacing here; or whether the reporter had violated an implicit or explicit understanding by asking a question that is really about her children, not about her.

Nor does Mrs. Fischer herself offer an explanation. Indeed, what seems to require an explanation *is* her surprising unwillingness or inability to explain herself in the presence of all these cameras. What Leacock's camera reveals, in revealing her unwillingness or inability to take these cameras into her confidence, as it were, is that Mrs. Fischer regards them as a threat. And there is no sign that she regards Leacock's camera as any less a threat than the others.

At this point, there is a cut to a doctor scrubbing his hands at a hospital sink. The narrator identifies him. "Mrs. Fischer's physician is Dr. James Berbos . . . An unusual general practitioner who does surgery and delivers babies. Dr. Berbos has become the third doctor in history to successfully deliver quintuplets."

As Dr. Berbos goes about his business, seeming to pay no attention to being filmed, he strides close to Leacock's camera (apparently, there is no other camera present). For a moment the frame is almost filled by his strikingly inexpressive face, half-hidden behind a surgical mask. Our impression, indeed, is that he is withholding expression from the camera, deliberately refusing to communicate with it, refusing even to acknowledge its presence.

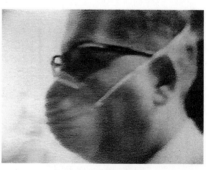

The camera follows Dr. Berbos into the room where the two-week old quints, born prematurely, have "taken up residence in isolettes." A series of close-ups brings what may be thought of as the film's prologue to a close. In these close-ups, which are the antithesis of the climactic vision of the dead child in *Land without Bread*, the infants, very much alive and kicking – are introduced one by one.

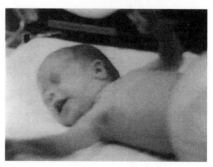

Except for the opening still and a single shot near the end of the film, these are the only views *A Happy Mother's Day* ever gives us of the five little innocents whose entrance into the world occasions the creation of the film. Although the narrator sustains his ironic tone even in this crucial passage, his bemused detachment is transcended by these views that invite us to ponder the awesome mystery of childbirth, the mystery of motherhood. (The mystery is not that every once in a while, somewhere on Earth, a human being becomes the mother of quintuplets. The mystery is that every human being has been born into the world, has been given birth to by a mother.)

As this series of close-ups makes clear, these infants, who never asked to be born into this world where they may be prey to prying eyes (and cameras), wish to be left alone. Yet Dr. Berbos's calling requires that he continually disturb them, intrude on their privacy, in order that they may be welcomed to life, successfully delivered into the world. *Chronicle of a Summer*, *Night and Fog*, *Land without Bread*, and even *Nanook of the North* compellingly demonstrate the camera's power to do violence to its subjects, the death-dealing aspect of the filmmaker's role. Can a filmmaker's calling, like a physician's, also be one of welcoming human beings to life, assisting in their birth, or rebirth?

The Death of Old Anai weaves the death of its subject into a myth of creation that is also a myth of the creation of death. A creation of death is at the heart of *Night and Fog* as well. *A Happy Mother's Day* is a film about creation, too. But it is a miracle of birth that attracts Leacock's camera to Aberdeen. If *Night and Fog* is about a city of death, *A Happy Mother's Day* is about a city in which life, not death, is created. Yet death – that is, the denial of life – is everywhere to be found in Aberdeen, a city that does not know how to celebrate the life that is born in its midst. The Aberdeen, the America, that is reality to Mrs. Fischer is itself dying, being transformed – the film identifies the media as the agents or catalysts of this deathly sea change – in ways that deny the life that has given birth to this world, the life to which this world has given birth.

There is a dissolve to a panoramic shot, taken from an airplane, of the landscape surrounding the Fischers' hometown. "Aberdeen, South Dakota, is a prairie town," the narrator says, speaking the obvious. "The land around it is flat. The roads are straight, and cross mile after mile of wheat and grasslands." There is a smooth cut to an aerial shot of neat rows of streets lined with neat rows of neat houses. "Aberdeen, with a population of twenty-three thousand, is the trading center for the vast agricultural area that surrounds it."

To enter the land of the Hurdanos, Buñuel and his companions ride donkeys over the high mountains that still isolate the region, divest themselves of their modern technology, and regress to the "primitive" state of their subjects. The Hurdanos believe that death is brought by an angel; allegorically, the camera, or the filmmaker behind the camera, unwittingly becomes the "exterminating angel" that steals upon its victims without awakening them. But it is on the wings of a modern airliner, not on the wings of angels or the backs of donkeys, and in the service of a major television network, that

128

Leacock and his crew enter the land of the Fischers. The endless flat farmland that once isolated Aberdeen no longer does so in this age of airliners and modern media.

There is a dissolve to a closer aerial shot of a street. Over the drone of the airplane motor, we hear a marching band. A parade is in progress. "Like most Americans, the people of Aberdeen love a parade. This one is in celebration of Gypsy Day."

No less than Dogon rituals, American parades invoke history (the World War I veterans playing "It's a Long Way to Tipperary"). Compared to a Dogon ritual, however, an American parade makes for a paltry theatrical spectacle. In a Dogon ritual, everyone has a part to play; no one simply watches; every gesture every participant performs has specific significance; knowledge is inscribed in every detail. When the residents of Aberdeen put on a parade, no detail is significant; all their parades are essentially the same, whether it be in celebration of Gypsy Day or the six-month anniversary of the birth of the Fischer quintuplets (the parade that provides *A Happy Mother's Day* with its ironically not-so-grand grand finale).

As we have seen, the logo with which the film opens envisions filmmakers as gypsies wandering who-knows-where to find subjects to film. The present-day inhabitants of Aberdeen are anything but gypsies, of course. The founders of the town once were pioneers, but they settled down as the frontier moved westward. Now that the frontier is no more, Americans love parades – is this also why Americans love films? – because they remind us of a time not so long ago when the nation was on the march, even as they allow us a place on the sidelines from where we are free to view the passing parade.

The camera picks out Mrs. Fischer in the crowd, her attention divided between watching the parade and tending to one of her children. The narrator wryly observes, "This is Mrs. Fischer two weeks after she created such worldwide interest." Part of his irony is that this woman is so manifestly ordinary that it is absurd for the media to take a special interest in her. An irony underlying this irony is that the people on display in American parades – the tuba players, the cheerleaders, the veterans of foreign wars – are no less ordinary than the spectators lining the streets. (And what of the ordinary Americans in Leacock's audience? Is it absurd for us to take a special interest in this ordinary American woman? Or is it absurd for us to find this absurd?)

There is a cut from Mrs. Fischer to her husband, who is hosing down a pair of cows. The cut intimates that Mr. Fischer is tending to his cows at the same time most of the townsfolk are enjoying the parade. Unlike his wife, he is not someone who "loves a parade."

"Mr. Fischer has always liked life on a farm," the narrator observes, "so although he works in the city, he rents a house and some land in the country so his children can have space to grow and animals to. . .make friends with." The narrator's slight pause suggests that the scene to follow will constitute an ironic illustration of his words. Indeed, there follows a charming incident in which one of the Fischer boys attempts to "make friends" with a reluctant cat by holding it down and forcing food into its mouth. Desiring the food but finding this invasion of privacy intolerable, the cat finally squirms away, dragging the food with it. With a delighted cry of "Ha ha, she took it away," the boy lumbers after it, his movements so clumsy that the cat effortlessly keeps its distance (as any self-respecting feline would).

The passage that follows is the most intimate, the most private, in the film. There is a cut directly to the dark interior of a barn. One of the Fischer boys, with great excitement, is leading his mother to something he is eager for her to see. "The babies are right over here," he says breathlessly. The camera reframes so we see that all the Fischer youngsters are gathered around whatever it is that is exciting the boy. We hear one of the boys say, "This one's lively, mom! This one's lively!" Finally we discover what the excitement is about when Mrs. Fischer, saying, "Aw, aren't they sweet," holds up a newborn kitten.

Mrs. Fischer lets one of her boys hold the little creature. Another asks, "How come they can open one eye, and the other one they can't?" (The human subjects of Leacock's camera don't literally have their eyes closed, but they're not fully open either. It is of the nature of human beings that "they can open one eye and the other one they can't." And no one can say "How come.")

Another of the Fischer boys, who has just finished counting, announces "Five kittens!" Another, with wonderment, repeats, "Five little kit-tons!" Having just given birth to her own litter of five, Mrs. Fischer laughs warmly at the sheer serendipity of this coincidence. (In so many grand cinéma-vérité moments, the filmmaker happens on situations so sublimely poignant, or so sublimely absurd, that we can hardly believe the miraculous stroke of fortune that reveals the world's astonishing genius for improvisation. Indeed, we never would believe it, if it were not "captured" on film.)

When her little daughter says, "I want to hold one, mommy," Mrs. Fischer moves toward the boy who is holding the kitten. With the words "No! Get another one out for Charlotte," he pulls it back. Gently but firmly, his mother takes it from him. There is a close-up of the little fur ball she is

cradling in her hands, the shot linking the squirming kitten, scratching and clawing with kittenish life, to the kicking and screaming Fischer quintuplets who had been on view moments before. This close-up conveys an intimate sense of the kitten's extreme cuddle-ability, and an equally intimate sense of the tenderness with which this mother – an old hand at nurturing – is cuddling it.

The narrator has told us that Mr. Fischer keeps animals so his children will be able to make friends with them, but we never see him take responsibility for teaching them what it takes to make friends, what friends are. It is Mrs. Fischer whom we see instructing the children, responding to them so as to teach them to be responsive, to respect the feelings of others, to imagine themselves in their places. Faced with this eruption of possessiveness on the part of her children, Mrs. Fischer – always teaching, always mothering, always teaching mothering – says that unless they put all the kittens back where they found them, "Mommy will come back and find them gone, and she's gonna cry." (Her implication is that the kittens' mother is going to cry not because she has lost prized possessions, but because she will be sad for them, sad that these babies will have lost the "mommy" devoted to providing the mothering they need.)

With these privileged revelations of the private realm, the realm of the Fischers' everyday life, the focus of the film abruptly shifts. We view a woman getting out of a yellow cab. "*The Ladies Home Journal* is preparing a special feature story on Mrs. Fischer," the narrator says. In the brief passage that ensues, there is a shot of Mrs. Fischer in which her face, no longer warm and open, is once again uncommunicative (uncommunicative as to her feelings about this *Journal* reporter, uncommunicative as to her feelings about Leacock's camera).

There is a shot of Mr. Fischer cranking up his "only luxury, a Model T Ford." One of the Fischer boys wanders into the frame and looks right at

the camera. At this moment, there is a cut to a photographer – the narrator identifies him as "the *Saturday Evening Post* photographer, Mr. John Zimmerman" – snapping a picture; a cut back to the Model T as its motor starts up; another shot of Zimmerman; then another of the car, already crammed with Fischers, into whose back seat Mrs. Fischer somehow squeezes.

This sequence of shots suggests, at least ironically, an equivalence between the shots taken by Leacock's camera and those taken by Zimmerman's camera. However, as Mrs. Fischer is squeezing into the Model T, her gaze momentarily meets the gaze of the camera. She shows no expression when this happens.

Like Dr. Berbos, at this moment Mrs. Fischer seems to be deliberately withholding expression from the camera. And it is very much Leacock's camera, not Zimmerman's, from which she seems to be withholding expression; it is Leacock's camera, not Zimmerman's, that reveals her withholding of expression. This passage thus also reveals a difference between the two cameras. And this revelation is at once Mrs. Fischer's (she is the one who casts this look at Leacock's camera) and Leacock's (his camera, not Zimmerman's, is searching for such a look, such a sign, such an affirmation of its difference).

The following shots again at once assert (at least ironically) and deny an equivalence between Leacock's camera and Zimmerman's camera. First,

there is an indescribably droll shot in which, at the outset, the Model T is in the left background and Zimmerman is in the right background of the frame. A moment later, three geese waddle into the foreground.

As the *Post* photographer gives directions to his subjects ("Move over, Julie and Eddie; come on, move over a little; that's good . . ."), the geese, in unison, shift position as if in response to his orders. Leacock's camera pans to follow the geese, excluding Zimmerman from the frame even as he continues to direct from offscreen ("O.K., daddy, you stay down very low now; I can't see Charlotte in back of you").

There is a cut back to Zimmerman, directing as he photographs. Then a cut to the Model T, which is turning around in a tight circle, the children in the car making such a racket that two dogs are attracted by the commotion. Leacock's camera begins reframing to follow the car, which is still circling. For a moment,

Zimmerman is framed together with the subjects he is directing/photographing.

This is a joke by Leacock at the expense of photographers who feel they have to direct their subjects, tell them what to do, in order to obtain the shots they desire. The joke is that in photographs taken this way people might just as well be geese. The joke is also that photographers who shoot human beings this way deny their own humanity as well; the *Post* photographer, too, might just as well be a goose. As this shot hilariously reminds us, photographers do not need to tell their subjects what to do, need not direct them, to capture the most remarkable revelations. Photographers need only be responsive to opportunities when they arise.

The sequence ends with a last view of the car. Again, the *Post* photographer is out of the frame; again, his camera is at least ironically linked with Leacock's camera. On the narrator's words "Mrs. Pieplow is taking Mrs. Fischer on a shopping trip," there is a cut to a clothing store. Mrs. Fischer is standing by, watching, as two women pick through a rack of suits and dresses. When the narrator adds, "Mr. Pieplow is the head of the Aberdeen Chamber of Commerce," his tone of voice insinuates that, however charitably intended this "shopping trip" may be, it is also motivated by the desire of the local business community to promote its own interest, to maximize its profit from the publicity attending the Fischer quints.

The ensuing dialogue is so hilarious – it could have been lifted from an Ionesco play – that I cannot resist reproducing it:

Shopkeeper: Something she could dress up or dress down, either way.
Mrs. Pieplow: You're talking about something like *this*.
Shopkeeper: Yes, this is what I'm talking about.
Mrs. Pieplow: But it seems to me that what she got yesterday would be more in *this* category than in *this* category.
Shopkeeper: Certainly, if she's going out dancing then she might want a dressy dress. But nothing we're looking at would be able to fit into this.
Mrs. Pieplow: What I'm talking about is something on this order.
Shopkeeper: Right, on that order, or on *this* order. I think it's something she could dress up, she could dress down, either way.

Starting and ending with "She could dress up, she could dress down, either way," this dialogue conveys a sense of the machinery of language idling (to use Wittgenstein's inspired metaphor), or going around in circles like Mr. Fischer's Model T. Complementing the circular form of the dialogue as a whole is the extreme indirectness of the individual remarks, most so garbled in syntax that they teeter on the edge of unintelligibility.

Mrs. Pieplow and the shopkeeper reveal themselves to share a Hurdanoesque obliviousness of how they are being revealed, how they are revealing themselves, in the camera's presence. However little Mrs. Pieplow and the shopkeeper are literally saying, their saying of this near-nonsense, in the presence of Leacock's camera, reveals each to be vying to appear more fashion-conscious, and more generous-spirited, than the other. Beyond this, their remarks are so wildly inappropriate that they completely deny who Mrs. Fischer is. (*Of course* this woman, given the life she lives, does not need a "dressy dress" for nights on the town. What would a "night on the town" be, in any case, when the town is Aberdeen?)

As Mrs. Fischer is contemplating her image in a full-length mirror, the narrator observes, "Mrs. Fischer has not had a store-bought outfit since her marriage." His words highlight the gap between the reality of Mrs. Fischer's life and any world – the worlds imaged in magazine ads or television commercials, for example – in which concepts such as "dressing up, dressing down" might possibly be applicable.

Turning away from the mirror, Mrs. Fischer looks almost at the camera, shrugs and laughs, as the narrator adds, "Manley Feinstein is giving her the pick of the store." The urbane Mr. Feinstein, who is not quite giving her the "pick of the store" after all, proceeds to drape a mink coat over Mrs. Fischer's shoulders. "Don't get any ideas, but this is how you should look, see? Don't you see how well the dress will take fur?" Mrs. Pieplow adds, with a laugh that lends her face an unflattering, rapacious aspect, "Look at yourself!"

Obligingly, Mrs. Fischer stares at herself in the mirror, walks toward the camera, and finally says, with a grin, "Here, here. Take it. *Quick!*" She is acting as if owning such a coat, conforming to the images of a glamorous

life that television commercials and magazines advertisements associate with mink, really were her innermost fantasy, her heart's desire, as Mrs. Pieplow and the shopkeeper take for granted it must be.

But the shot does not end here. It continues, enabling us to continue viewing Mrs. Fischer as her smile freezes and her face empties of spontaneous expression. On the earlier occasions in which Mrs. Fischer's face was conspicuously expressionless, I characterized her as withholding expression from Leacock's camera, refusing to reveal herself in its presence, denying it intimacy. When her face empties of expression in the present shot, by contrast, I take this to be a moment of intimacy with the camera, not a moment of withholding intimacy from it.

Within *A Happy Mother's Day* as a whole, this is a development of great significance. In their obliviousness, Mrs. Pieplow and the shopkeeper believe that Mrs. Fischer is oblivious. In the face of their astonishing obliviousness, the camera reveals Mrs. Fischer to be, she reveals herself to the camera to be, not oblivious at all, but, rather, inscrutable. When Mrs. Fischer's face becomes a mask in this shot, the camera reveals, she reveals to the camera, that she has been acting, that she has not revealed her private thoughts, her private feelings, that they have remained inaccessible, mysterious.

From Mrs. Fischer's inscrutable
face-turned-mask there is a dissolve
to Zimmerman, standing on a tall
ladder, barking orders ("Back a little
farther!") as he photographs, from a
height, what the narrator calls "a
representative selection of the gifts
that the Fischers have been offered."
Once again at least ironically identifying itself with Zimmerman's camera, Leacock's camera pans to take in

the array of "gifts" strewn across the yard, creating an image that is uncannily reminiscent of *Night and Fog*'s innocent-looking yet horrific images of
mounds of human hair, body parts, and images-painted-on-skin. These
objects appear absurdly lifeless and soulless when viewed *en plein air* in this
way, divorced both from their everyday use and from the glamorous aura
with which magazine ads and television commercials invest them.

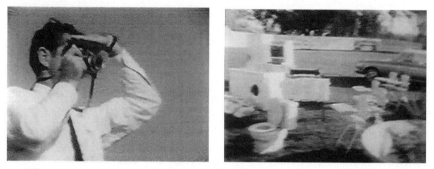

The narrator recites a litany – itself uncannily reminiscent of *Night and
Fog* – of the products on display, a summation of the commodities, the consumer goods, around which our society has come more and more to
revolve: "Automobiles, wading pools, high chairs, bathroom fixtures, wash-
ing machines, TV sets, toys, paint for their new house . . ."

There is a cut back to Zimmerman, still giving directions as he shoots
("Hold! Hold!"), then back to the products spread out on the lawn. Again,
Leacock's camera ironically simulates Zimmerman's as the narrator goes
on with his litany: " . . . A year's supply of milk, baby food, eighty pair of
shoes, tableware, clothing. Just about everything imaginable."

This is the moment at which the narrator first explicitly raises an issue of
central concern to the film. "Now all these manifestations of generosity and
public interest do pose certain problems," he observes, in a tone that suggests he is tactfully bringing up a matter of some delicacy. "All parents of
quintuplets are faced to a certain degree with . . ."

A cut back to the *Post* photographer, shooting from atop a ladder on the
products arrayed below him (the display Leacock's camera has just pre-

sented to us), intimates that the "problem" the narrator is about to name is some threat that these "gifts" pose to the Fischer family.

Some of these individual gifts, we suspect, may well come with strings attached, with a hidden price tag. But the greater threat, this series of shots implies, is that the Fischers, who have remained about as far removed from the consumerist mainstream as it is possible for contemporary Americans to be, will be suffocated by this veritable avalanche of commodities, buried under the weight of consumerism itself. The threat is that for the Fischer family, as for most Americans, "just about everything imaginable" will become reduced, their capacity to imagine will become reduced, to the self-contained universe of magazine ads and television commercials.

Surprisingly, the narrator's sentence concludes with the words "invasion of privacy." And these words are followed by a medium shot – it is as if this were the view Zimmerman was photographing in the preceding shot – of Mr. Fischer holding a son in his lap.

This father is exposing his son's privacy, as well as his own, to "invasion" by the *Saturday Evening Post*'s camera, a camera that not only views its human subjects as if they were geese, but views them as well as if they were consumers, as if they were cut to the measure of the products that they consume.

Having paid the family a substantial amount for exclusive rights to its story, the *Post* published two feature stories about the Fischer quints, elaborate spreads replete with wonderful color photographs (John Zimmerman turns out to be a very good photographer) and writing of a high professional standard.[45] Like the program ABC prepared from Leacock's footage, these montages of photos and text present the story from a variety of angles, including first-person narratives ostensibly written by Mr. Fischer ("with" John Bird, a *Post* writer) and Mrs. Fischer (also "with" the same writer). Overall, they convey a sense of journalistic "objectivity" or "balance" that *A Happy Mother's Day* can appear to lack. Aberdeen emerges in the *Post* articles as a town that affirms old-fashioned American values yet recognizes that it needs to change if only to keep those values alive, a town that is sincerely dedicated to respecting the Fischer family's privacy. Exemplary of the new world of modern mass media that Aberdeen so pragmatically embraces, the *Post* itself – fair and decent in all its dealings with the Fischers and their neighbors – emerges as upholding old-fashioned American values, too. The *Post* pictures an Aberdeen, an America, in which there is no one who is venal, no one who is foolish, no one who is oblivious, no one who is silent, and no one who is crying out in pain or anguish. There is no "endless cry." Everyone speaks in a rational voice. But it is the *Post* that provides all the words.

In his own not entirely rational voice, Mr. Fischer is saying, "It isn't something that happens every day of the week here. Once a year some place in the world." He raises his eyebrows in a funny way, almost a nervous tic, that reveals that he may not entirely believe, or even entirely understand, the words he is saying, that they represent a "line" he has been sucker enough to buy. "It's bound to make a big difference in the city of Aberdeen because nothing like this has ever happened here. It's always been a quiet town, and it's bound to liven it up tremendously, I think." As he goes on, clearly in this over his head, the camera pulls out to reveal his wife intently weighing every word. "As far as tourist trade and all this and that, you know as far as people showing interest and stuff like that are concerned," he continues. "Anybody within a hundred miles will surely drive in just to say that they've been in the town."

A cut to a new angle gives Mrs. Fischer more prominence in the frame. Her hapless husband continues, "Yeah, I suppose if there are lots of tourists coming in to see them, we're gonna have to let 'em in to . . ." Suddenly she interrupts. "No, no we're not. They're never gonna be on display to anybody as far as I'm concerned." As she speaks these last words, Mrs. Fischer looks almost at the camera in a way that declares that she means these words seriously, even as it leaves it unspecified whether she regards the camera that gives us access to this view as witnessing her vow, or as exemplifying the threat from which she is vowing to protect her children.

From offscreen, we hear a woman's voice ask, "To anybody?" Glancing almost imperceptibly in her husband's direction, Mrs. Fischer repeats, "To anybody." There is a cut to Mr. Fischer, his son in his lap. (This shot reprises the passage's initial framing, hence again identifies Leacock's camera, at least ironically, with Zimmerman's.)

From this shot, which conveys a sense of intimacy between father and son, the camera pans to Mrs. Fischer. She reiterates, "As far as I'm concerned that's the way it better be." The panning movement underscores that she recognizes, as we do, that both her husband and her son are vulnerable to a threat they are unwilling or unable to recognize (a threat represented by Zimmerman's camera, and perhaps by Leacock's as well).

This camera movement thus sets the stage for the next passage, which begins with a cut directly to a room in which a chamber of commerce meeting is in full swing. In absurdist humor, the ensuing discussion is a match for the earlier dialogue between Mrs. Pieplow and the shopkeeper. These men are no less Hurdano-like than their female counterparts, no less oblivious of the way they are being revealed, the way they are revealing themselves, in the presence of Leacock's camera. But these pillars of the business community, gathered to decide Aberdeen's response to the armies of media people and tourists descending on the town, are the closest Aberdeen comes to a patriarchal order. Throughout their discussion, conducted in Mrs. Fischer's absence and placed as it is immediately following her solemn vow, we are aware that these men wield power over her life, pose a serious threat to the privacy she is determined to retain for her family. (Mrs. Pieplow and the shopkeeper, equally foolish, are less powerful.)

There is general agreement that "an awful lot of tourists" will be coming in, hence that there will be "such things as, occasions when press conferences occur, or when there are certain instances in which people come to see" the quints. There is agreement, as well, that the Fischers will have to find a way to adjust "day by day by day" to the fact that "they can't possibly lead a normal life." And there is agreement that Aberdeen should do what it can – set up a mechanism that will "afford a place people who want to see them without busting in," for example – to enable the Fischers to live "as normal a life as possible under the circumstances."

Here agreement breaks down. One man asks, almost angrily, "Are they going to be put on exhibition?" "I don't see where it would necessarily work that way," another replies in a conciliatory tone. "But they're going to continue to be a point of interest, and Aberdeen, I would think, is going to benefit commercially simply because more people are going to come into the area than would have come here without them. Now there's nothing harmful in that." "I agree with you." Agreement restored, no one objects when the consensus is summed up thusly: "There's been so much over-stress on this commercial thing, as if there were something awful about the fact that more money is going to flow into the community. I see nothing harmful in it. It's the way you look at it, I think."

There is a cut to a woman informing Mrs. Fischer about a luncheon that the mothers of the town are planning ("We wanted a lovely and pretty and dignified luncheon, something that would be just specially for you, something that would compliment you and be your own fun time"). As the woman says, "We want you to be just as pretty as possible so your five children will just look at you and think, 'Oh, we're so proud of mommy, she looks so darling,'" there is a cut from Mrs. Fischer, inscrutable in the face of this astonishing display of obliviousness, to a group of men, sitting at a long table, planning the details of the parade they have decided to hold.

"They've been on sale for three days, and they aren't going well," one of the men is saying. "With people talking it up and telling where people can get it, we'll start selling this merchandise." Another asks, "What do you think of our running an ad in tomorrow night's paper saying 'Quint souvenir items can be purchased in any local store'? Think it would be too commercialized if we were to do that?" "I think if you run the ad you should be sure to indicate that the proceeds are going to go to the Fischer Foundation," the first replies. "But how are you going to say that? I mean, legally, how are you going to say that?" He adds, "We don't have a Fischer Foundation," providing the film with its biggest laugh lines. (It must be admitted that it is a bit of a cheap shot, if an irresistible one, to end the sequence with this line, knowing that it will inevitably give the misleading impression [perhaps only jokingly, to be sure] that these men are really planning to divide the profits among themselves, that the "Fischer Foundation" is a cynical fiction. In fact, a "Fischer Foundation" was already in the process of being set up, although as a legal entity it did not yet exist.)

There is a cut to one of the quints being weighed, then to a close-up. The close-up is held until the precise moment the infant appears to thumb (or pick) her nose as if summing up her judgment of this world into which she has been given no choice but to be born.

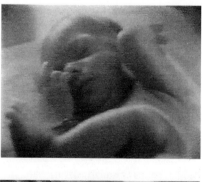

There is a cut to the exterior of the Fischer house, the camera panning across the many cars that are gathered. The narrator says, "The Fischers take part in a staged preview of the parade for the benefit of the newsmen whose headlines can't wait."

There is a quick succession of vignettes (an amusing scene in which the five older Fischer children are introduced to "Congressman Reiffel and Mrs. Reiffel," for example, and a shot of a nun snapping photographs), culminating in an exchange between a news photographer and a man in full Sioux feathered regalia. It begins with a shot of the photographer, gesturing and shouting, "Come on, get close to them, you're talking with *them*!" This is followed by a medium

close-up of the bewildered Sioux, who does not know which way he is supposed to look, as we hear, from offscreen, the photographer barking out in a brutally impatient, disrespectful voice, "Turn around and look at them, Chief! Turn around and look at them. Chief!" The "Chief," confused and embarrassed, awkwardly turns a full 270 degrees until he finally finds himself facing three Fischer children.

From this last shot, which is painful rather than amusing to view, there is a cut to the mayor of Aberdeen, looking distinctly uneasy as he is about to address the people gathered for the "lovely and pretty and dignified luncheon" that is supposed to be Mrs. Fischer's "own fun time."

The mayor begins:

Could I have your attention please. We are running slightly behind schedule so we will want to hurry along with this program. As the Mayor of the City of Aberdeen, it is an honor for me to bring a warm and sincere welcome to the Fischers and to all who are gathered here on this joyous occasion.

There would be nothing to mock in the mayor's speech if he had gone directly to his concluding lines ("Andrew and Mary Ann Fischer have the right to expect an opportunity to raise their family in privacy and dignity. It is our responsibility as a community to see that right is observed. And so today we pledge to the Fischers our cooperation that they will have the opportunity to raise their family in a community so dedicated to their welfare"). But the three intervening sentences, which are edited out of the ABC version, are so hyperbolic, and so tortured in syntax, that they lend the entire speech, for all its sincerity, a ludicrously pompous aspect ("I am sure that never in the history of the United States has a city official been so honored as I have this day. I am also sure that never in the history of the United States has a city official had the responsibility that has come to me and the other city officials. Never has a community had such a responsibility as we feel that we have here in Aberdeen today.")

Over applause – this audience does not find the speech absurd – there is a cut to a soprano singing (one of Grieg's *Norwegian Folk Dances*) with a perkiness she evidently takes for sophisticated sauciness.

As the maddeningly perky singing continues offscreen, there is a cut to Mrs. Fischer, who is stoically enduring this ordeal. Leacock's camera dwells on her masklike face.

We know that this woman knows this luncheon is a charade, that she is going along with it only because the family needs help to pay the expenses sure to be incurred by five new crying and hungry mouths. We know that she knows that the local businessmen and city officials and their wives have a vested interest in conspiring with the national media to put her family

on display. We know that she knows that her husband, a decent man, is not capable of understanding the seriousness of the threat to their privacy. We know that she knows that it is up to her to draw the line, to safeguard her family from the powerful forces that threaten it. We know that she knows that she stands alone. And we know that she knows that no one in Aberdeen, and no one among the reporters and photographers who are covering her story, really knows her. Like Stella Dallas and the other heroines of classical American melodramas of the thirties and forties, Mrs. Fischer is an unknown woman. What we do not know is how this woman, known to no one in her world, feels about being filmed by Leacock's camera, how she feels about being the central subject of this film, how she feels about our knowing her the way we do.

Leacock is a pioneer of a conception and practice of filmmaking that undertakes, by forsaking script and directing, to make filming itself an adventure. But now, as his camera continues to hold on Mrs. Fischer's face, it seems paralyzed, fixated, as if it were up to this woman to free it to move on. But what could Leacock's camera be searching for in this woman's face? What could it find there that might free it to resume its gypsy wandering?

All this time, Mrs. Fischer's eyes have been downcast, as if she were veiling the fact that she is not really listening to the singer. Suddenly sensing that Leacock's camera has been attending to her, thus revealing that it has been in her private thoughts, she shifts her eyes to sneak a glance at it.

Her suspicion confirmed, she furtively looks away, as if she could deceive Leacock's camera by pretending she had never been interested in its interest

in her. But then, no longer willing or able to continue this pretense, she deliberately meets the camera's gaze.

In this climactic confrontation, everything is at stake, and anything can happen. Mrs. Fischer's judgment on Leacock's camera, deferred until now, is finally to be passed. For all we know, she will thumb her nose at it, judge it really to be no different from all the other cameras that threaten her family's privacy. But she does not. Rather, her face lights up in a sly little grin. And it is at this joyful moment that Leacock's camera discovers, and declares, its freedom. It is at this moment that *A Happy Mother's Day* is born. It is at this moment that cinéma-vérité itself is born, or reborn, as a movement of independent film.

At the precise moment Mrs. Fischer's face breaks into a grin, Leacock's camera begins a circuitous panning movement in the course of which the camera comes to frame, in succession, Mr. Fischer, the mayor, Dr. Berbos, and the doctor's wife, finding obliviousness in the eyes of all these good people who are gathered to honor this woman they do not really know.

However often one views this shot, however closely one studies it, it is impossible to say which comes first, Mrs. Fischer's grin (her acknowledgment of the camera's capacity to acknowledge her) or the movement of Leacock's camera (its acknowledgment of her capacity to pass judgment). Our impression is that Mrs. Fischer's grin and the movement of Leacock's camera mutually provoke each other. Together, the camera and its subject authorize this shot's silent summation of her world, which is also a summation of the film. The vision they conspire to create has a nightmare aspect: It is into an oblivious world, a world of oblivion, that this mother's babies have been born. But it also has the aspect of an affirmation: This is a world capable of being viewed from a transfiguring perspective.

From the perspective that gives birth to this vision – a perspective the camera and its subject achieve together, in silence – everything is altered. Even the irrepressible voice of the perky soprano, which a moment before had been so maddening, now plays its part in animating the film's affirmation, in giving this luncheon, and the parade that concludes the film, an absurdly upbeat mood.

The parade, which features bands, baton twirlers, and floats we recognize from the Gypsy Day parade, brings *A Happy Mother's Day* full circle. "The Fischer family had a wonderful time," the narrator assures us. "And the people of Aberdeen turned out in force to honor their celebrated neighbors." There is a shot of the grandstand. Rain begins to fall in a deluge, and the Fischers, along with their less celebrated neighbors, scramble for cover. "It was a typical day of celebration in Aberdeen, South Dakota, USA."

The capacity to transfigure America, to celebrate the mythical in the typical, is the secret bond between Mrs. Fischer and Leacock's camera. And now this secret is revealed.

CHAPTER VI

Cinéma-Vérité in America (II):

Don't Look Back

That Monteverdi's first opera, as well as the two that preceded his initiating master-piece, and Gluck's masterpiece a century later, which brings the aria to the musical level of the recitative..., all work from the myth of Orpheus and Eurydice is almost too good to be true in establishing the myth of opera, of its origins – the story of the power of music, epitomized as the act of singing. So we might reemphasize the turn in the story, familiar but not universal, in which, after moving hell to release his wife, and despite charming tigers and stones, Orpheus at the last moment cannot redeem Eurydice for their everyday life together again; which makes the story one about the limitations of the power of voice. To draw morals from myths is an ancient practice, and which moral you draw from the Orpheus myth is apt to depend on how you understand "looking back." A sixteenth-century Italian translator of Ovid's *Meta-morphoses*, one of the sources of the myth, interprets it as "man's loss of the soul whenever he abandons reason and turns back: that is to pursue blameworthy and earthly concerns." This moralism is particularly striking in view of the ease with which the moral can be seen to be about skepticism, about the loss of the world through an impossible effort to certify its existence by means of the senses, especially through looking. (Freud's observation is pertinent here, that doubt is the emotion expressive of our essential uncertainty about what is happening behind us.)

– Stanley Cavell,
"Opera and the Lease of Voice"
(from *A Pitch of Philosophy*)

The highway is for gamblers. Better use your sense.
Take what you have gathered from coincidence...

– Bob Dylan,
"It's All Over Now, Baby Blue"

Donn Alan Pennebaker's *Don't Look Back*, a chronicle of Bob Dylan's 1965 British concert tour, represents the moment immediately following cinéma-vérité's break with, or expulsion from, network television. Unlike *A Happy Mother's Day*, it was conceived from the outset as a film to be shown in theaters. Because it was both an independent production and a "documentary," however, when it was released in 1967 its potential distri-bution was limited to art houses. It likely would have had no theatrical distribution at all had Dylan not by then become a star whose celebrity far outreached the folk music scene with which he had once been identified.

At the time of filming, Dylan was beginning to bridge not only the musical chasm between folk music and rock 'n' roll, but also the political chasm between Old Left "folkies" who protested for public causes and rock's rebels without causes who pursued liberation in their private lives. Inspired by the Beatles, Dylan in turn decisively influenced rock, playing a key role in the transition, of world-historical importance, from the alienation and civil rights protests of the early sixties to the counterculture that emerged in the late sixties.

The arrival of the counterculture that Dylan prophesied and helped goad into existence was announced in Pennebaker's landmark *Monterey Pop*, released in 1968; the counterculture's mythical high-water mark was registered in Michael Wadleigh's *Woodstock* (1970); its violent death was prematurely reported in *Gimme Shelter* (the Maysles brothers' 1970 film about the Rolling Stones' ill-fated Altamont concert); its early retirement was mourned in Martin Scorsese's elegiac *The Last Waltz* (1978); and its surprising continuing survival, at least to the end of the eighties, was celebrated in Pennebaker's and Chris Hegedus's remarkable 1989 film *Depeche Mode 101*.

The counterculture, evidently one of American cinéma-vérité's great subjects at this historical moment, was a political movement that turned half my generation of Americans into rebels with a cause (ending the war in Vietnam). At the same time, it was a utopian attempt to transform America by achieving a new philosophical perspective (it was also a perspective older than classical American cinema, as old, indeed, as the transcendental philosophy of Emerson and Thoreau), not by traditional political means.

In the aftermath of the events of May 1968, French intellectuals, in an effort to think more deeply about their failure to effect a second French Revolution, turned to Lacan, Derrida, Althusser, and Foucault. When American academics turned to the new French thought, for many it was less to think more deeply about America's traumatic experience of the sixties than to be released from thinking about it. It was in part to deny the necessity of thinking about itself, and thinking for itself, that American film study embraced the still dominant myth of its own origin, which envisions the field as born, or born again, through the saving grace of French theory. Within this myth, the events in Paris referred to as "May 1968," a historical moment that was not part of the American experience, became the decisive moment of the field's creation in America. This myth denies America's own experience of the late sixties, denies the true dimension of the reality of the world that gave birth to the counter-culture, denies the American way of thinking championed by Dylan (and by Pennebaker), as if it could have no fruitful role to play in the serious study of film.

■

Sara Lowndes, the woman soon to become Dylan's wife, had come to know Pennebaker when she worked as a secretary at Drew Associates. After who knows what conversations with Dylan, she suggested to Albert Grossman, his manager, that he invite Pennebaker to film the upcoming tour. Grossman was hoping for "promos" to help sell records. But Dylan seemed to have something else in mind. His boyhood idols had included James Dean and Marlon Brando, after all, as well as Hank Williams, Little Richard, and Woody Guthrie. He was intrigued that he might have what it takes to be a movie star. He was also intrigued that he might have what it takes to make movies. "This was a way to find out about films," Pennebaker has suggested. "He'd seen a couple of films that we'd done, so he knew a little that what we did was peculiar and different."[46] Who better to initiate him into the mysteries of filmmaking?

Pennebaker had wanted to make a film about the music scene. "I had talked to somebody who knew the Stones . . . but that didn't seem quite right. And then I thought of Baez . . . but that wasn't what seemed to me interesting. I had a definite idea in my head, but I didn't know about Dylan at all."[47] Grossman sent him a couple of Dylan albums. "The songs really hit me. From then on, I knew that by total chance I'd fallen into the place that I should be."[48]

Reviewing *Don't Look Back* at the time of its release, Andrew Sarris maintained that Pennebaker was only capable of making good films when he had good subjects, such as Dylan, hence that the filmmaker was no true "auteur," no artist in his own right.[49] But all artists need good subjects, subjects that are good for them. And what makes Dylan such a good subject for Pennebaker cannot be separated from what makes this filmmaker the "auteur" he is. (If Richard Leacock had made *Don't Look Back*, he might well have lost interest in Dylan and run off with Joan Baez.)

At their first meeting, Dylan and his friend Bob Neuwirth (road manager on the British tour) went through a couple of routines designed to test Pennebaker's coolness. Bob Spitz (not Dylan's most admiring biographer) describes the meeting as "a typical Bob Dylan burlesque." Dylan kept insisting, for example, that a woman at the bar was the singer Lotte Lenya, although Pennebaker knew perfectly well that she was not.

"It was an attempt to put me down," [Pennebaker] recalls. In fact, their routines had a completely opposite effect . . . I recognized instantly . . . that they had the same sense about what they were up to as we did about what we were up to, which was a kind of conspiracy. We felt as if we were out conning the world in some kind of guerilla action and bringing back stuff that nobody recognized as valuable and making it valuable.[50]

The way to film Dylan, Pennebaker thought from the outset, was "by having no expectations whatever." As the filmmaker puts it,

The thing that scared [Dylan] was that somebody was going to . . . say, "Here's what you have to do, because we're making this movie and it's got to be this way."

The idea that he could do anything he wanted, without any preconceived notions, really interested him.[51]

It also interested Dylan that Pennebaker envisioned filmmaker and subject as co-conspirators, like Flaherty and Nanook in the igloo-building sequence of *Nanook of the North*.

The first idea he came up with knocked me for a loop. Bob wanted to open the film with a song, only he wouldn't be singing it. It would be a track from one of his albums, during which he'd flip over cue cards displaying snatches of lyrics. It was fantastic, *exhilarating*! I remember thinking: What a strong, resonant character I have on my hands! . . . There was drama coming on. I could smell it.[52]

But drama is conflict. What "comes on" in *Don't Look Back* is something other than drama. *Don't Look Back*, like most Pennebaker films, is all but completely undramatic. First, because the primary focus is Dylan "hanging out," no conflict in sight. Second, because *Don't Look Back* is a film of ideas, and Dylan's ideas, and Pennebaker's, confront no formidable opposition within the film.

Don't Look Back is thus quite different from *A Happy Mother's Day*. Leacock's film *is* dramatic: The drama is rooted in the conflict between Mrs. Fischer and a world that does not know who she is, and revolves around her relationship with the filmmaker's camera. A condition of this relationship is Mrs. Fischer's complete isolation within her world. She alone perceives the presence of these cameras, Leacock's among them, as a threat. Her selfhood, and thus her relationship to her world, are at stake in the events *A Happy Mother's Day* "documents." And Leacock's identity as a filmmaker is at stake, too. In the making of the film, the fates of filmmaker and subject are joined. And their fates are sealed.

In Pennebaker's film, Dylan is not unknown. He is isolated, isolates himself, from the world represented by the mainstream media, but that is a self-contained universe, not the real world at all. Dylan tours with friends who know him, and there are millions out there who know him through his records and concerts. (Or do his fans know him? This question comes up repeatedly in the film.) There is no drama in Dylan's relationship to the camera. First, because the camera poses no threat. (In *Don't Look Back*, there is only one moment of visible tension between Dylan and the camera. Pennebaker describes it:

It's when he's playing with Alan Price – when he asks Alan if he's playing with The Animals any more, and he says, "no, it happens," and then Dylan starts to chord in those blues. And then he looked at me like he was kind of pissed that I was filming. . . . And then he looked away.[53]

Second, because the camera represents no hope of salvation to Dylan. From the outset, in *Don't Look Back*, Dylan is secure in his identity; he feels no need to be "saved." Neither does Pennebaker.

Neither Leacock nor Mrs. Fischer could have known, when shooting began, that in the presence of his camera she was destined to be set apart from all others in her world. Nor could either have known what was destined to set Leacock's camera apart from the other cameras threatening her family. But from the outset Dylan's sense of selfhood, his sense of who he is, what connects him to the world, what sets him apart, is a given, as is Pennebaker's sense of who he is as a filmmaker. From the outset, Pennebaker and Dylan recognize their affinity, their bond, in a way not possible for Leacock and Mrs. Fischer.

The drama of *A Happy Mother's Day* – there is a crisis in its subject's life; at any moment she might break down; she is walking a tightrope with no safety net and with the camera poised to film her should she fall – is thus nowhere to be found in *Don't Look Back*. In Pennebaker's film, the tyranny of the "crisis structure" is overcome by an idea of selfhood, exemplified by filmmaker and subject alike, that embraces the principle that human character is not fixed, that human beings are capable of changing, are incapable of not changing, are changing at every moment.

Prologue

Don't Look Back does, indeed, open the way Dylan had proposed. The first shot begins with a view of a nondescript London alley. A recording of "Subterranean Homesick Blues" is blasting away on the soundtrack. (Actually, the

first thing we view is "Academy leader," which counts down the number of seconds until the first shot. Ordinarily, this leader is not meant to be viewed; it is spliced onto the "head" of the reel to enable the projectionist to cue up the film's opening. In *Don't Look Back*, it *is* the opening.) The camera zooms out, disclosing the rakish figure of Dylan. A moment later, it zooms out further to disclose an unidentified man at the edge of the frame (we may or may not recognize him as the poet Allen Ginsberg).

Dylan is holding cue cards with words and phrases from the song, starting with "BASEMENT" ("Johnny's in the basement mixing up the medicine, I'm on the pavement thinking about the government. . .") and including, among others, "LOOK OUT!," "WATCH IT!," "HERE

148

THEY COME!," "LEADERS???," "GET BORN," "GET BLESSED," "SUCK-CESS," "DIG YOURSELF," "MAN WHOLE," "WHAT???" One by one, he presents the cards to the camera, unceremoniously letting each drop when it is time to move on to the next.

Spitz describes Dylan in the alleyway as "small and waiflike as a gypsy boy whose goal is eventually to lift your wallet, peering into the camera with a devilish glint in his eye."[54] In meeting one's gaze, however, a gypsy who wanted to lift one's wallet would hardly "peer" with a glint in his eye that disclosed his devilish intentions. Spitz's description implies that the camera is unmasking Dylan, that he is unmasking himself by the way he peers into it, that, thanks to the camera, we can rest assured our wallets are safe (as long as we are not fools enough to let Pennebaker film *us*), that it is Dylan's wallet – a stolen one, no doubt – really being lifted, figuratively speaking, by a camera with friendly intentions toward us but devilish intentions toward him. But what is "fantastic, *exhilarating*" about this prologue, I take it, is rather its declaration that we cannot take for granted our wallets are safe either with Dylan or Pennebaker.

This seems a strange opening for a film in which we are to view everything – are we not? – as unstaged. Yet its purpose – Dylan's as well as Pennebaker's – is to announce that the film that has begun is not really, or not merely, a "documentary," but (also?) a collaboration in which filmmaker and subject are co-conspirators.

As Dylan presents these cue cards, now and then he glances in the camera's direction, but always with a characteristic expression pitched between indifference and scorn. This expression is part of Dylan's act, his self-presentation. There is a glint in his eye as he performs this act, but we do not know what this glint reveals about him, whether he is looking to lift our wallets or is looking only to be our friend. (And do we know what a devil, or, for that matter, a friend, is, the difference between them? Is it possible for a friend to lift our wallets? for someone who lifts our wallets to be a friend? for a friend not to lift our wallets?)

It is no accident that Dylan chooses "Subterranean Homesick Blues" for this cue card treatment and not "The Times They Are A-Changin'," the other Dylan hit then climbing the charts in England (although he had recorded it months earlier). Later in the film, a fan tells Dylan she doesn't like "Subterranean Homesick Blues," that it doesn't "sound like him" the way "The Times They Are A-Changin'" does. What she means is that the latter makes her feel that Dylan is her friend, while the former makes her feel he has contempt for her.

In "The Times They Are A-Changin'," the singer calls upon "people, wherever you roam" to "come gather round." Like the old woman at the end of *Land without Bread*, like the narrator at the end of *Night and Fog*, he is offering all within earshot counsel that might save them. Without a trace of contempt in his voice, he is saying, "Admit that the waters around you have grown. . . You better start swimming or you'll sink like a stone, for the times they are a-changin'." Prior to "Subterranean Homesick Blues," there were Dylan songs in which his voice dripped with contempt, but they were addressed, rhetorically, to implied listeners Dylan's fans could easily dissociate from themselves. "The Lonesome Death of Hattie Carroll," for example, is disdainful of listeners it characterizes as "you who philosophise disgrace and criticize all fears," not the fans who take the song seriously.

At times, in "Subterranean Homesick Blues," the singer derisively mimics conventional voices of authority and mocks conformists who take them seriously ("Keep a clean nose," "Try to be a success" (the cue card spells it "suck-cess"), "Avoid scandals," "Don't be a bum," etc.). Other times, he admonishes the listener in his own voice ("Don't follow leaders!" "Dig yourself!" "Get blessed!" "Get born!"). At all times, the "kid" the singer is mockingly addressing is the Dylan fan who had always felt exempt from his scorn.

The singer in "The Times They Are A-Changin'" addresses listeners who already know what he is telling them; he is not *informing* them they'll sink like a stone if they don't start swimming, he is calling upon them to "admit" this. The singer in "Subterranean Homesick Blues" is addressing a listener who already knows which way the wind is blowing, already knows change is necessary, but has not yet taken the leap, not yet "jumped into the alleyway looking for a new friend," as the lyrics put it. To dig oneself, to get born, to get blessed, even only to stay afloat, requires more than knowledge. Like Lincoln staring down the lynch mob in *Young Mr. Lincoln*, the singer is cajoling, provoking, shaming his listeners into repudiating the lies society tells them, into aligning their lives with the truth they know in their hearts.

Even "Ballad of a Thin Man" (written immediately after the making of *Don't Look Back* and perhaps inspired by the encounter with the *Time* reporter immortalized by the film) intimates that Mr. Jones really knows that "something is happening here" and that he knows he does not "know what it is." By repeatedly asking "Do you, Mr. Jones?" the singer makes explicit his belief that the problem is not Mr. Jones's ignorance of some relevant fact, but his refusal to acknowledge something he knows. What Mr. Jones knows but fails to acknowledge is precisely that his knowledge has limits, that knowledge itself has limits. The contempt in the singer's voice reveals that he expects no honest answer from this man, expects him never to stop denying the truth. This refusal to acknowledge the truth is all that separates Mr. Jones from the singer, who makes no claim to know something the listener does not know. Dylan sees eye to eye with Samuel Beckett on this: The "something" that is "happening here" is not something that can be *known*.

In "Subterranean Homesick Blues," the singer bombards the listener with a headlong rush of words and phrases, some so vivid they stand out like neon signs. Many earlier Dylan songs – "A Hard Rain's A-Gonna

Fall," for example – had already taken the form of a succession of flashing images. But in "Subterranean Homesick Blues" this form takes on a mocking aspect, as if the singer were presenting the "kid" he is addressing with a series of cue cards in order to goad him into protesting being condescended to this way. The singer is not writing the listener off, he is trying to provoke him to "jump down the alleyway" – the alleyway on view in this shot? – "looking for a new friend." Pointedly, however, the singer does not promise *to be* this "new friend."

In this recording, the singer sounds like someone who is playing it cool, keeping his distance. This is exactly the figure Dylan cuts on-screen when he presents these cue cards that do nothing but point to the words and phrases being sung (words and phrases that in the song already function as cue cards, we have suggested). The on-screen Dylan treats these cards with an attitude of casual indifference, as if these words meant nothing to him, as if he had no special attachment to them, as if they were not his, as if he had contempt for anyone who believes he is revealed by them. Yet by presenting himself to the camera (with Pennebaker's complicity) as someone who has such an attitude, the slouching, leather-vested Dylan on view in this shot *is* revealed, *does* reveal himself; he *is* the very figure of cool, arrogant youth embodied or disembodied by the recorded voice.

The prologue ends with a quirky bit of business. As the sound begins fading out, Dylan exits the frame. Almost simultaneously, an unidentified man enters (Bob Neuwirth). Like Ginsberg, he is carrying a walking stick, which lends him a bohemian air. The two nod to each other, then stride off in opposite directions. (Something is happening here, but we don't know what it is, do we?) Fade out.

This conspicuously choreographed little rigmarole underscores that what we have viewed is a routine performed by Dylan and co-conspirators (Pennebaker among them) capable of putting us on if that is what they are looking to do. And what is true of this prologue is true of all that follows: The body of the film, too, is a performance by co-conspirators whose friendship we cannot take for granted, any more than we can take for granted that their intentions are devilish.

After a moment of darkness, we hear guitar chords. As if called into being by these sounds, a view fades in of Dylan, framed in close-up, his harmonica suspended in front of his face by a contraption he wears around his neck.

The camera zooms out to disclose that Dylan is in a dressing room preparing to make his stage entrance. As he stops strumming the guitar he is holding, the title "DON'T LOOK BACK" appears, one word at a time, superimposed over the left half of the frame, followed by the words "BY D. A. PENNEBAKER."

"Don't look back" is as good a way as any to paraphrase the singer's admonitions to the listener in "Subterranean Homesick Blues." Thus we understand from the outset that the film's title serves to sum up Dylan's attitude toward life. Dylan has jokingly suggested that "Don't look back" means "Don't look over your shoulder" (as in "Don't look over your shoulder, someone may be gaining on you," or as in Freud's observation that doubt is the emotion expressive of our essential uncertainty about what is happening behind us). But to Dylan, surely, "Don't look back" primarily means "Don't second-guess yourself," "Accept responsibility for your actions," "Acknowledge where you find yourself in the present, however you have arrived there," "Admit the necessity of change." If one looks down, one may fall; if one looks back, one may lose one's resolve to go on, because going on means leaving the past behind. "Don't look back" means recognizing that one has always already moved on, one has already left the past behind, there is no direction home. It means embracing the adventure of living. (The story of Lot is one pertinent myth. The story of Orpheus is another.)

Dylan walks toward the right foreground, the camera reframing with him. To offscreen applause, he goes through the stage door, which closes behind him, as the applause grows louder. (Again, I think of *Young Mr. Lincoln*.) Offscreen, we hear Dylan's guitar striking up. The camera pans across the closed door, making the frame go dark. More titles appear ("With Bob Dylan" – the name is written as a signature, as if this were a film *by* Dylan as well as *about* him – "and [in order of appearance] Albert Grossman, Bob Neuwirth, Joan Baez, Alan Price, Tito Burns, Donovan, Derroll Adams/London 1965").

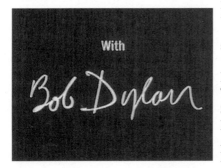

Over these titles, we hear Dylan singing

I ain't looking to compete with you,
To beat or cheat or mistreat you,
Simplify you, classify you,
Deny, defy or crucify you.
All I really want to do
Is baby be *friends* with you.

"All I Really Want to Do" is a perfect foil to "Subterranean Homesick Blues." Rhetorically, the singer is addressing a woman he assures of his friendly intentions. He recites such a vivid catalogue of the unfriendly things he says he is not looking to do, though, that the listener must recognize that this is a man who has done them all (who hasn't?) and is capable of doing them to her. He is making no promise not to do such things to the listener (for example, if he finds she is trying to compete with, to beat or cheat or mistreat, to simplify, classify, deny, defy or crucify *him*). He only says he is not *looking* to do them. (Who is?)

This is not the conventional scene in which by saying he is looking only to be friends a man assures a woman he is not looking to have sex with her. As he stretches "friends" into a word of many syllables, Dylan's voice is so insinuating, so seductive, it openly invites the listener to anticipate the satisfactions to be gained from being his friend. What "being friends" means, what being friends *is*, whether friends can remain friends if they become lovers, whether friends can remain friends if they do not become lovers, are matters to be worked out between them, within their friendship.

"Love is not love that alters when it alteration finds," Shakespeare writes. And friends are not friends, Dylan's song is implying, if they set limits in advance to their relationship. Friends are not friends unless they risk everything together, unless they embrace the principle "Don't look back." And so the Dylan of "Subterranean Homesick Blues" *is* the Dylan of "All I Really Want to Do." The Dylan of the prologue *is* the Dylan whose off-screen voice sings "All I really want to do is baby be *friends* with you," even as his signature appears on the screen.

"He's Only a Pawn in Their Game"

The song is cut off abruptly by a cut to Dylan and his entourage exiting an airport through throngs of fans, bobbies, and reporters. One asks, "Why do you think you're so big this time? What's changed?" "I have absolutely no idea," Dylan replies. "I'm doing just the same thing." There is a cut to a press conference. Dylan, carrying a giant light bulb, is asked, "What's the light bulb for?" "I thought you'd ask me that. I usually carry light bulbs."

Don't Look Back's most famous sequences are ones in which Dylan puts his interviewers on. These passages are reminiscent of the Maysles brothers' *Meet Marlon Brando*, which consists of virtually nothing but the star being interviewed by hopelessly outclassed television reporters – the Maysles's camera is just one among the battery fixed on him – while fulfilling a contractual obligation to promote the film *Code Name: Morituri*. Brando puts on reporter after reporter, knocks them for unthinkingly participating in the mendacity of the mass media. He alternates between propounding the thesis that human beings are violent by nature, hence that the media lie by repressing this truth their own mendacity confirms, and responding to his cynical interviewers, when they assume he is cynical, too, by stressing that unlike them he takes some matters seriously (the plight of Native Americans, for example). He allows male interviewers no comfortable position. And in his encounters with female interviewers, he also comes on to them, making them feel (not always wrongly) that in playing the roles the mass media allot them, they are literally prostituting themselves.

Dylan is contemptuous of some interviewers, too. But there is a crucial difference. Downplaying acting is part of Brando's self-presentation (he is not about to admit that anyone is better at it than he, though). Placing too high a value on acting, Brando implies, is one of the ways the media lie. But Dylan faults the media for placing too little value on what he does. Some interviewers wrongly believe Dylan is downplaying his own songs (when he asserts, for example, that people listen to him because they want to be entertained, or that his songs have no message, or that he has nothing to say about them). Brando denies that his acting exemplifies the philosophical perspective he articulates in his interviews; assessed from that perspective, acting *has* no value. But Dylan's songs, as he sings them, are statements of the same philosophy he articulates in his interviews. Brando's acting, hence his life, has no purpose; at least, that is the burden of his act. These songs are Dylan's purpose for living. And this is no act.

Like Hitchcock, Dylan has a knack for joking responses that deflate questions not worth taking seriously ("What is your real message?" "Keep a good head and always carry a light bulb."). And for telling the truth in such a way it passes for a mere joke ("Why do you think you're so big this time? What's changed?" "I'm doing just the same thing I was doing before." "Are you a folksinger?" "No, I'm not a folk.").

At the time of filming, whether he was a folksinger was a vexed issue for Dylan. This was the last tour in which, conforming to the conventions of the folk music concert, he performed alone, accompanying himself only with acoustic guitar and harmonica. On a couple of occasions before the tour, Dylan had already "gone electric" and brought a band onstage to make music with him. Purists castigated him for selling out, for "going commercial." But he had always felt constricted by the self-contained universe that was the folk music world. Hank Williams and Little Richard had been his idols no less than Woody Guthrie, and by 1965 the Beatles and other rock groups spoke to him more compellingly than any folksingers.

Calling him a folksinger, as the media were still wont to do, raised Dylan's hackles. To think of a song as a folk song is to think of it as having no author, or an author whose identity is unknown and of no consequence, as if the author were a "folk," not a person ("folk," unlike people, are interchangeable). Dylan is no "folk"; he is the individual human being he is: Dylan's songs, as he sings them, at every moment declare this. (The authors of the great traditional folk songs were not "folk," either; they were individuals whose names history, to its discredit, did not deign to record.) To call Dylan a folksinger, to think of his songs as folk songs, is to deny what it means that he *writes* these songs, that they give voice to his experience, that writing and singing these songs is his way of finding his own voice, his way of having a voice, his way of creating a voice for himself. And the Bob Dylan whose purpose for living is to sing these words, his words, in this voice, his voice, is the subject of the camera in *Don't Look Back*.

In the middle of this press conference, a thoughtful reporter asks Dylan, "Do you think a lot of young people who buy your records understand a single word of what you're singing?" Framed in tight close-up, she ends her question by looking challengingly at him.
She is not being hostile; she *wants* to be convinced he is serious. (I can't view this passage without thinking of Jean Seberg interviewing Jean-Pierre Melville in Godard's *Breathless*.)

We hear Dylan, offscreen, say "Sure," stretching the word out in a way that makes it unclear whether he is joking or serious. "You reckon they do?" "Sure," he repeats in the same manner. She looks relieved that his answer did not force her to dismiss the possibility he is being serious. And she looks intrigued, as if she had never seriously considered that there might be millions of young people who listened to Dylan because they understood his songs, not because they had been told it was a cool thing to do.

A male reporter is readier to be dismissive. "How can you be so sure?" The woman, hardly noticing his intervention, presses on. "They're quite complicated songs, aren't they?" "But they understand them." "How do you know they understand them? Have they told you that they do?" "They told me." She can't help laughing. The male reporter butts in, his voice now hostile. "Do you think they understand you because they go and see you?"

This sympathetic woman wants to think the best of Dylan (she is a listener, as becomes apparent when she asks him whether he reads the Bible, making clear she is asking because she finds biblical resonances in his songs). This unsympathetic man (he is not a listener) wants to think the worst of Dylan. To both it is a key question whether Dylan's listeners understand his songs. For Dylan this is no question. What comes through again and again in *Don't Look Back* is Dylan's faith that his fans enjoy his music because they listen to his songs, take them seriously, understand them.

This woman thinks Dylan's songs have a complicated message, and that she has clues although most fans do not. But what if the "message" were really no more complicated (but no less profound) than "All I really want to do is baby be friends with you"? The evident delight she takes in his answers – she smiles when he says "I'm not angry, I'm delightful, perfect" to a reporter who asks, "Are you protesting against certain things that you're angry about?" – reveals she is *perfectly* attuned to what Dylan's songs are saying. Then why does she assume that other listeners are less attuned, less responsive? (This male reporter is not responsive; nor is the man who terminates the press conference when Dylan makes his "I'm delightful, perfect" crack. But they are not listeners.)

Pennebaker's idea is not to be an "objective" observer, to have no point of view. But it is also not to advance claims about the world, to change the world by imposing ideas on it (except insofar as achieving a new perspective on the world is to change the world). His idea is to reveal the world on film, to allow the world on film to reveal itself. This is not an idea a filmmaker can impose on the world; it can only be revealed in the world, revealed by the world, that is, the world on film. The camera's "revelations" may turn out not to be true revelations. Behavior that seems candid, for example, may really be an act. Yet perceived *as* the act it is, it is nonetheless revealing. Pennebaker's idea, then, is to find a perspective from which the camera's revelations may appear perspicuous. As in the later philosophy of Wittgenstein, the goal is not knowledge, but acknowledgment (acknowledgment of the limits of knowledge). In the world of *Don't Look Back*, to aspire to such a perspective is to be on Dylan's side. For Dylan's guiding idea, which he is forever expressing in the film, is that his listeners cannot fail to understand his songs because they have no message that can be misunderstood. There is nothing they assert that the listener does not already know. Like classical movies, their mode is revelation, not assertion.

Dylan is asked the hostile question, "Would you say you care about people, particularly?" He answers, "You know, we all have our own definitions of those words. 'Care.' And 'people.'" "But surely we know what people are." "Well, do we?" Dylan is not claiming, as is a protest singer's wont, to care more about people than most people do. People who make such claims assume they know what "caring" means, what caring is, what counts as relevant criteria. They assume they know what people are, what a person, a character, a self, is. To assume a person is something fixed, unchangeable, knowable, is to deny the idea of selfhood Dylan's songs and Pennebaker's films affirm, the Emersonian idea that, as Katharine Hepburn puts it in *The Philadelphia Story*, "The time to make up your mind about people is never."

Responding to a question we do not hear, Dylan says, "This" – that is, when he is surrounded by press people – "is where I don't write. . . But when I'm living my own thing, doing what I do, this is never around me. I mean, I accept everything, I'll accept it." "Why?" "Because. . .it's real. It exists. . .I can't turn myself off to it, because. . .I'll just end up going insane faster than I eventually will go insane, if I do go insane." He speaks these last words in an exaggerated manner, mugging in a way he does at no other moment in the film. There is a cut to a nattily mustachioed photographer, who seems to point his camera directly at Pennebaker's. (At no other moment does anyone do anything like this, either.) This passage, as Pennebaker edits it, is reminiscent of the sequence in *A Happy Mother's Day* in which Leacock ironically identifies his camera with the *Saturday Evening Post* photographer's. But here it is the press photographer who seems ironically to be asserting a connection between his camera and the filmmaker's.

In any case, by saying "I accept everything," Dylan is affirming the reality of the one existing world, as cinéma-vérité does. Not to acknowledge what is real is insanity. Dylan's encounters with the press are real, although they are far removed from his "living his own thing," "doing what he does." In the midst of all these reporters, he is not writing or performing his songs, nor is he living the everyday life that gives rise to his songs, the form of life he writes about.

Yet Dylan's "normal" life is itself pitched on the edge of insanity, he jokes, implying it is only a matter of time before he goes over the edge. His mugging suggests that his joke is directed to the camera now filming him, as if he were jokingly implying that filmmakers and viewers live on the edge of insanity, too. Filming is real; being filmed is real; it is insanity not to acknowledge the reality of the camera. Yet life in front of the camera, life behind the camera, life that acknowledges the reality of the camera, is on the edge of insanity. Recognizing the edge may be all that keeps one from going over the edge.

A bit later, Dylan has a less joking encounter with a journalist. The passage begins with Dylan reclining on a sofa, reading. Offscreen, we hear a man say "This is for the African service of the BBC, Mr. Dylan." Putting his paper down, Dylan extends his hand. There is a cut to a well-tailored black Jamaican.

"The questions are four in number. For your approval before we ask them. What started it all for you? Just how do you see the art of the folk song in contemporary society?" The camera pans to Dylan, looking down at the written questions. "Has it a very real social impact?" Dylan nods, still studying the questions. "Something that will certainly interest our listeners in Africa, Bob, is your deeply humanitarian attitude to a number of public matters. For instance, you're quoted as saying, 'People talk about Negroes as if they were objects.' Does this sort of compassion, on your part, present any problems for you, in America? O.K.?" Dylan nods, smiling. The reporter adds, with casual urbanity, "By the way, you took part in a play in Britain some time ago written by a school friend of mine..."

Dylan has philosophical objections to these questions, of course (one calls upon him to look back, another assumes he is an artist of the folk song, yet another that he cares more about people than other people do). But he has no wish to embarrass this interviewer, who is being both professional and cordial (rather than trying to compete with him, to beat or cheat or mistreat him, or to simplify, classify, deny, defy, or crucify him, as so many journalists do). Dylan seems fascinated by this man who belongs to a world in which there exist blacks with all the trappings of privilege, fascinated that such a man, such a world, is real.

The interviewer speaks into the microphone. "How did it all begin for you, Bob?" "Um. . .," Dylan mumbles. A quick pan masks a cut to a visibly younger, shorter-haired Dylan at a civil rights rally in Greenwood, Mississippi – the footage was shot by Ed Emshwiller – singing "He's Only a Pawn in Their Game" to what seems to be a handful of young black men. Over the sound of a few clapping hands, there is a cut to a packed concert hall, ringing with applause, then to a medium close shot of Dylan, onstage, singing "The Times They Are A-Changin'."

And it is with this pair of clever and provocative transitions, which add up to a concise presentation of the way Dylan himself has changed, that Pennebaker introduces the first of the film's concert performance sequences.

The first transition (from Dylan being interviewed by this urbane Jamaican to Dylan singing "Only a Pawn in Their Game" for poor Mississippi blacks) may seem to be implying that the interviewer, however privileged he appears, is "only a pawn in their game," too. It may even seem to be implying that Dylan himself is a pawn (the "old" Dylan who sang protest songs on cue? the "new" Dylan many accuse of selling out?). The second transition complicates and clarifies the first by revealing how far Dylan has come since "Only a Pawn in Their Game."

This early Dylan protest song about the murder of Medgar Evers concludes that the murderer is himself a victim of the southern politicians who manipulate poor whites to set them against blacks. Assuming *he* is not a pawn (and, of course, not a player), the singer assumes he knows, assumes his listeners do not know, who the pawns and the villainous players are, and what the game is. The mode is assertion: The singer is conveying information to his listeners. In "The Times They Are A-Changin'," the singer no longer claims to know something his listeners do not. He is calling upon the people who may be listening to join hands in creating a new world. There are no more games, no more villains, no more pawns. We are all in the same boat, or, rather, bailing out of the same sinking ship, finding ourselves in the same swirling waters, having to swim to stay alive and sane.

Paul Williams, most eloquent of Dylan commentators, writes,

"The Times They Are A-Changin'" expresses a feeling that was in the air but had not yet been put into words (not in a popular. . . medium) that all these political and cultural (and personal) changes going on were part of one large Movement, a sea change. . . of historical proportions, the sort of thing spoken of in Biblical prophecy.[55]

In Dylan's own words, "I knew exactly what I wanted to say and for whom I wanted to say it."[56] But as with biblical prophecy, the mode of the "saying" is no longer assertion, it is revelation, as it is in "To Ramona," the other song in this first concert performance sequence.

"Ramona, come closer, shut softly your watery eyes," Dylan sings with tenderness and affection, the implied listener a woman who has come to him in tears. Williams describes the singer as "a sensitive, caring, big-brother shoulder-to-cry-on Dylan" who is "comforting a friend who's up against both circumstances (boyfriend problems?) and her own resultant self-doubts. He acknowledges feelings of desire for her (in order to be up-front, and maybe also to help her to feel better about herself), confusing us listeners into thinking this is a love song when in fact it's clearly a song of friendship."[57]

But in Dylan's songs there are never predefined boundaries between love and friendship, never preexisting rules for distinguishing them. Lines like "Your cracked country lips I still wish to kiss" and "Your magnetic movement still captures the moments I'm in" make it clear that the singer not only feels a more than brotherly love for Ramona, but that they once were lovers, or, at least, it is understood between them that he wished to be her lover. "To Ramona" is a song of friendship *and* a love song. It also stakes out a philosophical position.

Although the singer loves this woman, or because he loves her, when he sings her this song he is "closing the iron door" (as John Barrymore puts it in *Twentieth Century*). If she were weeping due to unhappy circumstances, he could try to cheer her up. What grieves his heart is that she is weeping, rather, because she is still trying "to be part of a world" – it makes no difference what exactly we imagine this world to be – "that does not really exist." So-called friends have fooled her by "hyping" her and "typing" her and making her feel she "has to be just like them." He can say to her, as he does, "There's no one to beat you, no one to defeat you 'cept the thoughts of yourself feeling bad." But he cannot make her acknowledge this truth she nonetheless knows – he knows she knows it – in her heart. She must acknowledge what is real, acknowledge the one world that exists, and that is something he cannot do for her. The singer grieves for her, because she keeps herself from acknowledging this truth; for himself, because the love in his song may be in vain; and for all human beings who think they are beaten and defeated when all they need is a new perspective.

To *Don't Look Back*'s developing picture of Dylan, this performance, placed here, reveals that his songs are "humanitarian" after all, if not in the way the BBC interviewer assumed. What makes them humanitarian is not Dylan's "attitude to public matters." "To Ramona" concerns a private matter, not a public one, and its singer strikes no attitude at all. What makes it humanitarian is the compassion we can hear in his voice. Compassion is not something one can extend, or fail to extend, to humanity in general, as if people were interchangeable folk, but only to particular people, oneself included. The real issue for Dylan is not the impact of his songs on "contemporary society," but on the individuals who listen, or keep themselves from listening, to his voice. The thrust of "To Ramona" may seem to be that the song falls on deaf ears, fails to achieve its desired impact on the woman to whom it is addressed. But this is not something the singer claims to know. Ramona will sink like a stone unless she changes, and for this the singer grieves. But people change. Her fate is not immutable.

To paraphrase the BBC interviewer, the singer's compassion may seem to present a problem for him; it makes him cast out this woman he loves so she might find her own freedom, leaving them both feeling like rolling stones. But feeling like a rolling stone is not the problem; it is the condition apart from which the real problem – not acknowledging reality – cannot be solved. At least, that is Dylan's faith. That we hear this faith in his voice reveals, first, that we feel he is singing for us, not just for Ramona. Second, that although she does not seem to hear his voice, we do. If we have faith in our capacity to become ourselves, to achieve the philosophical perspective apart from which there is no freedom, we can have hope for Ramona. If we can change, so can she.

This performance of "To Ramona" confronts the viewer of *Don't Look Back* with a firsthand experience of Dylan's ability, as Paul Williams puts it, to "penetrate a listener's reality and create an I-you relationship of startling, sometimes confusing, intimacy." It is provocatively followed by a passage in which a *Guardian* critic phones in his review.

He is not so much singing as sermonizing. Colon. His tragedy, perhaps, is that the audience is preoccupied with song. Paragraph. So the bearded boys and the lank-haired girls, all eye shadow and undertaker makeup, applaud the songs and miss, perhaps, the sermon. They are there. They are with it. But how remote they really are from sit-ins and strikes and scabs. And life.

This man has been moved, but his words get it wrong. Dylan's songs may be sermons, but we cannot grasp their moral without listening to them as songs. When Dylan is performing, to be "there," to be "with it," is not to be remote from life. Dylan's songs are as real as "sit-ins and strikes and scabs." The world on film is capable of revealing its own reality, and song is capable of revealing its own reality, too. If his audience is preoccupied with song, that is Dylan's triumph, not his tragedy. A tragic fate is fixed. Dylan's songs affirm that people change.

"Nothing Is Sacred, Right?"

"Are you aware of the fact," someone says to Dylan after the concert, "that tonight. . .you had a greater audience than has been seen here for many years? I mean, the applause was fantastic!" "That makes me feel good," Dylan mumbles, his expression guarded. "Are you religious?" "I don't know, what does that mean, 'religious'? Does it mean you bow down to an idol or go to church every Sunday or that kind of stuff?" "No, no, no. Do you believe in. . .?" "Why should I believe in anything?" "Are you cynical?" "No, I just can't see anything that anybody's offered me to believe that I might believe, that I might trust and have faith in. Nothing is sacred, right?"

In the long prose poem he wrote as liner notes for the 1964 album *Joan Baez in Concert: Volume 2*, Dylan speaks of his early idols, such as Hank Williams. "In later times my idols fell," he writes.

> For I learned that they were only men
> An had reasons for their deeds. . .
> But what I learned from each forgotten god
> Was that the battlefield was mine alone
> An only I could cast my stone

Dylan's idols were only men who had their own private reasons for their words and actions. But it is by learning these "forgotten gods" were only human that he learned he had to find his own voice. When Dylan says "I just can't see anything that anybody's offered me to believe that I might believe, that I might trust and have faith in," he means that there are no gods to be idolized. No one, and nothing, is better than he; no authority is "higher" than his own experience. Like "Don't look back," "Nothing is sacred" is a principle Dylan does trust and have faith in, but it is a principle he arrived at – how else can it be arrived at? – on the basis of his own experience. No one offered it to him to believe. Nor is he offering it to us as something to believe.

With Dylan's "Nothing is sacred, right?" still echoing in our minds, a flunky appears at the door of Dylan's hotel suite, announces there have been complaints about noise, and demands to know who is in charge. "In charge of what?" Albert Grossman replies, barely containing his fury. "Who is in charge of this room?" "What do you mean 'in charge of this room'?

It's rented to Bob Dylan." "Are you Bob Dylan's manager?" "Yes, but I'm not in charge of his room." "You're in charge of Bob Dylan?" "No, I'm not in charge of Bob Dylan." "We've had complaints about the noise." "That's unfortunate. We'll try to hold it down." "And if you don't in five minutes, I will ask you to leave." "There's been no noise in this room," Grossman says, taking back his conciliatory remark. "And you're one of the dumbest assholes and most stupid persons I've ever seen in my life."

When Grossman goes on in this vein, ultimately suggesting that the flunky should go see his "fop manager," Dylan seems deliberately to pass close by the camera so he can share a giggle with it. (This is the only moment in the film at which he openly claims a special friendship, as it were, with the camera.)

This juxtaposition of scenes reveals a surprising affinity, though with a difference, between Grossman and Dylan. "Nothing is sacred" is Grossman's faith as surely as it is Dylan's, although to the latter it means that nothing exists that is not sacred, while to the former it means that nothing exists that is not profane.

In Spitz's biography of Dylan, the characterization of Grossman ("cryptic, arrogant, condescending, shrewd, underhanded, cutthroat, even diabolical") is etched with acid. Spitz quotes the folksinger Dave Van Ronk, who considered Grossman "an astute but very cruel man" who played "a kind of Mephistophelian role" with his clients, guaranteeing "stardom in return for their integrity."[58] Pennebaker is more appreciative, and no doubt more accurate, when he simply observes, "Albert was one of the few people who saw Dylan's worth very early on, and played it absolutely without equivocation or any kind of compromise."[59] (When Grossman died some years after an acrimonious split with his client, Pennebaker wrote a letter to Dylan. "I said a lot of bad things had gone down between them, but I knew that basically Albert was extremely devoted to him and loved him – and I knew that Bob loved Albert; so it was really kind of sad that it had come to that. But. . .these things happen."[60])

What made their relationship so fruitful, as long as it lasted, was precisely their shared faith that nothing was sacred. It made Dylan literally incorruptible. And it enabled Grossman to realize it would not only be futile to try to corrupt this client, it would be like trying to kill the goose that laid the golden egg. "Image was an important feature of Grossman's management technique," Spitz writes. "Harnessing Bob's sense of inspiration, rebellion, exaggeration, peculiarity, posturing and conceit, Grossman intended to create a *legend*."[61]

But to transform Dylan into a legend was not to corrupt him. Transforming himself into a legend was Dylan's own goal. The legendary figure Dylan aspired to become – Grossman had to respect this – was not a god or an idol but a flesh-and-blood human being, a person in the world the man born "Robert Zimmerman" was capable of becoming. To say the legendary Bob Dylan (like the unlegendary Bob Zimmerman) is a person is to say he is capable of "a-changin'" – and of being filmed.

In Paul Williams's view, this legendary figure had "arrived" some months earlier when the album *Another Side of Bob Dylan* was released. What then arrived, he writes in a splendid passage,

> . . . is a sort of mythic being, "Bob Dylan" – the alter ego Robert Zimmerman began creating six or seven years earlier to help him express himself, call attention to himself, escape himself, and set his real self free – a stage identity, *nom de plume* and what Rimbaud called "the other." This being is now fully fleshed, holographic (you can look at the image from all sides), unselfconscious. . . and self-standing (the puppet walks by himself; the puppeteer no longer seems to exist).[62]

Joan Baez

Following a concert sequence – it features the film's longest uninterrupted performance of a single song, "The Lonesome Death of Hattie Carroll" – Dylan talks backstage to admiring young musicians. "It's very difficult to get them to listen to words," one says; "I just go out there and sing them," replies Dylan, who had no difficulty getting his audience to listen to the words of "Hattie Carroll." In "Only a Pawn in Their Game," as in most early Dylan topical ballads, a political issue takes precedence over the humanity of the characters. What makes "Hattie Carroll" so moving is that it dwells more on the life of the murdered woman, about whom Dylan seems to care and to want the listener to care, than on the miscarriage of justice that allows her wealthy young killer to get off almost scot-free.

There is a cut to Dylan's entourage making a dash through hordes of fans, the hand-held camera shaking; to the limousine plowing through the fans, one of whom is clinging to the top of the car as it drives away ("Will you please take the girl off the car," Dylan shouts, unable to keep from laughing); to approaching headlights, the glare blinding, viewed through slashing wiper blades (a shot reminiscent of *Psycho*). There is a sound overlap as we hear Joan Baez singing "Bad news, bad news came to where I sleep . . . ," and then a cut to a grainy, badly underexposed, frontal extreme close-up of the darkly beautiful Baez, singing in her achingly pure soprano, accompanying herself on the guitar, " . . . Turn, turn, turn again. Saying one of your friends is in trouble deep. Turn, turn, to the rain and the wind . . . " (The song is Dylan's "Percy's Song," a kind of companion-piece to "Hattie Carroll." Told in the first person by a friend whose plea to the judge falls on deaf ears, "Percy's Song" tells of a miscarriage of justice in which a young man, at the wheel

when four people died in an automobile accident, is sentenced too harshly.)

The camera lingers on this shot. It is so underexposed it is difficult to make out Baez's features, but that does not detract from the sense of beauty the shot conveys, a melancholy beauty that springs from the way this woman's voice melds with the way she looks. Her "looks," here, have as much to do with the interiority she projects as with her raven black hair, her cheekbones, her skin, her eyes. And yet "interiority" is a strange word to use to characterize the woman in this shot, whose face reveals no spark of expression. Her voice conveys the sense that the characters in the story, not her listeners or herself, are all that exist for her. Yet she does not act the story out as she sings, does not "become" these characters whose unhappy fates she is relating. There seems an invisible world inside her head, a world she makes no attempt to render visible, a world in which there is no trace of her or us, a world to which she abandons herself, a world within which she is abandoned.

Whenever Baez sings, Pennebaker's camera is drawn to frame her in extreme close-up, as if it wished to penetrate, or, perhaps, to preserve her mystery. For what is mysterious about Baez when she sings is her capacity to absorb herself completely in an invisible world from which her voice of unearthly purity seems to emanate. How better to meditate on this mystery than by revealing her ability to sustain her absorption no matter how close the camera comes to her face? Ordinarily, the camera's closeness threatens people's sense of privacy (Mrs. Fischer's, for example). But Baez seems to be daring the camera to come this close, as if she might thereby demonstrate her ability to fence out the visible world and thus prove the reality of the invisible world on the other side of the fence.

When Dylan sings, Pennebaker never frames him this way. But his singing never solicits such a framing. On film, Dylan always seems to be singing in the first person, always *to* a specific listener or listeners, but always *for* the camera. When Dylan sings about Hattie Carroll, for example, the murdered woman seems real to us, as she seems real to him; the listeners to whom the song is rhetorically addressed ("You who philosophize disgrace and criticize all fears. . .") seem real to us, as they seem real to him; and the singer seems real to us, and to himself.

Even when performing a song written in the first person, such as "Percy's Song," Baez seems to be singing in the third person, and to no listeners at all. When she sings, she seems as removed from the characters whose story she is telling as from the people in her presence, and from herself. This voice belongs to no character within the story. It does not exactly belong to the singer, either. The camera means the world to Dylan, but when Baez sings she seems to be trying, like Ramona, to be "part of a world that does not really exist." And yet the world on film, the world in which this woman is singing and Pennebaker's camera is filming, encompasses both the invisible and the visible realms. On film, the reality of the invisible world confirms the reality of the visible world, and vice versa. In the world on film, the mystery embodied or disembodied by Baez's voice is not that it is unreal, part of a world that does not exist, but that it is real. It emanates from this flesh-and-blood woman who inhabits the one existing world, not some "other" world on the other side of the fence. There is no fence separating the world on film from the real world. There is no world outside the world on film.

It is a widely shared intuition of opera, Stanley Cavell suggests, that "the intervention or supervening of music into the world" is "revelatory of a realm of significance that either transcends our ordinary realm of experience or reveals ours under transfiguration." Opera is predicated on

> . . . an encompassing sense of another realm flush with this one . . . Such a view will take singing . . . to express the sense of being pressed or stretched between worlds – one in which to be seen, the roughly familiar world of the philosophers, and one from which to be heard, one to which one releases or abandons one's spirit – and which recedes when the breath of the song ends.[63]

The one world on film encompasses both of these realms; Joan Baez, singing on film, is to be seen *and* heard. The medium of film also overcomes or transcends the convention, fundamental to opera, that singing is a figure for speaking. On film, singing, like speaking and being silent, is an action a human being performs for his or her own private reasons; singing is internal to our human form of life. Some moments in *Don't Look Back,* for her own private reasons, Baez speaks. Other moments, she is silent. When silence will not do but spoken words are out of reach, she sings.

When finally there is a cut from Baez, singing, to a close-up of Albert Grossman, his owl-like visage gives no sign of inner life. The camera lingers on his impassive face.

Our mood inflected by Baez's singing (". . . Tell me the trouble, tell me once to my ear . . . "), we find ourselves believing that even this man is attuned to the spell her voice casts. (This is confirmed a few moments later by a droll shot of Grossman, leaning back in his chair, one shoe ever-so-slightly beating time to Baez's singing.)

Meanwhile, we hear from off-screen the distracting "clack, clack, clack" of a typewriter. The camera pulls back, pans to include Dylan, then zooms in slightly to frame him,

from behind, in medium shot. It is he who is pecking away, one letter at a time – presumably writing or rewriting a song – as Baez's singing continues offscreen ("...Turn, turn, turn again..."). How can Dylan write, we wonder (the shot of Grossman invites us to wonder this), when Baez is singing? (It may occur only to the writers among us to wonder how she can sing when he is writing.)

Pausing, Dylan rubs his forehead. There is a cut to another extreme close-up of Baez, the camera lingering as usual ("...You're in prison for ninety-nine years. Turn, turn, to the rain and the wind. Tell me once how this came to be. Turn, turn, turn again..."). The clacking resumes. ("...It was manslaughter in the highest degree. Turn, turn, to the rain and the

wind...."). The camera pans to Dylan, empty wine glass and notebook beside him, and an unidentified woman (the singer Marianne Faithfull) in the left background of the frame.

Pausing again, Dylan bobs his head like a New Delhi taxi driver who is asked whether he knows where he is going and replies with a gesture that says "Yes" and "No" at the same time. When he resumes typing, Dylan's body is swaying a bit, and even the clacking seems in time with the music. (In an example of the remarkable serendipity characteristic of so many great cinéma-vérité moments, the words Baez is singing at this moment are "I sat down and wrote the best words I could write.") Dylan looks down and stops typing. Staring at his page, he listens ("...Turn, turn, turn again. Asked the judge to see me on Wednesday night. Turn, turn, to the rain and the wind..."). Whether he is hopelessly distracted by Baez's singing, or seeking inspiration from it, we cannot say.

The camera pans to Baez and lingers over yet another extreme close-up ("...Without a reply I left by the moon. Turn, turn, turn again" – in the middle of this line, someone passes in front of the camera – "I was in the judge's chamber the next afternoon. Turn, turn, to the rain and the wind...").

Eventually, the camera pulls away and pans to Dylan at the typewriter (this time without Marianne Faithfull; evidently, it was she who passed in front of the camera just before). Still not typing, still swaying to the music, he keeps looking at the page ("...Tell me now, I asked without fear. Turn, turn, turn again. How one of my friends could get ninety-nine years. Turn, turn, to the rain and the wind...").

Finally, the camera moves in such a way that for the first time it includes both Dylan and Baez, in the shadows, in one frame ("...A crash on the highway threw a car into a wheel. Turn, turn, turn again..."). The composition seems to sum up the situation: He hears her voice, but is turned away.

Still listening to Baez's voice (as we are), still not looking at her (as we wish to keep doing), Dylan gathers his concentration and resumes typing. (". . . Four people killed with him at the wheel. Turn, turn, to the rain and the wind. . .") Then, suddenly, there is an abrupt cut to Baez singing

Dylan's "Love is Just a Four-Letter Word." Evidently it is a bit later. The mood has shifted.

The camera in *A Happy Mother's Day* provokes a dramatic confrontation simply by dwelling on Mrs. Fischer's face. The camera in *Chronicle of a Summer* forces Marilou back on herself by continuing to film her when she is visibly breaking down. In both cases, there is a crisis in the camera's relationship with the woman. (From within that crisis, Rouch denies, Leacock embraces, the possibility of a happy resolution.) But when Pennebaker's camera dwells on Baez's face as she sings, their relationship does not assume a dramatic or melodramatic cast.

And yet, viewing these extreme close-ups of Baez under the spell of her singing, I have always found it irresistible to weave a romantic melodrama around these characters, a fiction in which Baez and Dylan are lovers whose affair is on the rocks. I imagine her singing for him, singing to him, singing out of her love for him, and singing, moreover, to prove her voice still has the power to turn him on, to distract him from his writing or claim her rightful place in it, to call upon him to acknowledge that to write the best words he can write he needs her to inspire him. I imagine her singing in the hope of winning a reprise for their relationship – why else sing this song about a too-harsh judge who fails to bend to a just appeal? – or, failing that, to remind him who it is he is rejecting, or to announce her intention to walk out on him if he does not change his tune. And I imagine Dylan savoring this moment in which, perhaps for the last time, it remains possible for him to listen to her voice without looking back.

Attuned to the spell cast by Baez's voice, I find myself savoring this moment, too. Far from being in a state of suspense I am anxious to have resolved, I find myself wishing this moment would never end. When I find myself weaving a melodramatic fiction around this moment, in other words, I also find myself absorbed by a mood that transcends, or overcomes, melodrama. The pleasurable mood of this passage would be different if it were not possible to weave a fiction around it. And yet the mood does not depend on the particular fiction we find ourselves weaving. Whatever may have brought this woman and this man to this crossroads, whatever their romance may have been or failed to be, whatever the "backstory," as screenwriters call it, the mood of this passage is what it is. As long as the breath of the song lasts, as long as the projector beams this sequence onto the screen, the mood is sustained. But knowing it must end is part of what makes it the mood it is.

In the world on film, everything is forever turning, turning, turning again. Film is a medium of the ephemeral, the never-to-be-repeated, a medium of the rain and the wind. That the world is forever changing is the only thing that never changes about the world, part of what makes the world a world. Hence film is also a medium of the unchanging. *Don't Look Back* enables us to return to this moment, fall under this spell, experience this mood, every time we view the film. What Pennebaker says about *Depeche Mode 101* (in the eloquent statement he wrote for the cover of the video cassette) he could also have said about *Don't Look Back*:

I don't think it's a documentary although it's about real people in real life. It's certainly not an acted film, although. . .there is in it every sort of performance. . .If I had to call it by any other name than a movie I would say it was a musical adventure, perhaps even a musical fantasy. It's not exactly what happened. . .For me it remains a dream memory, gone and over now but still visible like a fly in amber for all time.

(And, it might be added, the "fly on the wall" is for all time still invisible in this amber.)

"It never occurred to me to supply *information* in [*Don't Look Back*]," Pennebaker has remarked.[64] The film does not claim to tell the inside story. No effort is made to inform us about the intimacies of Dylan's private life. Nor does it claim we need to know such details in order for us to "get it" about what we are viewing. (It *is* necessary, though, for us not to deny that there are intimacies we are not privy to, that we are viewing a person with a private life.)

I had come to know *Don't Look Back* very well, almost as well as I now know it, long before I became aware that during the shooting Dylan was in the process of breaking up with Baez, with whom he had been having an affair that for two such private people had become painfully public. (Their affair was the subject, for example, of a *Newsweek* story that outraged and disgusted them both.) Having now sifted through much of the published literature on Dylan, I can say, not exactly with pride, that I have become relatively well-informed about Dylan's private life.

It seems to have been Grossman who suggested to Baez that she accompany the tour to England, and she did, perhaps not knowing that before the trip Dylan had begun seeing Sara Lowndes. During the tour, Baez walked out, upset that Dylan never invited her to sing with him, as she had invited him when he was unknown and she the queen of the folk world. "Think of what it must have been like for a performer of Joan's magnitude to be denied access to the stage," Spitz remarks, inviting us to pity Baez and pass a harsh judgment on Dylan. "To have to *watch*, of all things, while Bob played to packed houses of adoring fans. Fans she'd helped to cultivate for him."[65] In the face of such reproaches, Dylan more than once publicly defended his behavior, maintaining he had told Baez before the trip that she should not expect him to invite her to share his stage, and that in any case he owed her nothing at that point.

However grateful he may have been or should have been, Dylan did not owe Baez his fans, the listeners who take his songs seriously; they were not hers to give. In any case, for Dylan there was a philosophical as well as a personal issue at stake in his decision not to invite Baez to share his stage. Baez often said that Dylan songs spoke to her, spoke for her, enabled her to speak in ways she could not speak without them ("He can say it, but I can't write it, but I wish I could"). She found a voice singing Dylan songs. But she also found a voice singing folk songs. Indeed, she sings Dylan's songs as if they *were* folk songs. (Never having heard Dylan's version, I assumed, on the basis of Baez's rendition in *Don't Look Back*, that "Percy's Song," with its traditional melody and traditional-sounding repeated lines, actually *was* a folk song. To hear Dylan sing it is to know it as a Dylan song.) For all its beauty, Baez's voice is not her own, she does not claim it as her own, the way Dylan claims his voice as his. She absents herself from her singing as she absents the characters, the listener, the songwriter. She sings like a folksinger, in other words. But then how *can* she have a place singing Dylan songs on Dylan's stage?

And yet the beauty of Baez's voice meant a lot to Dylan. In the liner notes from which we have already quoted, Dylan meditates at length on the moment he first really listened to Baez's voice. In his early efforts to find a voice to "tell my tale," he writes, he turned to idols like Hank Williams.

> For he sang about the railroad lines
> An the iron bars and rattlin wheels
> Left no doubt that they were real. . . .
> An I'd judge beauty with these rules
> An accept it only 'f it was ugly
> An 'f I could touch it with my hand.

Time passed. Dylan learned his idols were only human, that he had to find his own voice, as they had. Then he met Baez.

> An many thoughts t me were taught
> By names an heads too many t count
> That touched my path . . .
> It is at this time I speak 'f one . . .
> Who like me strummed lonesome tunes . . .
> 'A thing of beauty' people said

'Wondrous sounds' writers wrote
'I hate that kind of sound' said I
'The only beauty's ugly, man . . .'
So between our tongues there was a bar . . . .
When I saw she was set t sing . . .
Sprang up like a protectin glass.

More time passed.

With friends scattered round the rooms . . .
An me crosslegged on the rug
I . . . gulped light red wine . . .
An the room whirled an twirled an sailed
Without one fence standin guard
When all at once the silent air
Split open from her soundin voice . . .
An I shook an started reachin for
That wall that was suppose t fall
But my restin nerves weren't restless now . . .
'Let her voice ring out' they cried . . .
An left me puzzled without no choice
Cept t listen t her voice . . . .
I felt my face freeze t the bone
An my mouth like ice or solid stone
Could not've moved 'f called upon . . .
An like others who have taught me well
Not about themselves but me
She laughed out loud as 'f t know
That the bars between us busted down . . .
An my head lay back upon the floor . . .
But I memorized the words t write
For another time in t'morrow's dawn . . .
As I passed out somewhere in the nite –

I did not begin t touch
Til I finally felt what wasn't there . . .
For the breeze I heard in that young girl's breath
Proved true as sex an womanhood . . .
An as long as fate an fatherhood
An like gypsy drums
An Chinese gongs
An cathedral bells
An tones 'f chimes
It jus held hymns 'f mystery
An mystery . . . shouldn't be called by a shameful name

By those who look for answers plain
In every book cept themselves.

When he finally stopped building a fence to keep himself from listening to her voice, what Dylan learned from Baez is a thought about reality, about beauty, about women, about this woman, about men, about himself, about the power, and the limits of the power, of the human voice raised in song. "I did not begin t touch," he says, "Til I finally felt what wasn't there" – what wasn't *there* as opposed to *here*, what was everywhere if it was anywhere, the breeze in the singer's breath. Baez's voice enabled him to touch, to be touched by, beauty whose reality he had always denied because it was not also ugly and because he could no more hold it in his hands than rain or wind (or the world on film).

The first time he really listened to Baez's voice, Dylan says, "the bars between us busted down." But he also says that he felt his face "freeze t the bone"; his mouth "like ice or solid stone could not've moved 'f called upon." When she is singing and he listening, his mouth is not "called upon" to move; he is not speaking, but neither is he failing to speak. But it doesn't take a weatherman to know that the moment the "breeze in her breath" died down, the bars would go back up. All the time he and Baez were lovers, Dylan confided to friend and biographer Robert Shelton, he felt he could not speak to her; she turned him to stone. ("You know, Bob, about Joan, I could never really talk to Joan. . . I clammed up. Like we made the concert tours, but I wouldn't talk to her."[66]) What Dylan says in his songs, he cannot *speak* to Baez, cannot speak *to* her.

The beauty Baez's voice reveals to Dylan is no illusion; it is real, although he cannot hold it in his hands. The voice raised in song "busts down the bars," transfigures the world: This is the "truth of song," as we might put it. It is this he says he learned from listening to Baez's voice. And Dylan's performances in *Don't Look Back* reveal that by the time of this British tour he had come to affirm the "truth of song" in his own songs and singing.

Having learned that he had to acknowledge the reality of "beauty that is not also ugly" in his own songs, his own singing, Dylan has nothing more to learn from listening to Baez's voice. And that is what comes through in this passage of *Don't Look Back*, I take it. When she sings, he listens, and he still hears those "hymns 'f mystery" in her voice. But Baez's voice no longer literally floors him. And, in the absence of conversation, song can no longer sustain their everyday life together. These things happen.

It cannot be said that *Don't Look Back* denies – how could it? – that Dylan and Baez have been lovers, that their affair is on the rocks, or that when she disappears from the film she also walks out, or is cast out, of his personal life. *Don't Look Back* does not assert that their relationship is platonic, or conflict-free, much less that they have no relationship. If the film asserted any such things, how could I have found it irresistible to imbed this passage within a fiction that turns out to be no mere fiction? *Don't*

Look Back asserts nothing about the off-camera relationship of Dylan and Baez, but neither does it make assertions about their on-screen relationship. The film's mode is revelation, not assertion, as we have said. The remainder of the sequence illustrates this.

It is later, and the mood has shifted, when Baez finds herself singing "Love Is Just a Four-Letter Word" ("... But I heard you say that love is just a four-letter word...").

The camera pans to Dylan, who is scratching his head, his back to the camera. He seems much less focused on her singing. As she nonetheless continues ("Outside a rambling storefront window cats meowed the break of day. Me, I kept my mouth shut, to you I had no words to say..."), there are cuts to a variety of setups (including the shot of Grossman beating time to the music).

Coming to the end of the last stanza she knows, Baez asks Dylan, "Do you know any more?" "I haven't finished it." "Oh god, you finished it about eight different ways! It's beautiful. If you finish it, I'll sing it for my record." Dylan rubs his eyes and mumbles inaudibly. Then he says to someone offscreen (a moment later we realize it is Neuwirth), "Have you ever heard 'She Died for Love at Three A.M.'? Bill Anderson wrote it. It's a great song." As Baez starts up another song ("...February brought us broken hearts..."), Dylan whispers, with a smirk that makes it clear his remark is really for Neuwirth's benefit, "Sing 'Long Black Veil!' Sing 'Long Black Veil!'" Offscreen, we hear Neuwirth say, "Hey, *don't* sing it."

There is an abrupt cut – again, time is elided – to a shot with Baez on one side of the frame and Dylan on the other.

Accompanying himself on the guitar, Dylan begins singing "Lost Highway," a great song written by Leon Payne and immortalized by Hank Williams's recording. The camera isolates him as he sings ("I was just a lad then at twenty-two, neither good nor bad, just a kid like you. Then I got lost too late to pray. I started going down that lost highway"). There is a pan to Baez, who hums along, harmonizing with Dylan's offscreen singing ("Now boys, don't start to ramble around on this road of sin or you're sorrow bound. And you'll get lost, just curse the day" – the camera reframes back to the two shot – "You started going down that lost highway").

This is how Bob Spitz describes the passage:

> There is a moment in *Don't Look Back* that serves to illustrate [Baez's] predicament. . .Joan harmonizes gaily with Bob to a medley of country and western songs. In between numbers, Bob prods her: "Sing 'Long Black Veil.'" Clearly, he didn't mean it. "Long Black Veil," like "Copper Kettle" and "Mary Hamilton," were leftovers from Joan's traditional folk repertoire. . .On more than one occasion, Bob had publicly ridiculed her dependence on those songs, so that by requesting "Long Black Veil" he was obviously making fun of her. In fact, Bobby Neuwirth accurately sums up the situation when he adds, "Hey, *don't* sing it." Joan, for her part, ignores them and continues singing a Hank Williams song, despite Bob's persistence: "Sing 'Long Black Veil,'" he demands. "She walks these hills in a long black veil." Finally he gives up and does a verse of "I'm So Lonesome I Could Cry."[67]

But Baez is not in the midst of "harmonizing gaily with Bob to a medley of country and western songs" (she has sung Dylan's "Percy's Song," and then, after a lapse of time, "Love Is Just a Four-Letter Word," another Dylan song). And she is in the middle of singing, not "between numbers," when Dylan and Neuwirth perform their little routine. By jokingly saying "Sing 'Long Black Veil!' Sing 'Long Black Veil!'" Dylan is not prodding Baez to sing it, much less demanding that she do so, and it is not "despite Bob's persistence" that she continues the song she is singing; we have no real evidence that Dylan wants her to do anything but go on. (That Dylan had publicly prodded Baez to shake her dependence on traditional folk songs like "Long Black Veil" doesn't mean he has contempt – how could he? – for the songs themselves, or for the way she sings them.)

For his own private reasons – Pennebaker makes no claim to know what they are – Dylan at this moment is conspiring with Neuwirth (who has his private reasons, too) to put Baez on. And she has her private reasons for ignoring them. Spitz claims to know that Dylan no longer wants (if he ever did) to be friends with Baez, that he is looking to compete with her, beat or cheat or mistreat her, simplify her, classify her, deny, defy, or crucify her. Something is happening here, and Spitz claims to know what it is. Not only does *Don't Look Back* not endorse his claim, it teaches us to be disdainful of it.

Dylan does not "finally give up" and do a verse of "I'm So Lonesome I Could Cry." The song he sings is "Lost Highway"; he begins after another lapse of time, not at the "next moment"; and nothing suggests he is singing for any reason other than that he loves the song and is in the mood to sing it now. Spitz characterizes this passage so negatively he misses its specific revelation, crucial to *Don't Look Back* as a whole, that, as Paul Williams puts it, Dylan makes music "because he loves it, not because it's expected of him."

Not that Dylan is completely comfortable singing "Lost Highway." A cool cat like him finds it daunting to express emotion so directly. But he sings it straight, allowing his voice to express the required feelings. When Dylan stops after two verses, Neuwirth reminds him there is another. "It's an ecstatic moment," Paul Williams astutely observes. "You can see it on Neuwirth's face. And he doesn't want it to end prematurely."[68] (Assuming he knows Neuwirth's intentions to be devilish, Spitz misses this loving, most undevilish, look.)

Beginning the "forgotten" verse ("I'm a rolling stone, I'm alone and lost. For a life of sin I've paid the cost"), Dylan muffs the words. But he gamely goes on, with Baez harmonizing ("Take my advice or you'll curse the day you started going down that lost highway"), to create what Paul Williams considers to be one of the two "transcendent musical moments" in *Don't Look Back*.

When this British tour ended, Dylan enjoyed an astonishing burst of creativity in which he wrote some of his greatest songs, including "Like a Rolling Stone," a song it is tempting to hear as a response to this experience of singing "Lost Highway." In "Lost Highway," the singer looks back with regret and remorse. The singer of "Like a Rolling Stone" accepts being "alone and lost," being "like a rolling stone"; he doesn't "curse the day" he started down the road on which he finds himself. He does not look back.

Dylan's songs chart a middle course between the metaphysics (as we might put it) of "Lost Highway," which laments the loss of a stable world of traditional values, and the skepticism of those who deny everything of value (who "philosophize disgrace," as "Hattie Carroll" puts it), who derisively dismiss love, for example, by calling it "just a four-letter word." (The title of Dylan's song refers not to something the singer is asserting, but something he had heard said by the woman he is addressing. For Dylan, "Nothing is sacred" means that no thing is less sacred than any other thing, that nothing that exists is *not* sacred. And insofar as "Love is just a four-letter word" is a principle Dylan himself can endorse, it means that love is something more, not something less, than it is conventionally held to be. For "love" to be a *four-letter* word – a word like "fuck" or "shit" – is for love to be the kind of thing whose true nature, and value, society denies. For "love" to be a four-letter *word* – a word like any other – is for love to be something everyday, something ordinary, something to be acknowledged for what it really is, not worshiped as something sacred, something that does not exist.)

Having come to the end of one great song, Dylan is itching to sing another. He begins singing "I'm So Lonesome I Could Cry," the signature song of his idol Hank Williams. Singing the first line ("Hear that lonesome whip-poorwill. . ."), he cannot keep a straight face. But he strives to sing this song, too, without mocking its emotion (". . .He sounds too blue to cry. That midnight train is rolling by. . .").

When Dylan comes to the refrain "I'm so lonesome I could cry," he seems especially embarrassed simulating Hank Williams's laughing-through-tears near-yodel (which itself mimics both his own and the whippoorwill's sobs), both because it is in such a high register he has to concentrate to hit all the notes, and because it is a daunting challenge to acknowledge his bond with a singer – not to mention a whippoorwill – capable of sobbing out loud without self-consciousness. But Dylan does make connection with the emotion (he sings the refrain the first time as farce, but the second time as tragedy).

There is an abrupt cut – again, some time has been elided – to a longer shot, from a different angle, in which Dylan is wearing shades. An offscreen voice (Grossman?) says (to whom?), "Welcome home. This is the first time that this room hasn't been filled with a bunch of insane lunatics, man." Dylan scratches his head. There is a cut to Baez, a white kerchief around her neck. She says, "Bobby, it was almost too nice. You don't know." There is a pan to Dylan. "It's the first time it's been cool around here." Baez says, "I'm sleepy. I don't know who fagged me out." She pulls her kerchief up to her face as if it were a Moslem woman's veil. (If she were not "fagged out," would she be luring him to the Casbah?)

Offscreen, in response to Baez's charade, we hear Neuwirth say, not without affection, "Scheherazade. . ." (As long as she was singing, her "execution" was deferred.) He adds, "You fagged out a long time ago. You fagged out before you even thought you were fagging out." She makes a face (at Neuwirth?) as Dylan crosses behind her in the frame. The camera reframes with her to Neuwirth, who is holding a guitar. "Oh my god, here she is: Fang!" Offscreen, Dylan briefly chants "Fang! Fang!" Neuwirth says, "Fang, you have one of those see-through blouses, blouses that you don't even wanna. . ." (As far as Baez's see-through blouse goes, I have always imagined that, although he may not admit it, Neuwirth *does* "wanna.")

Baez goes over to Dylan, again at his typewriter, his back turned to the camera. She puts her hands over his eyes, a provocative and ambiguous gesture. For his own private reasons, Dylan doesn't rise to this bait. She returns to Neuwirth and pummels him as if they were both children. Neuwirth, who seems to enjoy the roughhousing he pretends alarms him, says, "You wouldn't hurt a guitar, would you?" "No." There is a cut to Dylan at his typewriter, acting above the fray. We hear Baez's offscreen voice saying to Neuwirth, "Oh, pardon me." "I didn't mean to hurt you, sort of," Neuwirth says offscreen, as Dylan pecks at the typewriter, seemingly oblivious. Then we hear chords from Neuwirth's guitar, and Baez's voice saying

"God!" Then there is a cut to Baez unceremoniously departing (Spitz speaks of her as "sulking off," but I see no sulkiness in the way she goes out the door and closes it behind her).

Interviewing Pennebaker about the making of *Don't Look Back*, John Bauldie comments that Baez has made statements

...that she felt very alienated, treated very badly by Dylan at that time, and yet in the film – even for example in the scene where Dylan and Neuwirth are joshing with her about having the see-thru blouse you don't even wanna – there doesn't really seem to be any malice, or...[69]

Viewing Dylan's behavior in this scene, Bauldie sees innocent "joshing," not the malice Spitz sees. Then what of Baez's own assertions that she had felt abused? If Dylan was looking to cause her pain, "malice" would certainly be an apt word to characterize his behavior. And if he was oblivious of her pain, that would reveal a degree of indifference that, whether or not we would call it "malice," is little better in human terms. The fact is, Dylan's behavior here is not innocent. He is not simply joshing. He is casting this woman who loves him out of his life, and this causes her pain. But that doesn't prove he is being malicious or callously indifferent or hopelessly oblivious. (This man is the author – and singer – of "To Ramona," after all.) Whether he is looking to hurt her, is indifferent or oblivious, or feels he has no choice but to perform this act that causes her pain, is a question *Don't Look Back* doesn't claim to answer.

After Baez's exit, the camera pans back to Neuwirth, who strums his guitar as if to put a period to her departure. (I think of Hoagy Carmichael in *To Have and Have Not* playing a mock dirge on the piano when he discovers that Mr. Johnson – whose death will be mourned by no one – has been killed. But I also think of the newsmen in *His Girl Friday* who are sick at heart when they realize they had acted so heartlessly they had made Molly Molloy jump, apparently to her death.) For his part, Dylan continues pecking away at the typewriter. He rubs his eyes. There is a cut to a clock that reads "2:33." With the strumming continuing offscreen, there is a cut to the sheet of paper in the typewriter. Dylan goes on typing as if nothing had happened. (When a young boy dies in Renoir's *The River*, his parents go on as if nothing had happened, too.) As the sound and image fade out, we do not know what Dylan is thinking, what he is feeling, whether his heart is grieving.

Baez makes only two more brief appearances. In the first, Dylan and Baez are in a limousine, an unidentified man (John Mayall) between them. As Dylan says something to him about "just writing these things," Baez breaks into some lines of "It's All Over Now, Baby Blue" ("You must take what you want you think will last. But whatever you wish to keep, you better grab it fast") that could almost be the motto of a cinéma-vérité filmmaker. She peels a banana and, with a look of distaste, goes on with the song, parodying the last line ("Yonder stands your orphan with a gun, crying like a banana" – Dylan's word is "fire" – "in the sun").

Spitz writes that this scene "proves ominous as Joan sings a line about leaving. . . . The message, while most likely unintentional, was painfully explicit: Joan was leaving the tour. She'd had enough."[70] Messages are sent (whether consciously or not) by someone, to someone; messages *are* intentional. I can imagine that by singing these lines Baez may be sending Dylan the message (not that she expects him to be paying attention) that she was ready to split. I can also imagine that she may be sending this message (along with a message about Dylan's heartlessness, perhaps) to the camera (to Pennebaker, to us). And I can imagine that by including this passage here, Pennebaker may be relaying this message to us to clue us in on Baez's imminent disappearance from the film. Yet I can also imagine that Baez is sending no message at all (again, it is no message if it is not intentional). Even if she is not sending a message, though, her singing of these lines reveals (it does not *assert*) to anyone who accepts it as a revelation (as I do) that she is about to walk out of Dylan's life (and Pennebaker's film).

Baez last appears at the Birmingham Town Hall. Neuwirth is cracking up over something. Dylan is beside him, his back to the camera. Seemingly out of the blue, Baez sings, "Here comes the night, eeeee," climaxing in a shriek befitting a grand diva's mad scene. Neuwirth collapses with laughter (in response to Baez's cry? pretending obliviousness of it?). Baez performs an encore (making sure her message gets through? already in the grip of a nightmare and no longer even trying to make contact?). Dylan covers his eyes. Again, we do not know what he is thinking, what he is feeling, whether his heart is grieving.

The Science Student

The passage in Dylan's Newcastle dressing room in which he rakes a young interviewer over the coals is one of the most famous, or infamous, in *Don't Look Back*. In the film, we are never informed of his name (Terry Ellis). I will refer to him as the "science student." (It is an interesting footnote that he went on to found Chrysalis Records, abandoning science for the rock 'n' roll business.)

Following Baez's departure, Dylan makes his entrance onto a concert stage; Grossman and British agent Tito Burns negotiate over the phone with the BBC and Granada Television; Dylan admires electric guitars in a store window; Dylan, standing at an upright piano, thoughtfully works out bluesy chord progressions, the camera blessed to catch creation on the wing (Paul Williams finds this the film's other transcendent musical moment); fans on the street catch a glimpse of Dylan; finally, there is a cut to Dylan, his back to the camera as he strums his guitar, with a clean-cut young man in jacket and tie beside him – the science student.

"Do you think it would bother me one little bit if you disliked me? I've got my friends," Dylan is saying, having been asked by this man – who evidently is bothered when people don't like him – whether he worries what people think of him. Friends are the people whose feelings really matter, Dylan implies, leaving open who his friends are (whether his listeners are his friends is a question that keeps coming up, as we have noted). "What about before you had your friends?" "I wasn't worried about it, no. Were you worried when you didn't have many friends?" There is a cut to the science student framed in a mirror behind Dylan.

"That assumes I have many friends," the science student replies. "I reached the stage where I suddenly realized what a friend was. And then I probably had one or two." The camera moves in on Dylan, who seems to be passing harsh judgment on this man who claims to know what a friend really is.

"Now you know who your friends are, do you talk to your friends?" "There are one or two people I believe I *can* talk to." "That's how you know who your friends are?" "I think a friend is a friend because . . . they can understand me more than anyone else." "So that's how we differ," Dylan grins, jokingly implying that by this criterion he cannot be this man's friend (Dylan thinks friendship is a matter of attraction and feeling, not understanding; he cannot understand people who think otherwise). "We come from two different worlds. You come from England, I come from the United States."

By this point, Dylan is in the right foreground, doubled by his reflection in the mirror.

Flanked by these two Dylans, the science student protests, "But we're still human beings" – his tone is like young Charlie's in *Shadow of a Doubt* protesting her uncle's implication that wealthy widows deserve to die – "so there's *some* connection between us." As Dylan says "No, I'm just a guitar player," he rocks back and forth, repeatedly eclipsing his own reflection, and sometimes the science student's, in the frame. "Man, you're trying to knock me!" "I'd never try to do that," Dylan says with mock sincerity (he's not *trying*, he's *doing* it), the camera reframing with him to reveal Alan Price, obviously enjoying the exchange, at the piano.

"Why I came here I don't know, to be regaled with all this!" the science student muses. Perhaps implying it is up to his would-be interviewer to say why he *has* come here, Dylan asks, "Are you going to the concert?" "*This* is what I came to see, mostly. I came to see you. I thought I'd have a word with you first. I mean, when you meet somebody, what is your attitude towards them?"

"I don't like them," Dylan says jokingly, not accepting the question's premise. "You don't. . . ." "No." "I mean, when I come in here, what is your attitude towards me?" "Why should I have an attitude towards you? I don't even know you," Dylan says, making his objection explicit. "No, but it would be an attitude if you wanted to know me or didn't want to know me," the science student says, as if the only question were whether Dylan wants to know him, not whether he wants to know Dylan (it was he who came to see Dylan, after all). "Why should I want to know you?" "That's what I'm asking," the science student replies, exasperated. "Just give me a reason I should want to know you." "I might be worth knowing." The camera zooms and reframes, restoring the initial setup as it reveals we had been viewing, not the science student, but his mirror image.

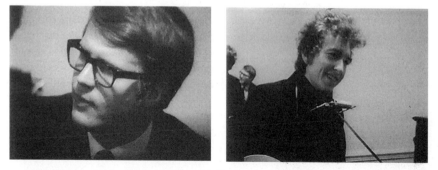

Dylan says, with a grin, "Why? Tell me, give me, name me one thing I'm going to gain." "You might learn something from my attitude to life." "What *is* your attitude to life?" "I can't explain that in two minutes!" "You're asking me to explain something in two minutes." "You're the artist, you're supposed to be able to explain it in two minutes." "Aren't you an artist?" "Oh no." "What are you?" "I'm a science student." "A what student?" "A *science* student." "What does that mean? What's your purpose in the world?" "What's my purpose?" "Yeah. How do you help?" "I'm in the world for me, just like everybody else." "Just like me? So we're just alike? We don't come from two different worlds?" "No. You were wrong."

Dylan does not reply to this, his silence speaking volumes. Desperate to avoid reading those volumes, the science student breaks the silence himself. "If I go to interview some groups, I don't think 'They couldn't care less about me.'" "Well, why don't you? Haven't you ever stopped to wonder why?" Dylan is joking, but also making a serious point. "Yeah, but it has nothing to do with me, because they don't want to know me before I go in." Implying it has everything to do with him, in particular with his assumption that all people are just like him, that they have no purpose in the world, Dylan asks, "What do you want with them? Can you write them up in your paper?" "I don't think of myself as necessarily a journalist." "Are you going to get something from them for science?" "I'm a *person*." "There's a million, thousand, billion, so *many* persons outside. You can't know them all." "But if I meet somebody and I speak to them a few minutes, I think that guy might be able to *give* me something."

Dylan leaps at this. "Oh ho!! Well!! What is it that you want?" "Everyone is out for what they can get. Well, I might be able to get something material." "You might be able to get a chick?" Following up the science student's suggestion that he hopes to get something material out of this encounter, Price hands him a harmonica. He refuses to accept it. "I don't want that thing, I can't play it." There is a noticeable pause before he again breaks the silence. "They may not be able to give me something material, but I'm not necessarily interested in. . . ." "What are they going to give you spiritually?" "I might learn something." "What don't you know that you might learn?" "I won't know if I don't try, will I?"

The camera keeps panning between them until it holds a framing in which Dylan is in the left foreground, with his back to the camera (our

impression is that he is staring, as we are, at his oblivious interlocutor), and the science student, vulnerable in his obliviousness, is in the center of the frame, caught squarely in the camera's – and Dylan's – sights. Gift wrapping the lesson, Dylan says, "Don't you ever just be quiet? In complete silence? And just watch? And don't say *one word?*" (Saying this, Dylan is all but explicitly assuming Pennebaker's position, all but explicitly pointing to the filmmaker behind the camera as the master of the requisite spiritual discipline.)

After a barely perceptible pause, all the silence he can bear, the science student goes on. "The whole thing that gets me about you is you're knocking from the minute I come in." "You don't even know when you're liked," Dylan says, beginning to knock in earnest this man who has no interest in learning how he thinks. "If we wanted to knock you. . . ." The camera zooms out to the science student, again flanked by Dylan and his mirror image. ". . . We would put you on." Dylan, rocking back and forth, again emblematically eclipses the science student in the frame. "Yeah, but, I mean, [Price] has just said I'm talking rubbish." Price interjects, "You're misquoting me already." "No, I interpreted you."

Dylan breaks in. "You interpreted him to your own thing? Your own rules, your own images?" "Trying to get some answer." "Why get some answer?" "To satisfy you," he says to Price. "You don't have to satisfy me," Price replies. Dylan again breaks in, now grilling unrelentingly. "You always try to satisfy everybody?" "No." "Do you every once in a while try to satisfy somebody?" "Somebody, but not everybody. Some people I can't satisfy. . . ." "Are you still friends with them even though you can't satisfy them?" "Friends. Not deep friends." "What's a deep friend?" "Somebody you're almost on exactly the same plane with." "Somebody just like you?" "No." "Looks like you?" "No." "Talks like you?" "Thinks the same way." "Like you both are happy about a green door?" "No. Thinks in the same language. So you can understand each other."

Dylan's tone hardens. "Let's try and understand each other." "That wouldn't be a bad idea. Then how are we going to tell about. . ." Dylan cuts him off. "You can ask your first question. Go ahead, have you got a question to ask?" "Well I didn't. . ." There is a knock on the door. Dylan says, with finality, "I think somebody's calling for you." "You want me to go? I'll go." Refraining from going for the jugular, Dylan softens. "No, you don't have to go," he says, relenting, as Price walks over to the door to answer it.

Don't Look Back calls upon us to do precisely what the science student cannot bring himself to do: just watch quietly, in complete silence, without saying one word. Viewing Dylan in *Don't Look Back*, it is impossible for us to satisfy him, hence impossible for us to fail to satisfy him. Thanks to the camera, thanks to the medium of film, we are able to watch and listen to Dylan without worrying whether we are satisfying him. Clearly, we get no material satisfaction from this; viewing *Don't Look Back* will not gain us harmonicas, or, for that matter, "chicks." If we stand to gain satisfaction, it is "spiritual," something – not a "message" – the film might teach us.

In the liner notes we keep invoking, Dylan speaks of "thoughts" he has been "taught well" by people who have touched his path. That "Only I can cast my stone" is a "thought" Dylan's songs teach. These songs are his purpose for living. When he performs them on stage, he is living his life in accordance with this "thought." That is why audiences idolize him. In *Don't Look Back*, the idol falls. Dylan's songs are forever declaring that he is only a man, a human being with his own private reasons for everything he says and does. *Don't Look Back* confirms that Dylan is a person, not a god. The film enables us to connect Dylan's songs, his voice, with the person he is in the world. He is real, and for real.

The power of *Don't Look Back* does not depend on facts it "documents"; the film is no more (but no less) a "documentary" than Dylan's songs are. But it does depend on who Dylan is. It depends on the fact that the person on view – one of the "million, thousand, billion persons" out there – is the one who sings these words, his words, in this voice, his voice, the person whose purpose for living is to affirm the "truth of song" in his own way. The "truth of song" Dylan affirms resonates with the "truth of cinema" Pennebaker's film affirms. Viewing *Don't Look Back*, the bars between us and Dylan "bust down," like the bars between Dylan and Baez when he listens to her voice. When the film ends, the bars come back up. But the world transfigured by film, like the world transfigured by song, is no illusion. The world on film is real: This is the "truth of cinema."

In *Don't Look Back*, what is, is; what happens, happens; the film enables us simply to "hang out" with Dylan when nothing is happening, dramatically speaking, whether he is in his hotel room, backstage, jousting with interviewers, writing, making music for the love of it, or performing on stage. The film's events, or, rather, its uneventful moments, succeed each other like the flashing images of a Dylan lyric. This tour is anything but ordinary, even for Dylan, yet what emerges in the film is a heightened sense of the ordinary. No moment is elevated above others; none is sacred, or all are. Every moment is charged, none more than others. What it is charged with is not drama, but its own particular quality, its distinctive mood or flavor, what classical Indian aesthetics calls "*rasa*," as if each moment sings its own song, sings in its own voice, which is to be savored.

Worth savoring, to be sure, is the ensuing visit of the "High Sheriff's Lady." The fact that the science student, allowed to remain in the room, now finally does bring himself to watch and listen without saying one word enhances our sense that the sequence is a textbook demonstration of the fruitfulness of Pennebaker's approach in capturing (or, rather, creating) on film scenes we could not have imagined, scenes we could not have scripted, scenes we value not for any "message" or dramatic impact but simply because they so completely are what they are.

The High Sheriff's Lady breezes in (from an Alec Guinness movie of the fifties, it would seem) with three teenage sons in tow ("They think you're so marvelous!"). All Dylan and his entourage can do – not to mention the three thrilled but mortified boys – is stand there, flabbergasted, as she says, in one breathless rush,

We are really very thrilled indeed to have you here, and, if you come after May again, then I'd have you as my guest in the mansion house. . . . I think the songs you sing are very wonderful. And you write them yourself, too, don't you, sometimes? Because they've got feeling and they're really marvelous. And I really mean this, I think you're a really good example for the youth.

Dylan introduces Alan Price ("He's my friend"), who gives the High Sheriff's Lady the harmonica the science student had rejected. She shakes his hand, saying "Oh, how very sweet! That's very lovely of you," and extends her invitation to him, too, to "stay in my mansion house. It's a beautiful place, really it is. After May, we shall be lord mayor, if God's willing, of this lovely city. And I want everyone to know what a wonderful city this is and what hospitality we give, and also want *you* to know how very thrilled we are to have you. Thank you very much. Goodbye. Goodbye," she says breathlessly, and then she is out the door. We hear a woman's voice say, off-screen, "She's charming!"

Also worth savoring is the passage in which Dylan, wiling away the time before his concert, is amused by Price's imitations of popular rock groups. Dylan finds out that Price isn't playing with the Animals any more. "It just happens," Price says, twitching his nose in a way that bespeaks a painful story he is not in the mood to tell. Picking up on the unstated emotion, Dylan plays a blues riff on the guitar. Price takes it up on the piano, improvises a while, before Dylan takes it up again.

This is the moment, perhaps the most intimate in the film, when Dylan (who wants the privacy of his friend's feelings to be respected) glares at Pennebaker's camera (which finds itself irresistibly drawn to the revelation of emotion). When someone appears at the door to summon him for the concert, Dylan says, "I really don't feel like singing," and trudges off as if to his doom. Ascertaining that only Neuwirth and the camera are watching (both acceptable co-conspirators), Price subversively opens a beer using the piano lid as a bottle opener. Before he can drink it, though, he has to remove splinters from the bottle. (I think of Clark Gable, in *It Happened One Night*, spitting like a tough guy after he frightens off a would-be blackmailer, then having to wipe spit off his own jacket.)

Worth savoring, too, is the inspired transition from this touching character study of Price, which doubles as a revelation of Dylan's character (he has feelings for his friend), to Dylan onstage performing "Don't Think Twice, It's All Right," perhaps the most beautiful song he had composed to that date, and certainly, to this point in the film, the performance that most single-mindedly aspires to, and achieves, "beauty that is not also ugly."

Ostensibly, the song is addressed to a woman the singer once loved, but whose voice he no longer hears ("An' it ain't no use in calling out my name, babe, like you never did before, an' it ain't no use in calling out my name, babe, I can't hear you any more"). But the singer is also meditating on himself ("I'm thinking and wondering, walking all the way down the road, how I once loved a woman, a child I'm told. I gave her my heart, but she wanted my soul" [does this last line mean that her intentions toward him were devilish, or that he failed to be her soulmate?]). So when the singer comes to the refrain "But don't think twice, it's all right," it is precisely ambiguous whether these words are addressed to the woman or to himself. Is he telling *himself* not to "think twice" (that is, not to look back), telling *himself* it's "all right" (all right that he is now thinking and wondering how he had loved her, all right that he is walking down this road on which he now finds himself)?

Equally inspired is the transition, effected by a sound bridge, from Dylan performing this song to Dylan looking out the window of a Manchester-bound train – thinking and wondering? – as drab industrial towns and suburbs pass by in monotonous succession. He yawns, tries to get comfortable, scratches his head, adjusts his shades, rubs his eyes, takes off his shades, rubs his eyes again, then covers his eyes with his hands (this last uncannily

echoing his gesture when Joan Baez signaled her departure from the film with her ear-piercing shriek, and her earlier gesture, before she walked out of his hotel room, of covering Dylan's eyes with her own hands).

Donovan

From Dylan on the train, there is a cut to the Manchester Victoria station, then to Dylan testing the acoustics in an empty, dark theater. In a complete change of pace, there is a shot that communicates a sense of real nervous tension in which Dylan and his entourage, followed by a shaky hand-held camera, run down a staircase, through a corridor, up another staircase, down another corridor, onto a street filled with screaming fans, and then to their

limousine. A cut to a poster highlighting the name "Donovan" serves to inform us – a rare moment it does occur to Pennebaker to supply information – that the young man on view in the next shot, smiling wanly, is Donovan himself.

Pennebaker feels the need to inform us who this is because Donovan has been a running joke throughout the film. Early on, Dylan is shown reading an article with the headline "Is Donovan deserting his fans?" "Who's Donovan?" Dylan asks. "A young Scottish bloke," Price explains. Dylan keeps repeating the word "bloke" until it becomes a vomiting sound. "Anyway," Price goes on, "he sings a bit of folk music and he's been around and he plays very good guitar. . . He's better than you, all right?" "Right away I hate him," Dylan says jokingly. Price replies, sincerely, "He's all right. I like him, anyway. He's not a fake." Dylan picks up the paper again. "'Is Donovan deserting his fans?' He's only been around for three months! Well that's what I call a loser!"

Somewhat later, a British agent says to Grossman, "We've got an award [for Dylan] for the most promising artist of the year and the best-selling pop record." Hearing this, Dylan interjects, "Tell them to give them to Donovan." And when Joan Baez leaves the hotel room and Dylan continues writing and there is a fade-out on the page in his typewriter, what next fades in is the headline "Dylan Digs Donovan! 'He's a Nice Guy. I Like Him.' Bob."

Donovan is sitting in Dylan's hotel room, which is filled with people. He turns around as there is a commotion at the door. Dylan enters, obviously in an agitated and feisty state. Demanding an answer from anyone in the room, Dylan angrily asks, "Who threw that glass in the street? If somebody don't tell who did it, you're all going to get the fuck out of here and never come back. I don't care who did it, I just want to *know* who did it." (It may occur to us to wonder whether Donovan's presence has anything to do with Dylan's mood, or, at least, his behavior. Is Dylan, at least in part, putting on a show for Donovan's benefit, to impress him in some particular way?)[71]

An obviously drunk young man expresses annoyance. "Don't tell me you're pissed, man. I'm the only one here who's pissed," Dylan says to him, his voice dripping with contempt. Still addressing him directly, he goes on, "Who threw the glass in the street? Tell me. You were there. If you know who did it, you just better tell whoever did it to get out there and tell the cats who come up here and ask who did it, to tell them who it was. I'm not taking no fucking responsibility for cats I don't know, man, I've got enough responsibility with my own friends and my own people."

Dylan announces, to everyone in the room, that if the young drunk doesn't clean up the glass, he will clean it up himself. Donovan says, "I'll help you, man." An unidentified older man (Derroll Adams, who was a friend of Jack Kerouac) assures Dylan that the young drunk is a good guy. But when the drunk pokes his finger at Dylan and says, very belligerently, "Listen . . .," Dylan makes it clear he has no intention of listening to a man who is refusing to take responsibility. "I know a thousand cats who look just like you, man, talk just like you," Dylan says. "Oh, fuck off. You're a big noise, you know?" "I know I'm a big noise," Dylan answers, "A lot bigger noise than you." "I'm a small noise, I'm a small cat." "That's right." "Listen, if I had thrown that fucking glass . . ." "You're anything you say you are, man." "I'm nothing." "I believe you." "I'm nothing. *Nothing.*" "I believe you, man."

With the air of an older brother, Adams leans on both their shoulders. "Boys . . ." But the drunk keeps insisting he did not do it and Dylan keeps asking him who did. Finally, though, the drunk agrees to face the music. Dylan tells him he does not have to clean up the glass, only tell the people downstairs that it will be taken care of. "I'll be groovy," the drunk promises.

"Dylan asked me if I could take out the fight in the hotel room," Pennebaker tells Robert Shelton. "He didn't want it to indicate that was the way he lived. I understood, but thought there were more important considerations. 'You are what you think you are.' What a marvelous thing to say! It's the fundamental existentialist concept. And Dylan's doing it, not like Norman Mailer, writing about it; that's what the film's about, so it couldn't be left out."

Pennebaker slightly misremembers Dylan's line ("You're anything you say you are," not "You are what you think you are"). In any case, Dylan is not advancing this as a general philosophical principle (saying "I am the King of England" will not make one King of England). What he means is that *these* things this man is saying about himself ("I'm a small noise," "I'm a small cat," "I'm nothing") do not just happen to be true. His saying these words here and now – saying them instead of taking responsibility for his actions – reveals their truth, all but makes them true.

It may seem unbecoming that Dylan, a "big cat," is picking on such a "small cat." But it is not Dylan who is acting like a bully. It is the drunk who is belligerently trying to force Dylan to listen to his phony excuses. Dylan is simply in no mood to listen to a man who is only "small" because he refuses responsibility for his actions, refuses to be the person he is capable of becoming, refuses to embrace change, refuses to live his life in accordance with the principle "Don't look back." This principle stands behind everything Dylan says; it defines the kind of person he aspires to be in the world. Pennebaker is right: This scene *is* essential.

Later, as Dylan is talking to Derroll Adams, he leans down to shake the drunk's hand. "I just didn't want the glass to hurt anybody," he explains. When a guitar begins to sound, Dylan says, astonished, "He plays like Jack [Elliott?], man!" And there is a cut to Donovan, who sings one of his own songs, accompanying himself on the guitar (which he does, indeed, play well), as Adams looks on, beaming.

> When the night has left you cold and feeling sad,
> I will show you that it cannot be so bad.
> Forget the one who went and made you cry.
> I'll sing a song for you.
> That's what I'm here to do.
> To sing for you.

Dylan exclaims, "Hey, that's a good song, man!" Buoyed, Donovan sings two more verses.

Donovan is no fake. He is good. But Dylan is better. Dylan knows this, and, I take it, Donovan knows it, too, accepts this reality with a melancholy grace. And so Dylan takes the guitar from Donovan, who requests "It's All Over Now, Baby Blue," knowing Dylan's performance will inevitably upstage his own. (How can Dylan not upstage Donovan without betraying himself?) The camera moving in on him, Dylan begins singing.

> You must leave now
> Take what you need you think will last
> But whatever you wish to keep you better grab it fast
> Yonder stands your *orphan* with his *gun* . . .

Singing these last obscure words, Dylan nods, laughing almost shyly, as if appreciating Donovan's appreciation of him. On the line ". . . Crying like a *fire* in the sun . . . ," the one Joan Baez had parodied, Dylan seems to nod in acknowledgment of the camera.

> . . . Look out! The Saints are coming through!
> And it's all over Now, Baby Blue . . .

There is a pan to Donovan. Puffing an outsized cigarette, looking young and vulnerable, he is staring at Dylan and smiling.

> . . . The highway is for gamblers. Better use your sense
> Take what you have gathered from coincidence . . .

On this last line (another that could serve as a cinéma-vérité filmmaker's motto), Donovan seems to turn inward.

> . . . The vagabond who's rapping at your door
> Is standing in the clothes that you once wore.
> Strike another match, go start anew.
> And it's all over now, Baby Blue.

Dylan smiles and laughs as he finishes. When the applause dies down, Donovan says, "Great, Dylan. That was nice, Bob. I used to . . ." But just as Donovan seems about to suggest another number *he* might perform, Dylan cuts him off. "You want to hear another song?" "Yes." There is a quick fade-out, the quickness seeming to underscore the deft, gentle way Dylan has just asserted, and Donovan acknowledged, his superiority.

Donovan's song assures the listener that "when the night has left you cold and feeling sad, I will show you that it cannot be so bad." To be shown that it "cannot be so bad" calls for achieving forgetfulness ("Forget the one who went and made you cry"). Donovan's singer envisions himself as always on call, always at the listener's service, as if the listener has a life but he has none, as if the night never leaves *him* cold and feeling sad. And he envisions his calling as an art of forgetting.

In Dylan songs like "To Ramona," "Don't Think Twice, It's All Right," or "It's All Over Now, Baby Blue," the singer's role is strikingly different. These songs never assure the listener it "cannot be so bad" (of course it can). In following his calling, the singer acknowledges that he, like his listener, is a human being in the world, not a god, a saint, or a selfless hero. For Dylan, the singer's calling is an art of wakefulness, not forgetfulness.

Donovan is not seen again, but his name comes up three more times.

The third occurs when Dylan is performing "Talking World War III Blues." He sings ("talking blues" style), "One time a crazy dream came to me. I dreamt I was walking in World War Three. I went to the doctor the very next day to see the kinds of things he had to say. He said it was a *terrible* dream." To loud laughter, Dylan ad-libs, "I looked in my closet. There was Donovan." This might seem a gratuitous put-down, but it strikes me more as an affectionate public acknowledgment that Dylan sees Donovan as a kind of alter ego.

In the second, Dylan and Neuwirth are backstage before the Albert Hall concert. Dylan asks if Donovan is there. Neuwirth answers, "I can't see. . . People like Donovan, they look just like ordinary people. . . ." This is followed by a big frontal close-up of Dylan, a cigarette in his mouth, studying himself in a mirror as an excited offscreen voice says, "The Beatles are here!"

In the first, Dylan is reading a newspaper as Grossman chats with the British agent handling Donovan's tour as well as Dylan's. They are in a limousine on the way to the Albert Hall concert. "Beautiful day," Grossman observes. "I've been in offices all day," the British agent replies, "Organizing my *other* tour." He adds with a snicker, "The *other* folksinger. Donovan." "How's that tour doing?" Dylan asks, putting down his newspaper. "Not so good," the agent answers. He goes on, speaking more to Grossman than to Dylan, "He says to me, 'What do you think if we booked a theater in Scarborough for a Sunday concert and put just Donovan all on his own?' I said, 'Well, you know, I can't see it.' He said, 'Do you think we should book one other act?' I said I think we should book about four other acts." Grossman and the agent share a laugh at this. Dylan lights up a cigarette and looks out the window.

Pennebaker describes this passage as one of

. . . the perfect scenes that you fall on – the moment when you can't make a mistake, and you know you're right in the center and you just shoot everything that moves, and you don't even think about why or how, you just shoot it . . . Going in the cab to the Albert Hall, when Fred starts talking about his "other" folksinger Donovan, and Bob says, "How's he doing?" and then Fred does the trashing of Donovan. And Dylan never cracks. He just looks out the window. It's just fantastic! Just one shot. You didn't have to edit anything; it told you everything. Those to me were really high moments of filmmaking . . . They don't come every film – just once in a while.[72]

Pennebaker is quite shrewd, as usual, in judging this deceptively simple passage to be a fantastic triumph of cinéma-vérité filmmaking. When Dylan looks out the window without "cracking" (what would it be for him to "crack"?), it indeed tells us everything. But it tells us everything by telling us nothing. We do not know, cannot say, what this man is thinking or wondering or feeling. Absolutely nothing is being asserted about, or by, the world on film. But absolutely nothing is being denied. Everything is revealed.

The *Time* Reporter

The interview with the *Time* correspondent – Judson Manning, *Time*'s London arts reporter, who had earned an enviable reputation as a journalist during the Second World War – is even more famous or infamous than the encounter with the science student.

It occurs immediately after a passage that helps establish the Albert Hall concert, which follows, as the culmination of the tour (and the film). Obviously impressed as he wanders the vast, empty hall, Dylan says, "This must be a very old theater!" There is a cut to the exterior, where people are already gathering, then to backstage. Grossman comes to get Dylan, and

there is a cut to the *Time* reporter, his eyes lowered. He looks up shiftily, veiling his gaze, as the camera, moving in on him, casts or unmasks him, even before he says one word, as a calculating villain.

There is a cut to Dylan speaking with great animation. "Are you going to see the concert tonight?" " Yes." "Are you going to hear it?" "Yes." "O.K., you'll hear it and see it and it's going to happen *fast*, and you're not going to get it all. And you might even hear the wrong words. And then afterwards, I won't be able to talk to you. . . I've got nothing to *say* about these things I write. . . If you want to tell other people that, go ahead. . . They're just going to think, 'What's this *Time* magazine telling us?' But you couldn't care less. . . You don't know the people that read you."

We hear the reporter mutter "Uh." There is a cut to him. "I've never been in *Time* magazine. . . " The reporter shifts his eyes, seeming uneasy under Dylan's, and the camera's, scrutiny. ". . . And yet this hall is filled twice. . . You'll probably call me a folksinger, but other people know better. Cause the people that buy my records, that listen to me, don't necessarily read *Time* magazine. You know the audience that subscribes to *Time* magazine? The audience of people who want to know what's happening in the world week-by-week, the people who work during the day and can read it small, and it's concise. And there are pictures in it. . . . I read it on the airplanes, but I don't take it *seriously*. If I want to find out anything, I'm not going to read *Time* magazine. I'm not going to read *Newsweek*. They've just got too much to lose by printing the truth. You know that."

We hear the reporter say "What kinds of truths are they..." Dylan talks right through him. "They'd go off the stands in a day if they printed really the truth." "What is really the truth?" "Really the truth is just a plain picture. Of, let's say, a tramp vomiting into the sewer. And next door to the picture, Mr. Rockefeller or Mr. C. W. Jones on the subway" – the "Mr. Jones" of "Ballad of a Thin Man"? – "going to work. Any kind of picture. Just make some sort of collage of pictures, which they don't do. There's no kind of *ideas* in *Time* magazine. There's just these *facts*."

Dylan goes on:

The article which you're doing...*can't* be a good article, because the guy who's writing the article is sitting at a desk in New York...He's just going to get these fifteen reporters and they're going to send him quotes. That's not really truth. He's going to put himself on, he's going to put all his readers on...I'm not putting that down, because people have got to eat and live. But let's at least be honest about it. You see, I know more about what you do...than you'll ever know about me....I could tell you I'm not a folksinger and explain to you why, but you wouldn't really understand. All you could do, you could nod your head.

The reporter asks, "Would you be willing to try?" "No," Dylan replies, "because it would be, you know, there are certain things which...Every word, every word has its little letter and big letter." "Pigeonhole." "That's not the word at all...You know, the word 'know,' 'k-n-o-w'?" "Yes." "Like, we all think we know things. But we really know nothing." "But you're saying you know more about what I do..." "No. I'm saying that you're going to die.... So am I. I mean, we're just going to be gone. The world's gonna go on without us...You do your job in the face of that. And how seriously you take yourself you decide for yourself, O.K.? And I'll decide for myself. Now you're not going to make me unhappy by anything you print about me...It couldn't offend me. And, I'm sure, I couldn't offend you," Dylan adds, again refraining from going for the jugular. "So all I could hope for you to do is, uh, you know, all your ideas in your own head, somehow..."

There is a pan to the *Time* reporter, who is looking away. After a long pause, he opens his mouth, clearly calculating the most effective moment to spring the line he has been composing in his head. When the moment arrives, he looks toward Dylan, then stares at him with a fixed, accusing glare. "Do you care about what you're saying?"

There is a pan back to Dylan, who says, his voice rising with (at once mock and real) outrage, "How can I answer that if you've got the nerve to ask me?! Do you ask the Beatles that?" "You have the nerve to question whether I can. . . ." "I'm not questioning you because I don't expect any answers from you." There is a cut to the reporter, then a pan to Dylan, who asks (something has been  elided here), "Who wants to go get whipped? And if you do want to get whipped, aren't you really being entertained? So do you really think someone who comes to see me is coming for any reason except entertainment?"

"They tell me they come for different reasons," the reporter replies. "Who cares what they tell you? Who cares what anybody tells you?" "They think they know why they're doing it." "Do you know why they're doing it?" "I know some of the things they say." "People say all kinds of things. You have to sort of weed it out. Can you weed it out?" The reporter's answer is inaudible.

Yet again, Dylan shows a surprising lack of killer instinct. He shakes his head and says, nonconfrontationally, "I have no idea. First of all, I'm not even a pop singer." "Surely you're in some sense a pop singer. Even if it's Caruso, he's. . . ." "He's a pop singer. . .," Dylan speaks over the reporter. ". . .I'm just as good a singer as Caruso. Have you ever heard me sing?" "I like Caruso better." "Right there we have a little disagreement," Dylan says, making a joke of his serious point. "I happen to be just as good as him. A good singer. You have to listen closely. But I hit all those notes. And I can hold my breath three times as long if I want to."

Clearly, in this case Dylan *is* "knocking from the moment he comes in," as the science student had charged. He does not like this man and does not want to know him. Then again, he claims he already does know him, at least knows what he does. Dylan claims to know what *Time* is, and he calls upon the reporter to acknowledge that he, too, knows that *Time* is guilty as charged. And the filmmaker, too, starts off with an attitude toward *Time*. Who knows better than Pennebaker, who had recently declared his independence from Drew Associates, a division of Time-Life, what *Time* is?

England is not his world, and Dylan is willing to joke with the British media. But the forces *Time* and *Newsweek* represent, and the power they wield, are no joke to Dylan. He is profoundly opposed to their impact on public matters he cares about. And he has felt firsthand the sting of the kind of journalism they shamelessly practice. (*Newsweek* had written a tabloid-style piece about Dylan's relationship with Joan Baez, which ended by intimating, of all things, that Dylan had not really written "The Times They Are A-Changin'" but had bought the song from a high school classmate.)

Given Dylan's contempt for *Time*, it is less surprising that he "knocks" this man that he refrains from going for the knockout. As Pennebaker puts it, "*Time* was a heavy enemy, it was detestable to Dylan, and Bob's way of dealing with someone he had no regard for was to play with him like a little rabbit. But he put Manning's nose into the turd, then very gently took him off the hook. . .I thought it was one of the kindest things I'd ever seen Dylan do."[73]

Dylan does care about the things he is saying, about the ideas that can be weeded out from what he says. For example, Dylan is joking when he claims he can hold his breath three times as long as Caruso. But he means it when he asserts he is just as good a singer. The simple fact is that he really does hit all those notes. (So does Pennebaker.) That so many reporters do not even consider this a possibility reveals that they do not really listen to his voice. They build walls to keep themselves from hearing him, and they are not honest about doing this.

And Dylan means it when he insists that "pigeonhole" is the wrong word to use to characterize *Time*'s kind of dishonesty. Dylan is not against pigeonholing. Without pigeonholing, without making or acknowledging distinctions, it is impossible to "weed it out," as Dylan prides himself on doing, impossible to recognize what people mean from what they say. But who we really are, who we are capable of being if we don't look back, cannot be identified with the pigeonholes we fit ourselves into. (It is because we are forever pigeonholing ourselves that the things we say have to be "weeded out.")

Time is not pigeonholing when it calls Caruso an "opera singer" and Dylan a "folksinger." Pigeonholes all fit pigeons, but *Time*'s distinctions impose hierarchies, place some people on pedestals, treat them as sacred, and demean others, treat them as profane. Their distinctions deny the reality of the one existing world, a world in which nothing is sacred, or everything is. (This is the point of Dylan's "big letter/small letter" distinction.)

When Dylan says to the science student, "Don't you ever just be quiet? In complete silence? And just watch? And don't say *one word*?" he is all but explicitly pointing to Pennebaker behind the camera as a master of the discipline of allowing the world to speak for itself, of acknowledging the realm of reality that cannot be asserted, only revealed. When Dylan tells the *Time* reporter that newsmagazines would present plain pictures rather than "facts" if they were really interested in publishing the truth, he again is all but explicitly pointing to Pennebaker's filming as exemplary. What better way to describe *Don't Look Back* than as a collage of plain pictures from which ideas emerge, truth is revealed? (When Dylan's songs take the form of successions of flashing images, they, too, aspire to being collages of plain pictures.)

This interview, placed immediately before the culminating Albert Hall concert, invites us to "weed out" what Dylan says, to check the truth of his claims against our own experience (Dylan's claim, for example, that things

192

happen fast in his performances; that he is a Caruso-class singer who has great breath control and hits all the notes; that he provides "entertainment" – pleasure, satisfaction – to listeners; that he really cares about what his songs are saying; that in his songs ideas emerge, truth is revealed, not by assertions, messages, but by the putting together of plain pictures that speak for themselves, at least to those who can "weed it out").

The Albert Hall Concert

The camera follows Dylan into the cavernous hall, ringing with applause, whose darkness is broken only by a circle of light around the microphone. Then there is a cut to an almost frontal medium shot of Dylan singing "The Times They Are A-Changin'."

After the first stanza, there is a dissolve to a slightly tighter shot of Dylan, viewed from the same angle, singing-speaking "Talking World War III Blues" ("One time a crazy dream came to me. I dreamt I was walking in World War Three. I went to the doctor the very next day to see the kinds of things he had to say. He said it was a *terrible* dream...."). There is another dissolve, again to the same setup ("...I looked in a closet. There was Donovan..."); then another ("...Some of the people can be half-right part of the time, all of the people can be part-right some of the time, half the people can be part-right all of the time, but all of the people can't be all right all of the time. T. S. Eliot said that. I'll let you be in my dream if I can be in your dream. I said that...").

Over the sound of applause, the camera zooms out, and there is a dissolve to another medium shot, this one from a slightly different angle (the camera is now screen right, not screen left, of its subject), as Dylan sings a couple of stanzas of a song he identifies as "It's All Right, Ma, I'm Only Bleeding Ho Ho Ho."

With the next dissolve, the camera returns to the original setup. Dylan is singing "Beneath the Gates of Eden." On the words "All except when 'neath the trees of Eden," there is a cut to a different angle, followed by a shot of the spellbound audience. As he nears the end of the song, the camera pans across the stage until it frames him from behind, silhouetted against the spotlight.

There is an abrupt cut to the stage manager on the house phone ("Limes out. House lights and the curtain"), to the applauding audience, then to Dylan, bowing. The camera pans and tilts up to the light, and there is a cut to backstage. "Actually, applause is kind of bull-shit," Dylan muses. "It would be something else if they just sat there and waved..."

The entire second half of the concert, devoted to an extended segment of one song, "Love Minus Zero/No Limit," is telescoped into two shots. It begins with a view of Dylan onstage, framed almost from behind, the camera to his left. The camera holds this framing for two entire stanzas.

In the dime stores and bus stations
People talk over situations,
Read books and repeat quotations,
Draw conclusions on the wall.
Some speak of the future.
My love, she speaks softly.
She knows there's no success like failure
And that failure's no success at all...

As his harmonica spells his voice, there is a stunning long shot, also almost from behind, of Dylan backlit by the spotlight.

On the words "The wind howls like a hammer," the camera zooms slowly out until Dylan is a small figure surrounded by darkness except for the spotlight that crosses the whole frame from top right to bottom

left. As he sings, "The night blows cold and rainy," the camera tilts up and to the right, until the light source and the now tiny figure of Dylan are at opposite corners of the frame, connected by a beam – I think of the projector beam in *Chronicle of a Summer* – that bridges the gulf between them, an emblematic picture of the artist, singled out for greatness, singing in his own voice, bridging the gulf between Earth and Heaven. Or is it the gulf between the underworld and Earth, between the hell-on-earth we are making of our planet and a world in which human beings might run free, that is bridged by the steep path of light this modern-day Orpheus ascends when he sings? Opera takes singing to express a sense of being stretched between two worlds, Cavell suggests. What more perfect picture of this condition? What more perfect picture of the one world on film encompassing both of these realms?

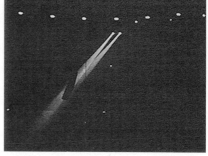

With infinite tenderness in his voice, Dylan sings the haunting final words, "My love, she's like some raven" – how can viewers of *Don't Look Back* not think of Joan Baez? – "at my window with a broken wing." (If he lets this raven in, if he opens the window, lets the bars between them fall, will he nevermore be free?) Singing these words, Dylan achieves a beauty even more breathtaking than his earlier performance of "Don't Think Twice, It's All Right." And, as the audience bursts into applause, the beauty of Dylan's song and singing is matched by the indelibly beautiful image the camera captures or creates when, in an ecstatic gesture, it tilts up even farther until it excludes the singer from a frame now empty and dark as night but for the flickering lights that perfectly evoke stars. Cinematically as well as musically, this is a transcendent moment, yet it is also a down-to-earth one. The camera, too, is ecstatically reaching for – and reaching – the heavens. But there is also a melancholy aspect to the camera's gesture, as there is to Dylan's voice at this moment. Here on Earth, both are acknowledging, the howling wind and the cold rain have not ended; we cannot yet look up and see the unreachable stars.

Throughout the film, Pennebaker has predominantly filmed Dylan in performance by framing him in medium shot, almost straight on. This is the technique he employs for most of the Albert Hall concert as well. Ordinarily, when Dylan is singing in *Don't Look Back*, viewing him in not-quite-frontal medium shots – he is neither too distant nor too close for comfort; he is singing *for* the camera but not *to* the camera – seems the ideal way to experience his performance. At once viewing him from this vantage and listening to his voice, our experience seems fuller than it would be if we were seated among the thousands in the hall, barely able to see him on the faraway stage, or if we were listening to a record, unable to see him at all.

Whenever Joan Baez sings, we suggested, Pennebaker's camera finds itself drawn to frame her in extreme close-up, usually frontally, because she seems to be abandoning herself to the invisible realm from which emanates her voice of purity and beauty. That we feel, viewing Dylan's performances in *Don't Look Back*, that these not-quite-frontal medium shots provide the ideal vantage, the best possible way to be his audience, means we feel not only that he is performing for the camera, but that he is performing *only* for the camera (which, for its part, only has eyes for him). Then why, when it is time to conclude this culminating performance sequence, does Pennebaker break decisively with the technique that served him well throughout the film? Why does he feel the need to capture or create this beautiful, emblematic image, to perform this extraordinary gesture of the camera?

Each of the films we have discussed incorporates a comparable gesture of the camera into its closing moments. I think of Flaherty cutting to Nanook's "master dog," the embodiment of the "melancholy spirit of the North," enduring the winter night as the family sleeps inside the igloo. I think of Buñuel cutting to the old woman walking the streets, crying out her warning to all who may be listening. I think of Resnais's camera pulling out from the death camp, reversing its movement from the film's opening, and abruptly stopping in its tracks as the music cadences, the narrator falls silent, and our view gives way to blinding white. I think of the magical transition in *Chronicle of a Summer* from the family singing at a picnic to the blinding projector beam piercing a swirling haze of cigarette smoke, the haunting singing a sound bridge linking the beam of light on-screen with the projector beam now carrying this image to our gaze. I think of Rouch's camera, in *The Death of Old Anai*, suddenly breaking free from the closed space in which the old priest is intoning the Dogon myth of Creation. And I think of Leacock's camera, fixated on Mrs. Fischer's face, freed by her smile to resume its gypsy wandering.

"Applause is kind of bullshit," Dylan muses during the intermission. He nods in agreement when Neuwirth, following Dylan's train of thought, wonders how different the world would be if audiences waved instead of applauded to express their appreciation. Before the breath of the last song ends, Pennebaker feels the need to express his appreciation of Dylan's performance. On more than one occasion, we have seen, Dylan all but explicitly expresses his appreciation of Pennebaker by acknowledging the filmmaker as a master of a spiritual discipline akin to his. Just as Dylan, in singing "I'm So Lonesome I Could Cry," acknowledges his bond with Hank Williams by expressing the song's emotion with his own voice, Pennebaker now acknowledges his bond with Dylan by performing a gesture of the camera that affirms, in the medium of film, the reality of the "beauty that is not also ugly" that Dylan affirms – never more powerfully than at this moment – in his songs and singing. What is required is a gesture of the camera which is Pennebaker's own the way Dylan's voice is Dylan's own, yet which conveys a sense that the "bars between them" have "busted down."

The framing sustained through most of the second half of the concert, in which Dylan is viewed almost from behind, already departs from the near-frontal medium shots that proved ideal vantage points for viewing his performances. In this framing, Pennebaker's camera assumes a place that seems to identify it more with Dylan than with his audience sitting in the concert hall. (But if the people sitting in the Albert Hall are beside themselves in ecstasy, perhaps they, too, can occupy such a place.) When it again frames him almost from behind and zooms slowly out until he is a tiny figure surrounded by darkness except for the beam of the spotlight, the camera sustains this identification with him even as it sums up Dylan's condition as an artist. At the moment the singer's words invoke a vision of his love, far yet not so far, separated from him only by a window, the camera tilts up even farther, excluding Dylan from a frame now empty and dark but for the lights that evoke stars in the night sky. On film, there is no longer any visible sign that Pennebaker's camera and Dylan occupy different places, that anything separates them. The bars between them have, indeed, busted down.

At the conclusion of my reading of *Night and Fog*, I found myself moved to observe that it is a recurring idea in my writing, an idea that is definitive of my sense of myself and my project, that a number of the greatest and most influential films that have ever been made have meditated on the mysterious barrier-that-is-no-real-barrier of the movie screen, and that their meditations have led them to envision this "barrier" as transcended or transgressed, as *Night and Fog* does in its privileged vision of the death-camp survivor no longer separated from us by the fence that made the camp a self-contained universe, and as *Don't Look Back* does in its culminating vision, its culminating gesture of the camera. Evidently, I locate my aspiration as a writer, too, in this vision, this gesture, that provides Pennebaker's film with its emotional climax – but not its ending.

The film ends with a tranquil coda. There is a cut to Dylan in a limousine slowly making its way through the crowd leaving the concert. He waves wistfully through the glass at the fans who are tapping at his window, so many ravens with broken wings. He says, "Go driver, go," but is still waving as the limousine pulls away into the traffic.

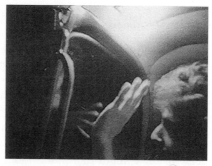

Neuwirth and Grossman agree this was a good concert, a beautiful concert, that everybody who was anybody was there. Still looking out the window, Dylan says, wonderment in his voice, "Goddamn, I feel like I've been through some kind of a *thing*! I mean there was something *special* about it." "They've started calling you an anarchist," Grossman remarks in a disingenuously offhand manner, subversively planting a thought in Dylan's head. "Who?" "The papers...Just cause you don't offer any solutions." "You're kidding. An anarchist!" Never more endearing than at this moment, Dylan takes off his shades and says to Grossman, with mock self-importance, "Give me a cigarette. Give the anarchist a cigarette." Looking out the car window again, Dylan repeats, "Anarchist...A figure such as I..." He takes a puff and blows out smoke. "It probably took them a while, man, to think of that name. In England, Communists really aren't..." Neuwirth finishes the thought. "It's cool being a Communist." "I don't think it's cool to be an anarchist,

though," Dylan says with mock seriousness. They all laugh their agreement. The title "DON'T LOOK BACK" appears at the bottom of the screen, followed by the final credits, as Dylan settles back into silently staring out the window, chin on his hand, at the fans on the other side of the glass who are now disappearing into the distance even as the concert itself is receding into the past. The bars have come back up.

And yet Dylan is not looking back, I take it, when the final credits appear on the screen. He is thinking and wondering what lies ahead, whether we will succeed in creating a new world in which there are no longer any bars, any fences. As the film draws to its close, and as this book approaches its ending, we, too, may well find ourselves thinking and wondering about what lies ahead – about our own future and that of our world, and about all that has transpired between *Don't Look Back* and the present, about what was then the future but is now the past.

Postscript: *Monterey Pop*

Throughout most of the performance sequences in *Don't Look Back*, as we have said, Pennebaker primarily frames Dylan in fixed, near-frontal medium shots. A number of conditions of Dylan's performances in this period are especially conducive to this technique. First, Dylan appears onstage alone, so there is no need to reframe or cut away to attend to other musicians or singers. Second, the people who fill the hall, except when applauding or (on rare occasions) laughing, sit in their seats in complete silence, so there is no need for the camera to attend to them, either. Third, Dylan does not throw himself viscerally into his performances in the manner of a Janis Joplin or a Jimi Hendrix, so the camera, in attending to him, has no need to roam below the belt or zero in on far-flung parts of his body. Fourth, Dylan's performances are not driven by a hard rock 'n' roll beat, so the camera is satisfied to remain sitting on its tripod, watching and listening, without an urge to get off its axis and dance.

For some time, however, Dylan had been finding these conditions increasingly frustrating. When he embarked on a world tour in 1966, accompanied by a group of musicians who then called themselves "The Hawks" (they were to gain rock 'n' roll immortality as "The Band"), these conditions no longer generally held. Dylan had broken with the mode of performance on view in *Don't Look Back*. Exacerbated by too many drugs and too little sleep, his lifestyle, too, had changed. Pennebaker was invited to film the British leg of this tour, but this time, for various reasons, the filming was problematic for all concerned. Dylan and Pennebaker never saw eye to eye on the new project. Assuming more and more directorial control during the shooting, Dylan also presided over the editing, creating a film of his own (*Eat the Document*, which has rarely been publicly screened) from footage shot by Pennebaker and Howard Alk. Pennebaker edited his workprint into his own version (*You Know Something Is Happening Here*, which has never been publicly screened).

In 1966, Dylan was at his height as a performer as well as a songwriter, and the concerts on this tour were among his greatest musical triumphs. They were also scenes of traumatic conflict. At every concert, elements of the audience vociferously rejected this new music that did not conform to their expectations of Dylan. By the time *Don't Look Back* was released in 1967 (he hesitated for a year before letting Pennebaker release the film), Dylan had for some time been seeking shelter from the storm. Indeed, following a near-fatal motorcycle accident, Dylan had gone into virtual seclusion. His career subsequently rebounded, but he never fully reclaimed – nor tried to reclaim – his extreme popularity or his status as prophet to a generation.

Dylan's performances on the 1966 tour, which broke with the conditions that made it possible for a static camera to provide the ideal vantage, challenged Pennebaker, shooting now with high-speed color stock, to develop new ways of filming and editing. Dylan's new mode of performance called for the camera to be responsive to the ever-shifting interplay among the musicians, to the pounding beat, and to the responses of audiences driven by the new music to react, or participate, far more viscerally than the quiet-as-a-churchmouse audiences of *Don't Look Back*.

In *Monterey Pop*, these new techniques are gloriously in evidence, most effectively in the sequences devoted to the performers (including Janis Joplin, Jimi Hendrix, and Ravi Shankar) who are worthy of them, who, like Dylan, "bust down the bars" between performer and audience.

When Joplin and her band (Big Brother and the Holding Company) perform "Ball and Chain," the sequence begins with a shot in which the camera pans to the left across the audience, the shot dominated by blue flowers, barely in focus, in the extreme foreground, as the band plays the bluesy opening of the song and Joplin starts to sing. There is a succession of shots,

the cuts always on the beat – several of his colleagues are shooting, as well as Pennebaker – of the drummer; a guitarist; another guitarist, who is mouthing along with Joplin's voice as if he were in a trance; both guitarists; then finally a tight close-up of Joplin.

In *Don't Look Back*, the extreme close-ups of Baez are frontal. In this shot of Joplin, the camera is placed somewhat to the singer's right, although sometimes, as she sings, she moves her face and body in such a way as to turn the setup into a frontal one.

Sometimes the camera zooms in so far that we are not so much viewing Joplin's face as feeling it with our eyes. Sometimes, indeed, our gaze oscillates between looking "through" the screen, as it were, and attending to the moving light-show-like patterns of color that splash on the screen's surface. And because Joplin throws her whole body into her performance in a way Baez does not, there are repeated cuts, on the beat, to shots that include all of her in the frame, or which zero in on her foot stamping emphatically, throbbingly, to the beat.

Unlike Baez, Joplin acts out her songs as she sings them. Rhetorically, she is singing here in the first person,

looking out her window at the rain
and addressing a lover who is absent
but is a vivid presence in her imagination, a lover who has a formidable
ability to arouse her sexually, who is
arousing her even now by every move
she imagines him making in passion-
ate response to her ever-more-pas-
sionate lamentations that love feels
like a ball and chain. She is singing
the blues, but she becomes ever more

aroused as she sings. And the camera, itself ever more aroused, is not only
witness and confidant but also an instrument of her arousal, as if with every
cut, every zoom, the camera is taking another little piece of her heart. The
guitars and drums of the band are themselves aroused and also instruments
of her arousal, too. So the camera is in synch with Joplin's verbal expostu-
lations, the wild gyrations of her body, and the quicksilver expressions that
animate her face; with the guitars and drums that give the music its pulsing
beat; and with an audience in ecstasy witnessing her ecstasy.

Understandably, Pennebaker has said that viewing Joplin through the
camera was one of the most exciting experiences of his filmmaking career.
The result might be accused of being pornographic, except that the whole
performance – Joplin's, the band's, the audience's, Pennebaker's – constitutes a powerful attack on the idea of pornography, an affirmation that
desire exists to be satisfied, not repressed, that (in the words of another
Joplin song) in making art as in making love, "You know you got it when it
makes you feel *good*. Oh yeah!"

The moment the breath of the song ends, Joplin awakens to the ground-
swell of appreciation from the stunned audience. With a delighted smile,
she turns and *runs* off the stage like a startled chicken. As soon as she is
out of sight of the crowd (but still within view of the camera), she gives a
spontaneous little-girl's leap into the air, so pleased is she with herself for
pulling off this incredible triumph. *Janis – Comin' Home*, a short film Chris
Hegedus (Pennebaker's collaborator for the past twenty years) edited from

footage Pennebaker and his colleagues shot of Joplin (including this sequence from *Monterey Pop*), ends with this leap, a freeze-frame stopping it just as her feet are about to land back on the ground.

This freeze frame casts into relief what the backstage leap at once reveals and acknowledges, that Joplin's singing onstage, for all its spontaneity and primal power, is also a sophisticated, seductive performance. The freeze-frame also casts into relief what the camera at once reveals and acknowledges by "capturing" this leap: Pennebaker's filming, for all its power and spontaneity, is a seductive, sophisticated performance, too.

No doubt, Jimi Hendrix's rendition of "Wild Thing" in *Monterey Pop* is a seductive, sophisticated performance as well. But in filming Hendrix, as in filming Dylan, the camera captures no gesture comparable to Joplin's joyful leap, no gesture that unambiguously reveals Hendrix's onstage performance *to be* a performance, an act.

Pennebaker films Hendrix mostly in a single fluid take, with only occasional cutaways to a backup guitarist and to an audience that becomes increasingly perplexed, troubled, and even alarmed as the act nears its climax. Mostly, the camera's attention is riveted on Hendrix himself.

In the original incarnation of "Wild Thing" as a pop hit by the British group The Trogs, the singer is addressing a woman ("Wild thing, you make my heart sing, you make everything groovy"). In Hendrix's rendition, the "wild thing" he is addressing, the "wild thing" that makes his "heart sing" and makes "everything groovy," is his electric guitar, from which, in a remarkable virtuoso display, he coaxes, and sometimes forces, a never-before-heard cacophony of shrieks, growls, wails, and machinelike hums and roars. This guitar does not stand in for a woman, like B. B. King's "Lucille," nor a lover of any gender. It stands in for Hendrix's own sexuality, for the organ that is the other "wild thing" that makes his heart sing and makes everything groovy.

The scene Hendrix is acting out is not one between lovers. Playing his guitar, he is not making love with a partner, he is playing with himself, masturbating. Hendrix turns the last line of the pop song ("Wild thing, I think I love you") into a refrain rather than a conclusion. Every time he sings this refrain, he adds, "But I need to know for sure," then follows this

with, "So sock it to me one more time," which triggers an even more gut-wrenching piece of virtuoso guitar-plucking, a more outrageous act of guitar picking, fondling and necking.

In poems, plays, novels, and movies, lovers often find themselves impelled by their passion to test the love of their beloved, as if the reality of another's love could be proved like a scientific hypothesis or mathematical theorem. But what Hendrix says he needs to "know for sure" is his own love. The idea that he can prove to himself that his love for this "wild thing" is real by experiencing one more time how he feels when it "socks it to him," by experiencing one more time the way it makes "everything groovy," the way it makes his heart sing, is a rich metaphysical joke. But it is no laughing matter. Having performed almost every carnal act it is possible to imagine performing with a guitar, perhaps having finally proved to his satisfaction that he does "know for sure" his love for this "wild thing" is real, Hendrix lays his instrument down, and, slowly and deliberately,

lights a match and drops it onto the guitar, setting it ablaze. Utterly without expression, he watches the fire consume this "wild thing" that is a part of himself he loves, not revealing what this sacrifice or self-sacrifice means to him, how it makes him feel. Then he picks up the flaming guitar and begins smashing it to pieces.

The sequence ends with a shot of audience members disturbed by what they have witnessed. From the outset, Hendrix performs as if he has no audience. His performance does not acknowledge that the people in the stadium play any meaningful role, not even the role of audience. They know they have been through an overwhelming experience, but they do not know what to make of this "wild thing" who made their hearts sing even as he symbolically immolated himself on stage. Hendrix does not claim to know what is to be made of his performance; all he claims is that this is what he loves. Nor does Pennebaker claim to know what to make of Hendrix's performance – in particular, how it relates to his own. (Pennebaker's camera, too, is a "wild thing" capable of making his "heart sing," capable of making "everything" – even self-immolation – "groovy.")

When this shot of troubled audience members is followed by a shot of Cass Elliot of the Mamas and the Papas singing, in easy-listening style, "Got a feeling I'm wasting time on you, babe," I always find myself thinking, "Truer words were never spoken." This forgettable number serves as a bridge between Hendrix's performance, the darkest passage in the film, and the film's brilliant and inspiring finale, transfigured by the transcendent music of Ravi Shankar.

Writing about the movies he calls "comedies of remarriage," Cavell observes, "It seems a firm commitment of the genre to make room for singing, for something to sing about and a world to sing in."[74] In a remarriage comedy, America as it stands is a world in which lovers with imagination find it possible to sing to and for each other, but not a world worth singing about. America remains a place in which most people do not live their everyday lives in a festive spirit, as the lead couple aspires to do. Thus this genre of comedy expects the pair to find happiness alone, unsponsored, in each other, out of their capacities for improvising a world, beyond ceremony. The couple, isolated from the rest of society, forms as it were a world elsewhere. Hence movies of this genre cannot conclude with a festival in which society celebrates its own renewal. For such festivals to be possible, society itself must be renewed. Society must go through a passage as from dreaming to waking, a passage Emerson and Thoreau call "dawn," the "winning of a new beginning, a new creation, an innocence, by changes that effect or constitute the overcoming of revenge."[75] Society has to let bygones be bygones, has to come to embrace the principle "Don't look back," in other words.

Cavell writes,

How can renewal come about? – the perennial question of reformers and revolutionaries, of anyone who wants to start over, who wants another chance. Even in America, the land of the second chance, and of transcendentalist redeemers, the paradox inevitably arises: you cannot change the world until the people in it change, and the people cannot change until the world changes.[76]

The way forward that remarriage comedies envision, in Cavell's understanding, is to "track the festive to its roots in the everyday, to show the festival to which its events aspire to be a crossroads from which a normal life, an unended diurnal cycle, may sensibly proceed."[77] In *Monterey Pop*, the event the film "documents" emerges as more than a concert; it is conceived as a demonstration – protesting nothing, affirming everything – of "what is happening here." America is changing, as Dylan had prophesied. This means America has already changed. It has become a place where a true festival is possible.

In the opening of the film, shots of last-minute construction and other preparations are intercut with shots of fans and performers pouring into Monterey for the festival that is about to begin. This montage is accompanied by such pop hits as "If You're Going to San Francisco" (with its visions of California as a mecca for innocent young hippies with flowers in their hair) and the Mamas and the Papas's "California Dreaming" (which asserts that "California dreaming is becoming a reality," but gives no hint that the likes of Jimi Hendrix, and not only gentle flower children, are an inalienable part of the reality this "California dream" – this dream of a new America – is becoming).

Within the geographical boundaries of America, *Monterey Pop* reveals, another America is already coming into existence, a new America worth singing about, an America renewed by a generation of Americans dedicated to living their everyday lives in a festive spirit, who are capable of singing, capable of celebrating song, capable of celebrating change. (The celebration is as yet unclouded by the drug-related deaths of Janis Joplin and Jimi Hendrix, the violence at Altamont, the commercialism of Woodstock, the killings at Kent State.) There is no fence separating the new America from the old; even a thirtieth birthday is not an unbridgeable barrier to making the leap. All it takes is to "tune in, turn on and drop out." All it takes is a change of perspective.

In a carnival, Bakhtin argued, everyday roles are reversed, hierarchies inverted, inhibitions released, only to be reinstated when the holiday ends and life returns to "normal" (at least until the next carnival). Carnivals, self-contained universes fenced off from everyday life, reduce the everyday to a self-contained universe, too. Unlike a carnival, the festival that culminates in Ravi Shankar's transcendent performance celebrates the dream of tearing down all the fences that separate the everyday, the diurnal cycle of our lives, from the festive, from the "groovy," from everything that makes our hearts sing.

As we hear the strains of Ravi Shankar's sitar on the soundtrack, the image of a pair of empty shoes fades in (one takes off one's shoes before entering Hindu temples), the camera zooming out to reveal that the shoes are sitting incongruously on the edge of a parking lot.

As the *raga* continues offscreen, there is a succession of shots of people waking up, unwrapping themselves from their sleeping bag cocoons, stretching, getting dressed, eating breakfast, gathering their children and belongings, and making their way toward the stadium where Ravi Shankar and his tabla accompanist are playing.

Another series of shots follows of the people gathering outside the stadium – a veritable National Portrait Gallery of hippies, flower children, and bikers; of weird hairstyles, outlandish costumes, and tattoos; of "normally" coiffed, dressed and un-made-up people of every race, ethnic group, and class; of families and friends and lovers and loners. Viewed under the ever-intensifying spell of the *raga* – we cannot tell whether it is only we who are falling under the spell of the music, or whether these people, too, are attuned to its mood – these shots constitute an eloquent demonstration of the principle of unity-in-diversity affirmed both by the Hindu religion and by the idea of America.

Characteristic of this kind of North Indian music, there is an incremental but inexorable musical progression, already well under way, starting from silence; to the near silence of tuning up; to the quiet, meditative early stages in which only the sitar is heard and there is not yet a clearly demarcated rhythm; to the entrance of the tabla and the ever more pronounced rhythmic patterns it marks; to the increasingly animated interactions between sitar and tabla that culminate in awe-inspiring displays of virtuosity no less wild than Jimi Hendrix's most frenzied guitar licks (and bumps and grinds). Ravi Shankar and his tabla player are masters at once of abandon and control; their music is spontaneous, improvised, not fixed in advance, yet it also conforms to the rigorous strictures of the particular *raga* being played.

Soon, the camera finds itself inside the stadium, where people of every stripe are responding, in ways as diverse as they are, to the deepening mood of the music. Finally, with a shrewdly composed close-up of the tabla play-

er – it is only when the camera pans and tilts to his hands that we know for sure that he is playing, not just listening to, this glorious music – and then a shot of Ravi Shankar, the camera makes the leap to the music makers themselves.

In the ensuing succession of shots, the camera attends to Shankar's eyes, to the smile that plays on his mouth, to his flying hands, to his bare foot count-

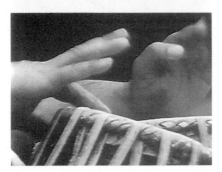

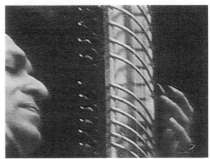

ing out the complex rhythmic patterns. Pennebaker cuts between the performers and members of the audience, some of whom seem at first not sure what they should be listening to, not sure how they should be responding, but all of whom appear to be falling more and more deeply under the ever-intensifying spell. Pennebaker also cuts between Shankar and the tabla player, attending both to their separate absorptions in their playing and to the assured glances that ping pong between them, culminating in their joyful exchange of looks when they recognize – and the camera recognizes that they recognize – that the musical climax is about to come. (I think of the look Jean Gabin gives the camera, in Renoir's *French Cancan*, when he recognizes it is time to enter the Moulin Rouge.)

When the music finally achieves its breathtaking, thrilling climax, the audience explodes with shouts and applause. There is a shot of Ravi Shankar acknowledging the audience by putting his hands together in the traditional Indian gesture of respect, followed by a panoramic shot taken from high in the stands – there is no other shot like it in the film – looking down upon musicians and audience framed together within the space of the stadium.

This bird's-eye view could well have ended the film. The shot could also have been followed by a tranquil coda that reversed the film's opening by showing performers and audience members departing, the festival facilities

being dismantled, the grounds returning to normal. Instead, the camera pans to the right so that the frame is completely filled with applauding audience members. This high angle extreme long shot is followed by a closer shot, from ground level, taken by a camera that now locates itself in the midst of the rapturously applauding throng. In this final shot, the camera moves from clapping hands to clapping hands to clapping hands, as if the whole world, the camera within it, were joined in ecstatic celebration. All creation, not a self-contained universe with a fence around it, is animated by the spirit that animates this festival.

As the opening of *Monterey Pop* makes clear, staging a rock festival requires constructing and readying all manner of facilities, making all manner of preparations. The early parts of the film echo the corresponding section of *Night and Fog*. Indeed, the staging of a rock festival, as *Monterey Pop* depicts it, is, on a small scale, like the construction and operation of a concentration camp as depicted in *Night and Fog*. In those cities of death, every aspect of the life of our ordinary cities had its counterpart. This is true of rock festivals, too. (Few accounts of Woodstock fail to cite the amount of food consumed, the number of portable toilets installed, and the marriages, births, and deaths that took place while the festival was going on.) Like Aberdeen, the town where the Fischer quintuplets were born, Monterey, transfigured by this festival, is a city of life, not a city of death. But the festival, as it emerges in *Monterey Pop*, is dedicated to celebrating, as Aberdeen was unwilling or unable to celebrate, the life in its midst, the life all around it.

In *Night and Fog*, we argued, Resnais's camera discovers a tangible sign of the true dimension of the world of the past (as well as a tangible sign of the author's own self) in the eloquent shot of the gas chamber ceiling, the stone scratched and clawed by the hands of countless victims who knew they were trapped, knew their dream of dying their own death was being denied. Pennebaker's camera discovers a tangible sign of the world of the present (as well as a tangible sign of the author's self) in the eloquent vision with which *Monterey Pop* concludes, the vision of a diverse multitude of clapping hands, the hands of human beings, each a separate individual, who are joined in applauding their freedom, affirming their dream of living their own life.

In reflecting on the place of *Don't Look Back*, *Monterey Pop*, and *Depeche Mode 101* within the history of "documentary" film, I have come to think of them as proposing an American answer to Leni Riefenstahl's *Triumph of the Will* (1935). *Depeche Mode 101*, to date the culminating work of the cycle, concludes with a concert-that-is-more-than-a-concert held in no less grand a venue than Pasadena's Rose Bowl. The veritable ocean of fans, expressing their appreciation not by clapping but by waving their hands (as Dylan had prophesied), is on an epic scale so vast it cannot but recall the multitudes in *Triumph of the Will* lining the streets of Nuremberg.

There are filmmakers who would have adopted an ironic or cynical attitude toward the spectacle of a hundred thousand rock 'n' roll fans in a football stadium waving their hands in unison, who would have assumed that these Americans must be as conformist, as mindless, as sheeplike, as their German counterparts, as much exemplars of inhumanity, not humanity. But that is not the attitude of Pennebaker and Hegedus. After all, these young people have not gathered to listen to Hitler rant about a master race building a Third Reich sure to remain standing for a thousand years. They are fans who have gathered to celebrate the music of a rock band, to celebrate being human, to celebrate living on Earth, where everything changes. In *Depeche Mode 101*, as in *Monterey Pop* and *Don't Look Back*, the "truth of cinema" and the "truth of song" come together in celebrating a shared dream of a world in which no fence separates the everyday from the festive. In reality, this world is a dream. But in the world on film, in these quintessentially American works, this dream is also a reality. And the world on film has a reality of its own; there is no real fence separating it from the one existing world. For the dream these films affirm to become real, all it would take is for the world to stop denying reality.

In search of food, Nanook and his family penetrate deeper and deeper into the frozen wilderness until they reach its veritable heart. There the spirit of the North fully reveals itself. And it is upon reaching this geographical and spiritual place that *Nanook of the North* ends, in a melancholy mood, without envisioning a way home.

Land without Bread follows a similar trajectory. The narrator and his companions depart from Alberca and cross high mountains into the land of the Hurdanos. They penetrate deeper and deeper into this impoverished region until the horror that is the Hurdanos' existence fully reveals itself. Once the camera arrives at this place, too, it envisions no way out. But the mood is not melancholy; it is horror.

Triumph of the Will also follows this trajectory, it might be noted. Geographically and spiritually, the camera penetrates deeper and deeper into the land of the Nazis until it reaches the place where the horror fully reveals itself (but does not recognize itself for the horror it is). Yet again, once the camera arrives at this place, it envisions no way out.

Night and Fog follows this trajectory as well. The camera enters the death camp by crossing the fence it means death to cross; once within the city of death, it penetrates deeper and deeper until the true dimension of its reality reveals itself in the marks scratched in the stone ceiling of the gas chamber by the bleeding fingers of the trapped and dying victims. This must remain the camera's place until all the doors have been opened, all the fences torn down, all the dead mourned.

The Death of Old Anai likewise follows this trajectory. The camera penetrates ever deeper into the land of the Dogon, until it arrives at the place that holds all the mysteries of Creation. Once there, it is free to roam to the far reaches of the Dogon universe. But it despairs of returning home.

In *A Happy Mother's Day*, the camera crosses the endless plains to enter the land of the Fischers, then penetrates deeper and deeper into this territory until it arrives at the pre-parade luncheon that, Aberdeen tells itself, is meant to be Mrs. Fischer's own "fun time." There the absurdity of existence in Aberdeen, absurdity of existence in an America that takes the self-contained universe of the media to be the real world, fully reveals itself. Once it arrives at this place, the camera finds itself fixated on the face of the one person capable of recognizing the absurdity. Just when it appears it will never be free to move on, Mrs. Fischer's grin releases the camera, or condemns it, to wander like a rolling stone in an absurd world that has lost its bearings, as Aberdeen has.

From the outset, *Don't Look Back* embraces the condition of being a rolling stone, as Dylan's songs do. Not looking back, on philosophical principle, it looks ahead to the new world Dylan prophesies in which people will gather round to acknowledge, not deny, the reality of their condition. And it is with the purpose of affirming the principle "Don't look back" that the finale of *Monterey Pop* precisely recapitulates the trajectory familiar from the films we have studied. Attracted and animated by the music emanating from the stadium, the camera enters this alien yet strangely familiar region, then is drawn deeper and deeper until it penetrates to the place where the spirit of this music, the spirit of this film, the spirit of cinéma-vérité, fully reveals itself. Once the camera reaches this place, it envisions no way out, no way back, no direction home. There is no world outside the world transfigured by Ravi Shankar's music, no world outside the world transfigured by Pennebaker's film. But this is not a cause for melancholy, for horror, for mourning, or for despair. It is a cause for a festival.

Notes

1 In addition to numerous journal articles, I am thinking of such recent books as William Guynn, *A Cinema of Nonfiction* (Rutherford, NJ: Fairleigh Dickenson University Press, 1990); Bill Nichols, *Representing Reality: Issues and Concepts in Documentary* (Bloomington: Indiana University Press, 1991); P. J. O'Connell, *Robert Drew and the Development of Cinéma Vérité in America* (Carbondale: Southern Illinois University Press, 1992); Michael Renov, ed., *Theorizing Documentary* (New York: Routledge, 1993). I am also thinking of two important books that call into question some of the assumptions, or conventions, of most academic film study: Charles Warren, ed., *Beyond Document* (Middletown: Wesleyan University Press, 1996) and Carl Plantinga, *Ordered Images: Rhetoric and Representation in Nonfiction Film* (New York and Cambridge: Cambridge University Press, forthcoming).

2 Thomas W. Benson and Carolyn Anderson, *Reality Fictions: The Films of Frederick Wiseman* (Carbondale: University of Southern Illinois Press, 1989) and Barry Keith Grant, *Voyages of Discovery: The Cinema of Frederick Wiseman* (Urbana and Chicago: University of Illinois Press, 1992). Alan Cholodenko's brilliant but unpublished 1987 Harvard doctoral dissertation, *The Films of Frederick Wiseman*, is also worthy of note.

3 Gilberto Perez, "The Documentary Image," a chapter of *The Material Ghost: Films and their Medium* (publication forthcoming from Johns Hopkins University Press). Perez's essay, which contains lucid and insightful discussions of *Nanook of the North* and *Land without Bread*, among other classic documentary films, probes a number of issues that are of central concern to the present volume.

4 Georges Sadoul (translated, edited, and updated by Peter Morris), *Dictionary of Films* (Berkeley and Los Angeles: University of California Press, 1972), p. 185.

5 Stanley Cavell, *The World Viewed: Reflections on the Ontology of Film* (Enlarged Edition) (Cambridge and London: Harvard University Press, 1979), p. 39.

6 Cavell, p. 233 (note to p. 41).

7 Cavell, pp. 40–1.

8 Jay Cantor, "Death and the Image," in Charles Warren, ed., *Beyond Document* (Middletown: Wesleyan University Press, 1995), p. 27.

9 Cantor, p. 28.

10 It is a much commented-on feature of *Night and Fog* that the narration never explicitly addresses the fundamental connection between the death camps and the "Jewish problem," makes no mention either of the anti-semitism that was pervasive throughout Europe or of the Nazis' genocidal project of exterminating the Jewish people. Ilan Avisar gives a thoughtful assessment of this omission in his eloquent remarks on

Night and Fog in *Screening the Holocaust: Cinema's Images of the Unimaginable* (Bloomington and Indianapolis: Indiana University Press, 1988), pp. 6–18.

11 Resnais also worked closely with Jean Cayrol on *Muriel*, perhaps the greatest of the director's "fiction" films. Like other major writers with whom Resnais has collaborated (Marguerite Duras and Alain Robbe-Grillet, for example), Cayrol is noted as a theorist of literature as well as a literary figure. There is a very helpful discussion of the influence on Resnais's work of Jean Cayrol's literary theories in René Prédal, et al., *Etudes Cinématographiques* 64–8 (1968), pp. 103–20. André Pierre Colombat draws on this study in his insightful and informative extended analysis of *Night and Fog*. See André Pierre Colombat, *The Holocaust in French Film* (Metuchen, NJ, and London: The Scarecrow Press, 1993), pp. 121–66.

12 Cantor, p. 29.

13 Cantor, p. 29.

14 Cantor, p. 28.

15 Cantor, p. 28.

16 Cantor, p. 28.

17 Cantor, p. 27.

18 Cantor, p. 30.

19 Cantor, p. 30.

20 Cantor, pp. 29–30.

21 William Rothman, *The "I" of the Camera: Essays in Film Criticism, History and Aesthetics* (Cambridge and New York: Cambridge University Press, 1988), p. 47.

22 Rothman, p. 151.

23 Rothman, pp. 150–1.

24 William Rothman, *Hitchcock – The Murderous Gaze* (Cambridge: Harvard University Press, 1982), p. 255.

25 Rothman, p. 255.

26 "*Jean Rouch – Les aventures d'un nègre blanc*," interview with Rouch by Philippe Esnault, in *Image et Son*, no. 249, April 1971. Quoted by Mick Eaton

in "The Production of Cinematic Reality," in Mick Eaton, ed., *Anthropology – Reality – Cinema: The Films of Jean Rouch* (London: British Film Institute, 1979), p. 51.

27 The transcribed text of the film – including several sequences cut from the final version as it was shown in theaters – was contained in a volume on *Chronicle of a Summer* (number one in the series "Domaine Cinéma") published in Paris in 1962 by Interspectacles. A slightly modified version was published in English translation in Steven Feld, ed., *Studies in Visual Communication* 11, 1 (Winter 1985), pp. 38–70.

28 Feld, p. 53.

29 Feld, p. 53.

30 Feld, p. 53.

31 Feld, pp. 53–4.

32 Eaton, p. 51.

33 Paul Stoller, *The Cinematic Griot: The Ethnography of Jean Rouch* (Chicago: University of Chicago Press, 1992), pp. 2, 100–4, 193–218.

34 Stoller, p. 100.

35 Jean Rouch, "On the Vicissitudes of the Self: The Possessed Dancer, the Magician, the Sorcerer, the Filmmaker and the Ethnographer," in *Studies in the Anthropology of Visual Communication* 5, 1978, pp. 2–8.

36 Rouch, p. 8.

37 Stoller, p. 168.

38 Stoller, p. 169.

39 Stoller, p. 102.

40 Cited in S. Feld, "Themes in the Cinema of Jean Rouch," *Visual Anthropology* 2, 1989, p. 233.

41 Stoller, pp. 170–1.

42 Jean Rouch and E. Fulchignoni, "Conversation between Jean Rouch and Professor Enrico Fulchignoni," *Visual Anthropology* 2, 1989, pp. 265–301. Cited in Stoller, p. 172.

43 William Rothman, *The "I" of the Camera: Essays in Film Criticism, History and Aesthetics*, (Cambridge and

New York: Cambridge University Press, 1988), pp. 69–70.

44 The pioneering text on the emergence of cinéma-vérité in America is Stephen Mamber's *Cinema-Verite in America* (Cambridge: MIT Press, 1974). An overview of the Drew productions is P. J. O'Connell's *Robert Drew and the Development of Cinéma Vérité in America* (Carbondale: Southern Illinois University Press, 1992). See also Jeanne Hall's illuminating essay "Realism as a Style in Cinéma-Vérité: A Critical Analysis of *Primary*," *Cinema Journal* 30, 4 (Summer 1991), pp. 24–50.

45 *The Saturday Evening Post*, November 16, 1963, pp. 25–48. Also *The Saturday Evening Post*, May 2, 1964, pp. 18–28.

46 "D. A. Pennebaker Interviewed by John Bauldie," in John Bauldie, ed., *Wanted Man: In Search of Bob Dylan* (New York: Citadel Press, 1990), p. 46.

47 Bauldie, p. 47.

48 Bauldie, p. 44.

49 Andrew Sarris, "Don't Look Back," *Village Voice*, September 21, 1967, in Elizabeth Thomson and David Gutman, eds., *The Dylan Companion* (New York: Delta Books, 1991), p. 88.

50 Bob Spitz, *Dylan: A Biography* (New York: Norton, 1989), p. 280.

51 Spitz, pp. 280–1.

52 Spitz, p. 281.

53 Bauldie, pp. 48–9.

54 Spitz, p. 282.

55 Paul Williams, *Bob Dylan: Performing Artist 1960–73* (London: Omnibus Press, 1994), p. 91.

56 Cited in Williams, p. 90.

57 Williams, pp. 114–5.

58 Spitz, p. 177.

59 Bauldie, pp. 52–3.

60 Bauldie, p. 53.

61 Spitz, pp. 179–80.

62 Williams, p. 116.

63 Stanley Cavell, *A Pitch of Philosophy: Autobiographical Exercises* (Cambridge and London: Harvard University Press, 1994), p. 144.

64 Quoted in Robert Shelton, *No Direction Home: The Life and Music of Bob Dylan* (New York: William Morrow, 1986), p. 299.

65 Spitz, p. 299.

66 Shelton, p. 296.

67 Spitz, pp. 291–2.

68 Williams, p. 143.

69 Bauldie, p. 51.

70 Spitz, p. 292.

71 Upon reading a draft of this chapter, Jay Hollenbach wrote a letter spelling out his reading of this sequence, which complements mine, but is rather darker. For Hollenbach, the key to this passage is that it is an instance of the kind of conspiracy between filmmaker and subject that I insist on in my discussion of the film's opening. He sees Pennebaker and Dylan as conspiring to set Donovan up, and to set the viewer up, for the little "spontaneous" demonstration that culminates and concludes this sequence, in which, as we shall see, Dylan asserts – and Donovan ruefully acknowledges – that he is the superior artist. And in pondering why Dylan feels compelled to assert his dominance over Donovan in this way, Hollenbach finds a dark side to the film's subject, a disturbing gap between who Dylan really is and who he claims to be, and a dark side to Dylan's relationship with Pennebaker, as well.

72 Bauldie, p. 48.

73 Spitz, p. 295.

74 Stanley Cavell, *Pursuits of Happiness: The Hollywood Comedy of Remarriage* (Cambridge and London: Harvard University Press, 1981), p. 248.

75 Cavell, p. 261.

76 Cavell, p. 257.

77 Cavell, p. 237.

Index

215